JEFFERSON READER

By FRANCIS COLEMAN ROSENBERGER

VIRGINIA READER

JEFFERSON READER

Jefferson at 78.

LARGE FULL LENGTH BY THOMAS SULLY, 1822

(Jefferson gave sittings to Sully at Monticello in 1821.)

Courtesy of the United States Military Academy, West Point, New York

JEFFERSON READER

A Treasury of Writings About Thomas Jefferson

EDITED WITH AN INTRODUCTION BY

FRANCIS COLEMAN ROSENBERGER

Illustrated with Fifteen Life Portraits of Jefferson

E. P. DUTTON & COMPANY, INC.

New York, 1953

LIBRARY OF CONGRESS CATALOG CARD NUMBER: 52-10424

CONTENTS

Contents

Contents

Contents

ILLUSTRATIONS

◇◇

INTRODUCTION

In his *History of the United States,* which is not notable for any partiality for Jefferson, Henry Adams wrote with a perception which warrants its frequent quotation: "Almost every other American statesman might be described in a parenthesis. A few broad strokes of the brush would paint the portrait of all the early presidents with this exception . . . Jefferson could be painted only touch by touch, with a fine pencil."

This is true, but more: no one pencil has wholly succeeded in presenting a complete or final portrait. There is for Jefferson, perhaps more than for any other great American, justification for a volume such as this: an anthology which brings together what many writers, with their various points of view and abilities, have had to say. Jefferson, in Paris in 1789, caught up in his admiration for a great draftsman, wrote: "I do not feel an interest in any pencil but that of David." But for Jefferson himself there has been no single David to the exclusion of all others.

If such a volume as this is well worth doing, I am not unmindful of the difficulties of doing it well. Any anthology must stand or fall upon the sense of selectivity which it exhibits. The more abundant the choices the more demanding is the editor's work. I have, off and on, been reading about Mr. Jefferson since my student years at the University of Virginia. But to read with the thought of choosing one selection above another, and to choose those which may be brought together to make a volume of some balance and proportion, is a rather different matter. A wiser man than I would have hesitated to make the attempt. I had not long been at the task when I realized full well why no such volume has before been published.

This is not to suggest that I have looked into, or even know of the existence, of all the writing about Jefferson. Such a disclaimer is quite unnecessary for the reader who knows the field. The total amount of writing about Jefferson is staggeringly large. There is not in existence anything like a complete bibliography. More than ten years ago, in an engaging paper on *Some Aspects of Jefferson Bibliography,* William Peden wrote: "Only the barest preliminary steps have been taken in the publication of Jefferson bibliographies. . . . Nor can I believe that there will be a successful attempt in this generation to issue a general bibliographical work on Jefferson. . . . Of writing about Jefferson it has been estimated that it would take ten years simply to assemble the materials for a bibliography and another five to digest them. Men like Chinard and Malone and perhaps a dozen others would have the ability to accomplish this, but I doubt that any of them would have the patience." No one has yet come forward to prove Mr. Peden wrong.

What I have hoped to accomplish here is to bring together, within the limits of a single volume of manageable size, and with some attention to a balance between the undeservedly little-known and the deservedly well-known, a selection of the more readable and illuminating writing about Jefferson from his own time to the present. In number of authors, I have allotted the lion's share to the reports and reminiscences of those who had the great good fortune to know or visit Jefferson in life. In number of pages, I have given it to later writers who, in an age of specialization, have written ably on one aspect or another of the many-sided Jefferson. Poems are included, and political comment, and a taste of contemporary calumny, and evaluations of Jefferson's life by various hands through the years.

II

It may be well to state one thing which this book does not attempt to be. It is not a composite biography of Jefferson. Such a volume could, assuredly, be assembled. There have been many biographies of Jefferson since the first, by George Tucker, Professor of Moral Philosophy at the University of Virginia, appeared in 1837. The card catalogue of the Library of Congress contains some four hundred entries with Jefferson as the subject. Among a number of worthy biographies have been those by James Parton (1874), John T. Morse (1883), David S. Muzzey (1918), Albert J. Nock (1926), Francis Hirst (1926), Claude Bowers (1925, 1936, 1945), Gilbert Chinard (1929), Saul Padover (1942), and Nathan Schachner (1951).

The piecing together of a composite biography, however, has particular point and reason only where one biographer and another have written with especial insight about one period and another of a great man's life. Paul M. Angle has edited an admirable composite narrative of this sort in *The Lincoln Reader* and Stanley F. Horn has in *The Robert E. Lee Reader*. But such a volume for Jefferson would be less rewarding than for Lincoln or for Lee. Jefferson biography has been a thing of mountains and valleys, or one mountain and valleys. The great monument for nearly a hundred years has been *The Life of Thomas Jefferson* by Henry S. Randall, published in 1858. For all of its belonging to the nineteenth century, and to the antebellum nineteenth century, it has been to Randall that the reader must go for the most thorough and satisfactory narrative of Jefferson's life.

Subsequent biographers, providing their own interpretations, have relied heavily upon Randall for the facts. It has not been until the immediate present that the work of Jefferson biography has been undertaken afresh on a comparable scale. Randall is now being matched by two modern multi-volume biographies of Jefferson, the works in progress by Marie Kimball and Dumas Malone. Three volumes of Marie Kimball's biography have now appeared, carrying her account of Jefferson to the year 1789. Dumas Malone, in what promises to be the finest biography of Jefferson, has now published two volumes of his projected five-volume, *Jefferson and His Times.*

No, the volume in your hands does not undertake to be a composite biography of Jefferson. But if, for the narrative of Jefferson's life, there is no substitute for Randall, or for Malone for the years which Malone has covered, there is elsewhere immensely rich and rewarding writing about Jefferson—presenting glimpses and aspects of him "touch by touch, with a fine pencil." The *Jefferson Reader* is an anthology of that writing. If a volume comparable in purpose should be sought on the shelf of Lincoln books, it would not be Paul

M. Angle's *The Lincoln Reader* but more nearly Edward Wagen-
knecht's anthology, *Abraham Lincoln*. In its approach to its subject,
the *Jefferson Reader* is nearer still to the editor's own *Virginia Reader:
A Treasury of Writings from the First Voyages to the Present.*

III

After Henry Steele Commager's brief and admirable summary of
Jefferson's importance today, which was published on the appearance of the first volume of the great Princeton project for a definitive
edition of *The Papers of Thomas Jefferson,* I have begun with the
first-hand accounts of those who knew Jefferson. The first of these is
that of the Florentine Philip Mazzei, who saw Jefferson as a young
man of thirty. (Mazzei erroneously makes him two years older in
the reminiscences.) The second, and far more valuable, is the excellent account by the Marquis de Chastellux of his visit to Monticello
in 1782. Jefferson was then not quite forty—"an American, who without ever having quitted his own country, is at once a musician, skilled
in drawing, a geometrician, an astronomer, a natural philosopher,
legislator, and statesman"—and de Chastellux's is the earliest perceptive description of Jefferson and of the mansion which he was
building on his Virginia mountaintop. And few, if any, writers have
ever better described Jefferson in a sentence than de Chastellux does
in his final words.

A letter by Abigail Adams provides a fleeting glimpse of one of
Jefferson's dinners in Paris, but regrettably says little of the host.
The Duc de la Rochefoucauld-Liancourt and the English visitor
Isaac Weld, in their accounts of their travels in North America, give
descriptions of their visits to Monticello in 1796—that of the Duke
de la Rochefoucauld-Liancourt, full and detailed, an especially interesting one. Of Jefferson as President, there is perhaps no more engaging description than that of Margaret Bayard Smith; and the dour
John Quincy Adams concedes to his diary "one of the *agreeable*
dinners I have had at Mr. Jefferson's."

A grandson of Thomas Jefferson, an overseer at Monticello, and
one of Jefferson's slaves, each from his own point of vantage, have
left descriptions and reminiscences which help us to see Mr. Jefferson more fully. When Jefferson retired from the Presidency, Monticello became the goal of innumerable visitors, invited and uninvited.

Of those who put their impressions on paper, included here are the accounts of five: two young Bostonians, Francis Calley Gray and George Ticknor, in 1815; the English visitor Francis Hall in 1817; Daniel Webster in 1824; and Duke Bernhard of Saxe-Weimar Eisenach the year before Jefferson's death. At eighty-two (the last visitor quoted here, like the first, gives Jefferson's age erroneously), Duke Bernhard found him, as they sat before the evening fire, lively in spirits and wide-ranging and enthusiastic in conversation: "one would have taken him for a man of sixty."

Of the numerous popular political songs of Jefferson's day which had him as the subject and hero, I have chosen two of the most widely known: "The People's Friend" and "Jefferson and Liberty." The excerpt from "The Embargo" by the youthful William Cullen Bryant (which forecast the later Bryant's poetic abilities if not his political sentiments) is a more competent than average example of the broadsides in verse which attacked the President; and the satire from *The Port Folio* on the President's day, it seems to me, reaches in places something very near to true wit. Few men in public life have ever been more viciously assaulted than was President Jefferson and it has seemed proper to include a sample of the calumny in the selections from Callender and one of the Federalist newspapers. The texts here of "The People's Friend" and "Jefferson and Liberty" are as they appear in printed versions clipped and pasted in a Jefferson Scrapbook, which is now in the Alderman Library of the University of Virginia. Jefferson wrote of the Scrapbook, in a letter to John Adams on February 25, 1823: "I was in the habit, also, while living apart from my family, of cutting out of the newspapers such morsels of poetry, or tales, as I thought would please, and of sending them to my grandchildren, who pasted them on leaves of blank paper and formed them into a book." As a morsel clipped by Jefferson, I have not resisted the temptation to include here one other item from the Scrapbook, the bit of verse, "On Defamation."

To illuminate Jefferson's enormously wide-ranging interests I have chosen nine essays: the number might well have been very considerably extended. The paper by John W. Davis on Jefferson as an attorney is marked with the scholarship and eloquence which have made Mr. Davis a leader of the bar of our own day. Until Edward Dumbauld gives us his promised book on Jefferson and the law, Mr. Davis's paper, which deserves better than to be left in a volume of bar association proceedings, is likely to remain the most thorough consideration of this aspect of Jefferson.

Julian P. Boyd, in his introductory essay to the monumental and meticulously edited Princeton edition of *The Papers of Thomas Jefferson,* has provided one of the finest of commentaries on the significance of the heritage of Jefferson papers. A central point which Mr. Boyd makes, the purposefulness of Jefferson's inquiries and activities, is one which should by no means be missed. Gilbert Chinard's wise and felicitous "Thomas Jefferson as a Classical Scholar" is mellow scholarship at its best. Of Jefferson and science, a subject which has been considered in greater detail in the recent volume, *Thomas Jefferson: Scientist* by Edwin T. Martin, I have chosen the paper by the distinguished biologist, Austin H. Clark. The perceptive consideration of Jefferson and religion is from the first volume of Marie Kimball's biography, and to the passage Mrs. Kimball has generously made an addition to round it out for this anthology. I have included a long, but it seems to me all too brief, selection from Edward Dumbauld's pioneering and engaging volume, *Thomas Jefferson: American Tourist.* Hugh H. Bennett, America's most widely known soil conservationist, writes ably on Jefferson as a farmer and a friend of the land. One could hope, I think, for no more expert paper than Fiske Kimball's "Jefferson and the Arts" or more eloquent one than John Dewey's "Thomas Jefferson and the Democratic Faith."

Of later poems which take their inspiration from Jefferson I have included five. Hezekiah Butterworth's Victorian "The Death of Jefferson" belongs to a time whose tastes in rhetoric are not our tastes, but it has seemed to me to deserve a place here as a period piece if on no other grounds. There follows evocative work by four distinguished American poets of the present day: Allen Tate's epigrammatic "On the Father of Liberty," which here appears in book form for the first time, and moving poems by Lawrence Lee, Archibald MacLeish, and Karl Shapiro.

In the selection of comments by specifically political figures on Jefferson and his significance, and of such comments there is a great abundance, I have been severe, limiting the number to four. Abraham Lincoln's letter of June 6, 1859, which might have been a routine note declining an invitation to speak, is, it seems to me, one of the great statements on Jeffersonian principles. The other three Presidential opinions, the Woodrow Wilson address of 1912, Herbert Hoover on Jefferson and the Bill of Rights, and Franklin D. Roosevelt's brief and memorable address at the dedication of the Jefferson Memorial in Washington, are each of them more than ephemeral political comments.

The final section of the anthology, for which there was a very wide range of choices, presented very hard decisions. I am altogether satisfied with the inclusion of each of the seven selections which are here, but I am less than satisfied with the exclusion of the many which might well be here. The estimate of Jefferson in Nicholas Biddle's *Eulogium*, delivered before the American Philosophical Society in 1827, is of all that I have seen the finest of the many tributes to Jefferson which followed his death. Lord Macaulay's letter, rightly seeing that the principles of Jefferson are the foundations of democratic society, but damning both, is an item of very great interest, and I am grateful to Lyman H. Butterfield except for whom it would not have come to my attention. Henry Adams' judicious weighing of the qualities of Jefferson, with his grudging admiration, is a selection which could not be omitted. "The Return of a Virginian" is a fine passage, and one well calculated to stand alone, from Dumas Malone's masterly biography in progress. Adrienne Koch's "The Earth Belongs to the Living," revised by Miss Koch for this anthology from her *Jefferson and Madison: The Great Collaboration*, and Bernard Mayo's "A Peppercorn for Mr. Jefferson," are valuable and engaging papers. Dixon Wecter's "Thomas Jefferson, the Gentle Radical," the essay with which I bring this anthology to a close, is one of the very finest general discussions of Jefferson of which I know.

I V

If I should list the selections which might have been included here, this Introduction would exceed all practicable limits. But in the hope that this anthology may whet rather than slake an interest in Jefferson, a few guideposts to further reading may be put up. Another rewarding account of a visit to Monticello was left by the British diplomat, Sir Augustus John Foster, and appears in the extracts from his "Notes on the United States," edited by Margaret Bailey Tinkcom,

in the January 1951 issue of the *William and Mary Quarterly*. Thomas
Moore's satirical comment in verse on Jefferson and the District of
Columbia might have been included, but the reader has its flavor—
and the most biting lines—in the quotation included in Dixon Wecter's essay here. The two poems are readily available (Moore's *Poet-
ical Works,* Boston, 1856, II, 75, 82; and later editions). The reader
who has especially enjoyed Gilbert Chinard's paper here will find
Thomas Jefferson: American Humanist by Karl Lehmann (1947) a
highly rewarding volume. The reader who has found particular interest in Marie Kimball's discussion of Jefferson and religion will want to
read Henry Wilder Foote's able introduction to his edition of Jefferson's *The Life and Morals of Jesus of Nazareth Extracted Textually
from the Gospels of Matthew, Mark, Luke and John* (1951). Jefferson
the bookman, an aspect of Jefferson which is not the chief concern of
any one of the essays here, is the subject of Randolph G. Adams' excellent "Thomas Jefferson: Librarian" in his volume *Three Americanists*
(1939). To add to the sheaf of modern poems on Jefferson, the reader
may seek out Gamaliel Bradford's "Thomas Jefferson" and his "Ode to
Thomas Jefferson," Rosemary and Stephen Vincent Benét's "Thomas
Jefferson," Ruth H. Hausman's "Monticello," and Lawrence Lee's fine
"The Tomb of Thomas Jefferson." The reader who has found the selection of comments by political figures too brief may continue in the
books by Senator John Sharp Williams (1913) and Senator Elbert
Thomas (1942) and in the papers and addresses of Daniel Webster
(address of August 2, 1826), Grover Cleveland (address of April 27,
1889), William Jennings Bryan (*The North American Review,* June
1889), and Harry S. Truman (accepting the first volume of *The Papers
of Thomas Jefferson,* May 17, 1950). Two special Jefferson issues of
periodicals will repay the reader's examination, the Spring 1943 issue
The Virginia Quarterly Review and the July 14, 1943 issue of the *Proceedings of the American Philosophical Society.* Of recent periodical
articles there are none better than "The Agrarian Democracy of
Thomas Jefferson" by A. Whitney Griswold in the August 1946 *American Political Science Review* and "The Reconciliation of Adams and
Jefferson" by Lyman H. Butterfield in the Winter 1951 *Yale Review.*
A provocative discussion of the personalities of Jefferson and Hamil-
ton is contained in Gerald W. Johnson's *American Heroes and Hero-
Worship* (1943). The text of Sidney Kingsley's stirring play, *The
Patriots,* originally entitled *Jefferson,* is available as a book (1943).

An entertaining imaginary dinner with Mr. Jefferson is included in *Van Loon's Lives* by Hendrik Willem Van Loon (1942).

v

What Jefferson's actual appearance was is a fascinating matter. I am grateful for the generosity of the publishers in permitting the reproduction here of fifteen life portraits of Jefferson, bringing them together for the first time in one book. For a careful discussion of Jefferson portraiture the interested reader should go to Fiske Kimball's "The Life Portraits of Jefferson and Their Replicas" (in the *Proceedings of the American Philosophical Society*, December 28, 1944). Two of the life portraits reproduced in this anthology have come to light since the appearance of Mr. Kimball's article, the bust by John Coffee (discussed by Anna Wells Rutledge in the *Gazette des Beaux-Arts*, November 1945) and the profile by Edme Quenedey (discussed by Howard C. Rice, Jr., in the *William and Mary Quarterly*, January 1949). Rounding up copies of the fifteen portraits with permission to reproduce them was something more of a chore than I had anticipated, and I am grateful to all those who co-operated in the matter. Specific acknowledgments accompany each of the illustrations.

With the *Jefferson Reader*, as with the earlier *Virginia Reader*, I owe a debt of gratitude to the publishers for their patience and understanding. I am especially indebted to Mr. Nicholas Wreden and Miss Louise Townsend Nicholl for their enthusiasm for Mr. Jefferson and for this anthology.

FRANCIS COLEMAN ROSENBERGER

Fairfax County, Virginia

JEFFERSON READER

'THOMAS JEFFERSON STILL SURVIVES'

Henry Steele Commager

Jefferson is the central figure in American history and—if freedom and democracy survive in our generation—he may yet prove to be the central figure in modern history. He was not only one of the Founding Fathers, the source and inspiration of much of American democracy and of American nationalism; he was, too, a world figure. Certainly no other public man contributed so richly to so many chapters in modern history.

He was, of all the Founding Fathers, indeed of all the men of the eighteenth century, the most contemporary. Both in his public and his private life he addressed himself continuously to problems of permanent and universal interest. What he wrote and what he did— about the nature of society and of government, the relations of man to government, the meaning of republicanism and democracy, the significance of education and of toleration and of experimentation to democracy—is as relevant today as it was in the eighteenth century. It is, notwithstanding profound changes in politics and economy, as relevant for France and Germany and Italy as it was for the young United States.

Nor has any other American revealed himself or illuminated the history of his age more fully in his writings. Even his public writings constitute a record of incomparable importance: imagine our history without the Declaration of Independence, the Virginia Statute of Religious Freedom, the Ordinance of 1784, the Bill for the Diffusion of Knowledge, the Kentucky Resolutions, the First Inaugural Address, the Louisiana Treaty.

These, however, represent only a small part of Jefferson's total contribution to our history. His writings are essential, too, for an understanding of many things which he did not himself create or sponsor. Thus, for example, the Northwest Ordinance, the Bill of Rights, the Virginia Constitution, the Monroe Doctrine; thus, too, such institutions or movements as the political party, the attack on slavery, the role of the judiciary in our constitutional system, and a variety of humanitarian and reform movements.

When to all this are added private writings on almost every aspect of American society and culture, and correspondence (a correspondence singularly elevated and felicitous, with hundreds of public men at home and abroad), we can see that Jefferson furnished both the soil and the seed from which many of our national institutions grew.

No one has yet exhausted the richness of that mind, a mind in many respects the most interesting of modern times. Jefferson's versatility is by now a familiar, almost a hackneyed, subject. He was a scientist and an inventor; he was the greatest American architect of his day; he was a farmer, experimenting endlessly with crops and stock; he was a man of letters; he was a bibliophile, collecting not one but two of the greatest private libraries in the country; he was something of a philologist; he was a student of the classics—as who was not in that age—and of the Bible, compiling his own for good measure; he was a lawyer and a collector of law reports.

Also, he was something of a musician, playing the fiddle and collecting music and musicians; he was the first great educational statesman, not only the founder of the University of Virginia but the sponsor of far-reaching educational reforms; he was a horticulturist, and his garden book has permanent value. What was he not? Even in an age of versatility his catholic interests are a matter of perpetual astonishment.

Fortunately he was, too, an indefatigable letter-writer. His famous epistolary record runs to over six hundred closely written pages. Nor were his letters merely the hasty scrawls of a hurried man; many of them were minor treatises on politics or law or religion or education or philosophy.

How he found time for it all, even in a life of eighty-three years, is one of the mysteries of history; perhaps it was that he was untroubled by modern labor-saving devices and innocent of those squads of secretaries with which every modern statesman and business man surrounds himself.

Nor were all these interests, so richly revealed in his writings, the expression of dilettantism. It was said of one of the Lord Chancellors of England that if only he knew a little law he would know a little of everything. That could not be said of Thomas Jefferson. He was curious about almost everything, but his curiosity was rarely irrelevant.

Whatever he learned, whatever he knew, fitted into and enriched his philosophy. For of all American statesmen, Jefferson was the most philosophical. One abiding purpose runs through his whole life, one pervasive philosophy dominates it. He insisted that man should be free and he was persuaded that, once free, mankind would progress toward happiness and virtue. He was enraptured with the vision of mankind free from political tyranny, from the bondage of superstition and of ignorance, from the sins of the past, from poverty, from war. He had an eighteenth-century faith in the perfectibility of man, but it was not merely a visionary faith; it was faith rooted in the reality of New World experience.

For here in the New World mankind had been given a new chance—mankind free from the tyrannies and oppressions, the poverty and ignorance of the Old World. Here men could live close to nature, cultivate the soil, raise large families, keep what they earned, benefit from learning and from science, escape war, advance—as was said in the great First Inaugural Address—"rapidly to destinies beyond the reach of mortal eye."

And as America was to be a model for the world, to prove what man was capable of when free, Jefferson devoted himself passionately to strengthening this nation, expanding its territory, building up its resources, maintaining its security, fostering its culture and its virtue. The first strokes of his mature pen were a call for freedom; his last written words recalled that earlier faith.

It is eminently fitting that "The Papers of Thomas Jefferson" should be launched as a national enterprise. All who cherish American traditions, all who are zealous for the maintenance of freedom and democracy in the world, all who retain their faith in reason and morality, will rejoice at this reaffirmation of devotion to the principles to which Jefferson dedicated his life. "Thomas Jefferson still survives," said John Adams on his deathbed; it was a prophecy which each generation must justify anew.

MR. JEFFERSON FACE TO FACE: SOME VISITS AND REMINISCENCES

REMINISCENCES OF JEFFERSON IN 1773

Philip Mazzei

I struck up a friendship with Franklin and, through him, with various other persons from the colonies, which now form the Republic of the United States. One of these persons was Mr. Thomas Adams, a Virginian, who, being a close friend of Jefferson, made it possible for Mr. Jefferson and me to know a great deal about each other some years before we actually met. . . .

Having procured everything I wished to take with me from Florence to Virginia, I sent it all ahead to Leghorn in a stout barge, with Vincenzo in charge. When I reached Leghorn myself, I found the farmers from Lucca and Genoa and the tailor from Piedmont waiting for me. After purchasing provisions there too, I said good-by to my friends and relatives. I took with me enough *pesos duros* not only to support me for a reasonable length of time, but also to enable me to undertake some business project after my arrival, since I did not wish to risk any money until after I had arrived on the spot and had studied the best course to follow. I finally set sail on September 2, arriving in Virginia toward the end of November, 1773. . . .

We arrived off capes Henry and Charles one morning before dawn, and soon a coastal pilot came on board. From him I learned that the Assembly of the colony was still in session at Williamsburg, but that it was about to conclude its business. I knew that Williamsburg was not far from the James River. The pilot told me that between the river and the city was the home of Mr. Eppes, where I could rest. We were about forty miles away, but the wind and tide were in our favor, so that we soon arrived. Mr. Eppes's house was about four miles from the river and as far from Williamsburg. The pilot had his cabin boy accompany me there. Everyone was at table having lunch. I took nothing, as I had already eaten. Mr. Thomas Adams, Mr. Thomas Jefferson, and Mr. Samuel Griffin had already spoken of my

From *Memoirs of the Life and Peregrinations of the Florentine Philip Mazzei, 1730-1816*, translated by Howard R. Marraro. Copyright 1942 by Columbia University Press, New York. Reprinted by permission.

approaching arrival to several persons, among them Mr. Eppes, whose wife was Jefferson's sister-in-law. . . .

Williamsburg might really be called a township rather than a city, although the governor's palace, the Assembly Hall, the college, and the court were located there, and all the deputies of the colony lived there when the Assembly was in session. There were many persons in the capital when I arrived, because of the session, which, however, ended that same day. Several deputies, who were getting ready to leave, stayed a day longer to meet their new countryman, of whom Mr. Thomas Adams had already spoken too favorably.

Before the latter's arrival, two other persons had come to bid me welcome. The first was Mr. George Washington, who later distinguished himself through his command of the American Army during the Revolutionary War, which gave birth to the Republic of the United States, of which he later became the first president. The other was Mr. George Wythe, Jefferson's legal preceptor, a resident of Williamsburg, and one of the greatest personalities the world has ever produced, eminent in law, and a former teacher of Mr. Jefferson. Mr. Adams called the attention of several persons to the fact that I had undertaken to ship a large supply of grain back to Leghorn, to which port no Virginian ship had ever sailed. . . .

I had told Mr. Adams, before his departure from England, the kind of soil required for planting vines. He had obtained 5,000 acres of land for me from the Assembly. But I could not accept this property, as it was divided into many parcels, at some distance from one another.

Mr. Adams had sold the house where he lived and its furnishings and had bought property of greater extent about 160 miles north of Williamsburg, in Augusta County, and about 20 miles from the Blue Ridge Mountains, so called by the first European emigrants because from a distance the atmosphere surrounding them appears to be of that color—an effect which occurs elsewhere also. These mountains separate Augusta County from Albemarle County, where Mr. Jefferson resides, some 20 miles from the mountains.

I set out with Mr. Adams to visit his new property. He wished to look around, to see where it would be best for him to build a house, and I wanted to see whether I could buy a parcel of land near his, if the location suited me. We agreed to spend two or three days with Mr. Jefferson on our way.

Mr. Jefferson was thirty-two years old, that is, eleven years younger than I. He had married a widow, twenty-three years of age, and they had a little girl only a few months old. We arrived in the evening, and the following morning, while the others were still asleep, Jefferson and I went to take a walk in the neighborhood. He took me to the house of a poor man, who owned a cabin and about 400 acres of land, which bordered on his own, and of which about one-eighth had been deforested and cultivated.* The man wanted to sell the place, because he had several children and, by going inland about 100 miles, he could buy, with half of the sale price, a tract of land large enough to enable him to leave more than 400 acres to each of his sons. I decided to purchase the place he had for sale.

The cabin was more than large enough for the farmers I had brought with me. It was on a small plain, with higher land on two sides. On one side the land was level, while on the other, which was much longer and higher, formed a hill, on which we decided I could have a frame house built for myself. As Mr. Jefferson's estate was adjacent to this property and as he had much more land than he needed, he said he would give me a tract of about 2,000 acres. He had other estates in an adjoining county. Every year he sold the produce of the land, over and above what he needed for his own consumption and that of his household, receiving about £2,000 for it.

By the time we returned home, everyone was up. Looking at Mr. Jefferson, Mr. Adams said, "I see by your expression that you've taken him away from me. I knew you would do that." Jefferson smiled, without looking at him, but, staring at the table, said: "Let's have breakfast first and then we'll see what we can do."

After breakfast, he dispatched a man with a letter to Mr. Eppes, his brother-in-law, asking him to send on my men and the effects I had listed in a note he enclosed. He also asked him to tell Mrs. Martin that after the arrival of the men and our belongings, Mr. Adams and I would go to get her and her daughter.

Mr. Adams left at once for Augusta and had not yet returned when my men arrived. Jefferson understood the Tuscan language very well, but he had never heard it spoken. Nevertheless, he could converse with my men in Italian, and they were so pleased by the fact that he could understand them that I was touched. Among his slaves,

---

* Over there, a poor man is one who is forced to till his land himself, since he is not in a position to buy slaves.

there were many skilled workmen of all trades, but no tailors. As soon as he saw our spades and bill hooks, he ordered some made for use on all his estates. He liked our hunting coat, and adopted it too. The neighbors imitated him, with the result that it became very popular. This was advantageous for the tailor, since, in accordance with our agreement, he was required to work for me and my group, and in return I was to supply him with all his needs. But he alone was to profit from all the other work he did.

While I awaited Mr. Adams, I put my men to work on deforesting the land, from the tilled part of the property to a point beyond the hill on which I wished to build my house. To speed the work, I hired two strong Negroes. In this task of deforestation, I did not follow the custom of the country. As a measure of economy of labor, instead of uprooting the trees and cutting them out well underground, they had them cut so much above ground that a woodsman did not have to bend over at all to apply his axe. The landowners who were required to do all this work themselves did not cut the trees down at all, but merely removed about six inches of bark all the way round, which caused the trees to dry out and, after many years, to fall.

I continued clearing my land for four winters, engaging more men every year. From the windows of my home and from those of Mr. Jefferson's, I was spared the ugly sight of withered trees, which looked like skeletons, and of stumps of trees standing three feet above the ground, because, since the neighborhood had been under cultivation for more than half a century, they had rotted away. . . .

Jefferson at 43.

PORTRAIT BY MATHER BROWN, LONDON, 1786

(Earliest portrait of Jefferson. Replica, painted by Brown for
John Adams, of the lost original which belonged to Jefferson.)

*Courtesy of Hon. Charles Francis Adams, Boston, and the
Frick Art Reference Library, New York*

Jefferson at 44.

DETAIL FROM THE DECLARATION OF INDEPENDENCE
BY JOHN TRUMBULL, PARIS, 1787

Courtesy of the Yale University Art Gallery, New Haven

A VISIT TO MONTICELLO IN 1782

The Marquis de Chastellux

From the moment the French troops were established in the quarters they occupied in Virginia, I formed the project of travelling into the upper parts of that province, where I was assured that I should find objects worthy of exciting the curiosity of a stranger; and faithful to the principles, which from my youth I had lain down, never to neglect seeing every country in my power, I burned with impatience to set out. The season however, was unfavourable, and rendered travelling difficult and laborious; besides, experience taught me that travelling in winter never offered the greatest satisfaction we can enjoy; that of seeing nature, such as she ought to be, and of forming a just idea of the general face of a country; for it is easier for the imagination to deprive a landscape of the charms of spring, than to clothe with them, the hideous skeleton of winter; as it is easier to imagine what a beauty at eighteen may be at eighty, than to conceive what eighty was at eighteen. —Monsieur de Rochambeau being absent likewise during the month of February, and Monsieur la Chevalier de la Luzerne having chosen the month of March to pay us a visit, politeness and my duty obliged me to wait till April, before I could begin my travels. —On the 8th of that month I set out with Mr. Lynch, then my aid-de-camp and Adjutant, now General; Mr. Frank Dillon, my second aid-de-camp, and Mr. le Chevalier d'Oyré of the engineers: six servants and a led horse composed our train; so that our little caravan consisted of four masters, six servants, and eleven horses. I regulated my journey by the spring, and gave it time sufficient to precede us. For though in the 37th degree of latitude, one might expect to find it in the month of April, I saw no trace of it in the wood through

From *Travels in North-America, in the Years 1780 -81 -82*, by the Marquis de Chastellux, one of the forty members of the French Academy, and Major-General in the French Army, serving under the Count de Rochambeau. Translated from the French, by an English Gentleman, who resided in America at that period. . . . New York, 1827.

33

which we passed; the verdure being hardly discoverable on the thorns, the sun notwithstanding was very ardent, and I regretted to find summer in the heavens, whilst the earth afforded not the smallest appearance of the spring. The eighteen miles through which we passed, before we baited our horses at Bird's tavern, were sufficiently known to me, for it was the same road I travelled last summer in coming from Williamsburgh. The remaining sixteen, which completed our day's work and brought us to New-Kent court-house, offered nothing curious; all I learnt by a conversation with Mr. Bird was, that he had been pillaged by the English when they passed his house in their march to Westover, in pursuit of Monsieur de la Fayette, and in returning to Williamsburgh, after endeavouring in vain to come up with him. It was comparatively nothing to see their fruits, fowls and cattle carried away by the light troops which formed the vanguard, the army collected what the vanguard had left, even the officers seized the rum, and all kinds of provisions, without paying a farthing for them; this hurricane which destroyed every thing in its passage, was followed by a scourge yet more terrible, a numerous rabble, under the title of Refugees and Loyalists, followed the army, not to assist in the field, but to partake of the plunder. . . .

*   *   *   *   *

The night was already closed in, when we arrived at the house of Colonel Boswell, a tall, stout Scotsman, about sixty years of age, and who had been about forty years settled in America, where, under the English government, he was a colonel of militia. Although he kept a kind of tavern, he appeared but little prepared to receive strangers. It was already late indeed, besides that this road, which leads only to the mountains, is little frequented. He was quietly seated near the fire, by the side of his wife, as old, and almost as tall as himself, whom he distinguished by the epithet of "honey," which in French corresponds with *mon petit coeur.* These honest people received us cheerfully, and soon called up their servants, who were already gone to bed. Whilst they were preparing supper, we often heard them call Rose, Rose, which at length brought to view the most hideous negress I ever beheld. Our supper was rather scanty, but our breakfast the next morning better; we had ham, butter, fresh eggs, and coffee by way of drink: for the whiskey or corn-spirits we had in the evening, mixt with water, was very bad; besides that we were perfectly reconciled to the American custom of drinking coffee with meat, vegetables, or other food.

We set out the next morning at eight o'clock, having learned nothing in this house worthy of remark, except that notwithstanding the hale and robust appearance of Mr. and Mrs. Boswell, not one of fourteen of their children had attained the age of ten years. We were now approaching a chain of mountains of considerable height, called the South-West Mountains, because they are the first you meet in travelling westward, before you arrive at the chain known in France by the name of the Apalachians, and in Virginia by that of the Blue Ridge, North Ridge, and Allegany Mountains. As the country was much covered with woods, we had a view of them but very seldom; and travelled a long time without seeing any habitation, at times greatly perplexed to choose among the different roads, which crossed each other. At last we overtook a traveller who preceded us, and served not only as guide, but by his company helped to abridge our journey. He was an Irishman, who though but lately arrived in America, had made several campaigns, and received a considerable wound in his thigh by a musket ball; which, though it could never be extracted, had not in the least affected either his health or gaiety. He related his military exploits, and we inquired immediately about the country which he then inhabited. He acquainted us that he was settled in North-Carolina, upwards of eighty miles from Catawbaw, and were then 300 from the sea. These new establishments are so much the more interesting, as by their distance from all commerce, agriculture is their sole resource; I mean that patriarchal agriculture which consists in producing only what is sufficient for their own consumption, without the hope of either sale or barter. These colonies therefore must necessarily be rendered equal to all their wants. It is easy to conceive that there is soon no deficiency of food, but it is also necessary that their flocks and their fields should furnish them with clothing, they must manufacture their own wool, and flax, into clothes and linen, they must prepare the hides to make shoes of them, &c. &c.; as to drink, they are obliged to content themselves with milk and water, until their apple-trees are large enough to bear fruit, or until they have been able to procure themselves stills, to distil their grain. In these troublesome times we should scarcely imagine in Europe, that nails are the articles the most wanted in these new colonies: for the axe and the saw can supply every other want. They contrive however to erect huts, and construct roofs without nails, but the work is by this means rendered much more tedious, and in such circumstances every body knows the value of time and labour. It was a natural question to ask such a cultivator what could bring him four hundred miles from home, and we learned from him that he carried on the trade of horse selling, the only commerce of which his country was susceptible, and by which people in the most easy circumstances endeavoured to augment their fortunes. In fact these animals multiply very fast in a country where there is abundant pasture; and as they are conducted without any expense, by grazing on the road, they become the most commodious article of exportation, for a country so far from any road or commerce. The conversation continued and brought us insensibly to the foot of the mountains. On the summit of one of them we discovered the house of Mr. Jefferson, which stands pre-eminent in these retirements; it was himself who built it and preferred this situation; for although he possessed considerable property in the neighbourhood, there was nothing to prevent him from fixing his residence wherever he thought proper. But it was a debt nature owed to a philosopher and a man of taste, that in his own possessions he should find a spot where he might best study and enjoy her. He calls his house Monticello, (in Italian, Little Mountain,) a very modest title, for it is situated upon a very lofty one, but which announces the owner's attachment to the language of Italy; and above all to the fine arts, of which that country was the cradle, and is still the asylum. As I had no farther occasion for a guide, I separated from the Irishman; and after ascending by a tolerably commodious road, for more than half an hour, we arrived at Monticello. This house, of which Mr. Jefferson was the architect, and often one of the workmen, is rather elegant, and in the Italian taste, though not without fault; it consists of one large square pavillion, the entrance of which is by two porticos ornamented with pillars. The ground floor consists chiefly of a very large lofty saloon, which is to be decorated entirely in the antique style: above it is a library of the same form, two small wings, with only a ground floor, and attic story, are joined to this pavillion, and communicate with the kitchen, offices, &c. which will form a kind of basement story over which runs a terrace. My object in this short description is only to show the difference between this, and the other houses of the country; for we may safely aver, that Mr. Jefferson is the first American who has consulted the fine arts to know how he should shelter himself from the weather. But it is on himself alone I ought to bestow my time. Let me describe to you a man, not yet forty, tall, and with a mild and pleasing countenance, but whose mind and understanding are ample substitutes for every exterior grace. An American, who without ever having quitted his own country, is at once a musician, skilled in drawing, a geometrician, an astronomer, a natural philosopher, legislator, and statesman. A senator of America, who sat for two years in that famous Congress which brought about the revolution; and which is never mentioned without respect, though unhappily not without regret: a governor of Virginia, who filled this difficult station during the invasions of Arnold, of Phillips, and of Cornwallis; a philosopher, in voluntary retirement from the world, and public business, because he loves the world, inasmuch only as he can flatter himself with being useful to mankind; and the minds of his countrymen are not yet in a condition either to bear the light, or to suffer contradiction. A mild and amiable wife, charming children, of whose education he himself takes charge, a house to embellish, great provisions to improve, and the arts and sciences to cultivate; these are what remain to Mr. Jefferson, after having played a principal character on the theatre of the new world, and which he preferred to the honourable commission of Minister Plenipotentiary in Europe. The visit which I made him was not unexpected, for he had long since invited me to come and pass a few days with him, in the centre of the mountains; notwithstanding which I found his first appearance serious, nay even cold; but before I had been two hours with him we were as intimate as if we had passed our whole lives together; walking, books, but above all, a conversation always varied and interesting, always supported by that sweet satisfaction experienced by two persons, who in communicating their sentiments and opinions, are invariably in unison, and who understand each other at the first hint, made four days pass away like so many minutes.

This conformity of sentiments and opinions on which I insist, because it constitutes my own eulogium, (and self-love must somewhere show itself,) this conformity, I say, was so perfect, that not only our taste was similar, but our predilections also, those partialities which cold methodical minds ridicule as enthusiastic, whilst sensible and animated ones cherish and adopt the glorious appellation. I recollect with pleasure that as we were conversing one evening over a bowl of punch, after Mrs. Jefferson had retired, our conversation turned on the poems of Ossian. It was a spark of electricity which passed rapidly from one to the other; we recollected the passages in those sublime poems, which particularly struck us, and entertained my fellow travellers, who fortunately knew English well, and were qualified to judge of their merit, though they had never read the poems. In our enthusiasm the book was sent for, and placed near the bowl, where, by their mutual aid, the night far advanced imperceptibly upon us. Sometimes natural philosophy, at others politics or the arts, were the topics of our conversation, for no object had escaped Mr. Jefferson; and it seemed as if from his youth he had placed his mind, as he had done his house, on an elevated situation,from which he might contemplate the universe.

A DINNER WITH MR. JEFFERSON IN PARIS

Abigail Adams

A LETTER TO MISS LUCY CRANCH

Auteuil, 7 May, 1785

I presume my dear Lucy would be disappointed, if her cousin did not deliver her a line from her aunt. Yet it is hardly fair to take up an exhausted pen to address a young lady, whose eager search after knowledge entitles her to every communication in my power.

I was in hopes to have visited several curiosities before your cousin left us, that I might have been able to relate them to my friends; but several engagements in the company way, and some preparation for his voyage, together with the necessary arrangements for our own journey, have so fully occupied me, that I fear I shall fail in my intentions. We are to dine to day with Mr. Jefferson. Should any thing occur there worthy of notice, it shall be the subject of my evening pen.

Well, my dear niece, I have returned from Mr. Jefferson's. When I got there, I found a pretty large company. It consisted of the Marquis and Madame de la Fayette; the Count and Countess de —; a French Count, who had been a general in America, but whose name I forget; Commodore Jones; Mr. Jarvis, an American gentleman, lately arrived, the same who married Amelia Broom, who says there is so strong a likeness between your cousin and his lady, that he is obliged to be upon his guard, lest he should think himself at home, and make some mistake; he appears a very sensible, agreeable gentleman; a Mr. Bowdoin, an American also; I ask the Chevalier de la Luzerne's pardon,—I had like to have forgotten him; Mr. Williams, of course,

From *Letters of Mrs. Adams, the Wife of John Adams,* with an introductory memoir by her grandson, Charles Francis Adams. Fourth edition. Boston, 1848.

as he always dines with Mr. Jefferson; and Mr. Short; though one of Mr. Jefferson's family, as he has been absent some time, I name him. He took a resolution that he would go into a French family at St. Germain, and acquire the language; and this is the only way for a foreigner to obtain it. I have often wished that I could not hear a word of English spoken. I think I have mentioned Mr. Short before, in some of my letters; he is about the stature of Mr. Tudor; a better figure, but much like him in looks and manners; consequently a favorite of mine. They have some customs very curious here. When company are invited to dine, if twenty gentlemen meet, they seldom or never sit down, but are standing or walking from one part of the room to the other, with their swords on, and their *chapeau de bras,* which is a very small silk hat, always worn under the arm. These they lay aside whilst they dine, but reassume them immediately after. I wonder how the fashion of standing crept in amongst a nation, who really deserve the appellation of polite; for in winter it shuts out all the fire from the ladies; I know I have suffered from it many times. At dinner, the ladies and gentlemen are mixed, and you converse with him who sits next you, rarely speaking to persons across the table, unless to ask if they will be served with any thing from your side. Conversation is never general, as with us; for, when the company quit the table, they fall into *tête-a-tête* of two and two, when the conversation is in a low voice, and a stranger, unacquainted with the customs of the country, would think that everybody had private business to transact.

Last evening, as we returned, the weather being very soft and pleasant, I proposed to your uncle to stop at the Tuileries and walk in the garden, which we did for an hour; there was, as usual, a collection of four or five thousand persons in the walks. . . .

A VISIT TO MONTICELLO IN 1796

The Duc de la Rochefoucauld-Liancourt

Monticello is situated four miles from Milford, in that chain of mountains which stretches from James-River to the Rappahannock, twenty-eight miles in front of the Blue-Ridge, and in a direction parallel to those mountains. This chain, which runs uninterrupted in its small extent, assumes successively the names of the West, South, and Green Mountains.

It is in the part known by the name of the South-Mountains that Monticello is situated. The house stands on the summit of the mountain, and the taste and arts of Europe have been consulted in the formation of its plan. Mr. Jefferson had commenced its construction before the American revolution; since that epocha his life has been constantly engaged in public affairs, and he has not been able to complete the execution of the whole extent of the project which it seems he had at first conceived. That part of the building which was finished has suffered from the suspension of the work, and Mr. Jefferson, who two years since resumed the habits and leisure of private life, is now employed in repairing the damage occasioned by this interruption, and still more by his absence; he continues his original plan, and even improves on it, by giving to his buildings more elevation and extent. He intends that they should consist only of one story, crowned with balustrades; and a dome is to be constructed in the center of the structure. The apartments will be large and convenient; the decoration, both outside and inside, simple, yet regular and elegant. Monticello, according to its first plan, was infinitely superior to all other houses in America, in point of taste and convenience; but at that time Mr. Jefferson had studied taste and the fine arts in books only. His

From *Travels Through the United States of North America, the Country of the Iroquois, and Upper Canada, in the Years, 1795, 1796, and 1797,* by the Duke de la Rochefoucault Liancourt. Second Edition. London, 1800. Volume 3.

travels in Europe have supplied him with models; he has appropri-
ated them to his design; and his new plan, the execution of which is
already much advanced, will be accomplished before the end of next
year, and then his house will certainly deserve to be ranked with the
most pleasant mansions in France and England.

Mr. Jefferson's house commands one of the most extensive prospects
you can meet with. On the east side, the front of the building, the eye
is not checked by any object, since the mountain on which the house
is seated commands all the neighbouring heights as far as the Chesa-
peak. The Atlantic might be seen were it not for the greatness of the
distance, which renders that prospect impossible. On the right and
left the eye commands the extensive valley that separates the Green,
South and West Mountains from the Blue-Ridge, and has no other
bounds but these high mountains, of which, on a clear day, you dis-
cern the chain on the right upwards of a hundred miles, far beyond
James-River; and on the left as far as Maryland, on the other side of
the Potowmack. Through some intervals, formed by the irregular
summits of the Blue-Mountains, you discover the Peaked-Ridge, a
chain of mountains placed between the Blue and North Mountains,
another more distant ridge. But in the back part the prospect is soon
interrupted by a mountain more elevated than that on which the
house is seated. The bounds of the view on this point, at so small a
distance, form a pleasant resting-place; as the immensity of prospect
it enjoys is, perhaps, already too vast. A considerable number of cultivated fields, houses, and barns, enliven and variegate the extensive
landscape, still more embellished by the beautiful and diversified
forms of mountains, in the whole chain of which not one resembles
another. The aid of fancy is, however, required to complete the enjoyment of this magnificent view; and she must picture to us those
plains and mountains such as population and culture will render
them in a greater or smaller number of years. The disproportion existing between the cultivated lands and those which are still covered
with forests as ancient as the globe, is at present much too great: and
even when that shall have been done away, the eye may perhaps
further wish to discover a broad river, a great mass of water—desti-
tute of which, the grandest and most extensive prospect is ever desti-
tute of an embellishment requisite to render it completely beautiful.

On this mountain, and in the surrounding valleys, on both banks
of the Rivanna, are situated the five thousand acres of land which Mr.

Jefferson possesses in this part of Virginia. Eleven hundred and twenty only are cultivated. The land left to the care of stewards has suffered as well as the buildings from the long absence of the master; according to the custom of the country it has been exhausted by successive culture. Its situation on declivities of hills and mountains renders a careful cultivation more necessary than is requisite in lands situated in a flat and even country; the common routine is more pernicious, and more judgement and mature thought are required than in a different soil. This forms at present the chief employment of Mr. Jefferson. But little accustomed to agricultural pursuits, he has drawn the principles of culture either from works which treat on this subject, or from conversation. Knowledge thus acquired often misleads, and is at all times insufficient in a country where agriculture is well understood; yet it is preferable to mere practical knowledge, in a country where a bad practice prevails, and where it is dangerous to follow the routine from which it is so difficult to depart. Above all, much good may be expected, if a contemplative mind, like that of Mr. Jefferson, which takes the theory for its guide, watches its application with discernment, and rectifies it according to the peculiar circumstances and nature of the country, climate and soil, and conformably to the experience which he daily acquires.

Pursuant to the ancient rotation, tobacco was cultivated four or five successive years; the land was then suffered to lie fallow, and then again succeeded crops of tobacco. The culture of tobacco being now almost entirely relinquished in this part of Virginia, the common rotation begins with wheat, followed by Indian corn, and then again wheat, until the exhausted soil loses every productive power; the field is then abandoned, and the cultivator proceeds to another, which he treats and abandons in the same manner, until he returns to the first, which has in the meantime recovered some of its productive faculties. The disproportion between the quantity of land which belongs to the planters and the hands they can employ in its culture, diminishes the inconvenience of this detestable method. The land, which never receives the least manure, supports a longer or shorter time this alternate cultivation of wheat and Indian corn, according to its nature and situation, and regains, according to the same circumstances, more or less speedily the power of producing new crops. If in the interval it be covered with heath and weeds, it frequently is again fit for cultivation at the end of eight or ten years; if not, a space of twenty years is not sufficient to render it capable of production. Planters who are not possessed of a sufficient quantity of land to let so much of it remain unproductive for such a length of time, fallow it in a year or two after it has borne wheat and Indian corn, during which time the fields serve as pasture, and are hereupon again cultivated in the same manner. In either case the land produces from five to six bushels of wheat, or from ten to fifteen bushels of Indian corn, the acre. To the produce of Indian corn must also be added one hundred pounds of leaves to every five bushels, or each barrel, of grain. These leaves are given as fodder to the cattle. It was in this manner that Mr. Jefferson's land had always been cultivated, and it is this system which he has very wisely relinquished. He has divided all his land under culture into four farms, and every farm into six [seven] fields of forty acres. Each farm consists, therefore, of two hundred and eighty acres. His system of rotation embraces seven years, and this is the reason why each farm has been divided into seven fields. In the first of these seven years wheat is cultivated; in the second, Indian corn; in the third, pease or potatoes; in the fourth, vetches; in the fifth, wheat; and in the sixth and seventh, clover. Thus each of his fields yields some produce every year, and his rotation of successive culture, while it prepares the soil for the following crop, increases its produce. The abundance of clover, potatoes, pease, &c. will enable him to keep sufficient cattle for manuring his land, which at present receives hardly any dung at all, independently of the great profit which he will in future derive from the sale of his cattle.

Each farm, under the direction of a particular steward or bailiff, is cultivated by four negroes, four negresses, four oxen, and four horses. The bailiffs, who in general manage their farms separately, assist each other during the harvest, as well as at any other time, when there is any pressing labour. The great declivity of the fields, which would render it extremely troublesome and tedious to carry the produce, even of each farm, to one common central point, has induced Mr. Jefferson to construct on each field a barn, sufficiently capacious to hold its produce in grain; the produce in forage is also housed there, but this is generally so great, that it becomes necessary to make stacks near the barns. The latter are constructed of trunks of trees, and the floors are boarded. The forests and slaves reduce the expence of these buildings to a mere trifle.

Mr. Jefferson possesses one of those excellent threshing-machines, which a few years since were invented in Scotland, and are already very common in England. This machine, the whole of which does not weigh two thousand pounds, is conveyed from one barn to another in a waggon, and threshes from one hundred and twenty to one hundred and fifty bushels a day. A worm, whose eggs are almost constantly deposited in the ear of the grain, renders it necessary to thresh the corn a short time after the harvest; in this case the heat, occasioned by the mixture of grain with its envelope, from which it is disengaged, but with which it continues mixed, destroys the vital principle of the egg, and protects the corn from the inconveniences of its being hatched. If the grain continued in the ears, without being speedily beaten, it would be destroyed by the worm, which would be excluded from the eggs. This scourge, however, spreads no farther northwards than the Potowmack, and is bounded to the west by the Blue Mountains. A few weeks after the corn has been beaten, it is free from all danger, winnowed and sent to market. The Virginia planters have generally their corn trodden out by horses; but this way is slow, and there is no country in the world where this operation requires more dispatch than in this part of Virginia. Besides the straw is bruised by the treading of horses. Mr. Jefferson hopes that his machine, which has already found some imitators among his neighbors, will be generally adopted in Virginia. In a country where all the inhabitants possess plenty of wood, this machine may be made at a very trifling expense.

Mr. Jefferson rates the average produce of an acre of land, in the present state of his farm, at eight bushels of wheat, eighteen bushels of Indian corn, and twenty hundred weight of clover. After the land has been duly manured, he may expect a produce twice, nay three times more considerable. But his land will never be dunged as much as in Europe. Black cattle and pigs, which in our country are either constantly kept on the farm, or at least returned thither every evening, and whose dung is carefully gathered and preserved either separate or mixed, according to circumstances, are here left grazing in the woods the whole year round. Mr. Jefferson keeps no more sheep than are necessary for the consumption of his own table. He cuts his clover but twice each season, and does not suffer his cattle to graze in his fields. The quality of his dung is therefore in proportion to the number of cattle which he can keep with his own fodder, and which he intends to buy at the beginning of winter to sell them again in spring; and the cattle kept in the vicinity of the barns where the forage is housed, will furnish manure only for the adjacent fields.

From an opinion entertained by Mr. Jefferson, that the heat of the sun destroys, or at least dries up in a great measure, the nutritious juices of the earth, he judges it necessary that it should be always covered. In order therefore to preserve his fields, as well as to multiply their produce, they never lie fallow. On the same principle he cuts his clover but twice a season, does not let the cattle feed on the grass, nor encloses his fields, which are merely divided by a single row of peach trees.

A long experience would be required to form a correct judgement, whether the loss of dung which this system occasions in his farms, and the known advantage of fields enclosed with ditches, especially in a declivous situation, where the earth from the higher grounds is constantly washed down by the rain, are fully compensated by the vegetative powers which he means thus to preserve in his fields. His system is entirely confined to himself; it is censured by some of his neighbours, who are also employed in improving their culture with ability and skill, but he adheres to it, and thinks it is founded on just observations.

Wheat, as has already been observed, is the chief object of cultivation in this country. The rise, which within these two years has taken place in the price of this article, has engaged the speculations of the planters, as well as the merchants. The population of Virginia, which is so inconsiderable in proportion to its extent, and so little collected in towns, would offer but a very precarious market for large numbers of cattle. Every planter has as many of them in the woods, as are required for the consumption of his family. The negroes, who form a considerable part of the population, eat but little meat, and this little is pork. Some farmers cultivate rye and oats, but they are few in number. Corn is sold here to the merchants of Milford or Charlotte-Ville, who ship it for Richmond, where it fetches a shilling more per bushel than in other places. Speculation or a pressing want of money may at times occasion variations in this manner of sale, but it is certainly the most common way. Money is very scarce in this district, and, bank-notes being unknown, trade is chiefly carried on by barter; the merchant, who receives the grain, returns its value in such commodities as the vender stands in need of.

Mr. Jefferson sold his wheat last year for two dollars and a half per bushel. He contends, that it is in the district whiter than in the environs of Richmond, and all other low countries, and that the bushel, which weighs there only from fifty-five to fifty-eight pounds, weighs on his farm from sixty to sixty-five.

In addition to the eleven hundred and twenty acres of land, divided into four farms, Mr. Jefferson sows a few acres with turnips, succory, and other feeds.

Before I leave his farm, I shall not forget to mention, that I have seen here a *drilling machine,* the name of which cannot be translated into French but by *"machine à femer en paquets."* By Mr. Jefferson's account, it has been invented in his neighbourhood. If this machine fully answers the good opinion which he entertains of it, the invention is the more fortunate, as by Arthur Young's assertion not one good drilling-machine is to be found in England. This machine, placed on a sort of plough-carriage, carries an iron, which gently opens the furrow as deeply as is required. Behind this iron and, in the upper part of the machine, is a small trough, containing the grain which is intended to be sown. This grain is taken out of the trough by a row of small receivers, sewed on a leather band, or ribbons, and turning round two pivots placed above each other at the distance of from seven to eight inches. The small receivers take the grain from the trough, and turn it over into a small conduit, which conveys it into the furrow made by the iron. The distance of one of those receivers from another determines that of the places in which the grain is deposited in the ground; and a harrow, fixed on the machine behind the conduits through which the feed falls into the furrow, covers it again. The *endless* chain of the receivers, which forms the merit of the machine, may be compared with that which is used for drawing water from a great depth, or still more properly with a heaver of flour in Evans's mills. It is put in motion by a light wheel, which moves along the ground as the machine advances, and is fixed in such a manner that it is not obstructed in its movements by the inequalities of the ground, nor even by the stones which it may find in its way. If this machine really answers the intended purpose, it is difficult to conceive why it should not have been invented before, as it is extremely simple, composed of movements well known, and of powers frequently employed. In my opinion it admits, however, of great improvements.

My readers will undoubtedly find that I bestow peculiar attention on agriculture, by speaking of Mr. Jefferson as a farmer, before I mention him in any other point of view.

They must be very ignorant of the history of America, who know not that Mr. Jefferson shared with George Washington, Franklin, John Adams, Mr. Jay, and a few others, the toils and dangers of the revolution, in all its different stages; that in the famous congress which guided and consolidated it, he displayed a boldness and firmness of character, a fund of talents and knowledge, and a steadiness of principles, which will hand down his name to posterity with glory, and ensure to him for ever the respect and gratitude of all friends of liberty. It was he, who in that famous congress, so respectable, and so much respected—in that congress, ever inaccessible to the seduction, fear, and apparent weakness of the people—who jointly with Mr. Lee, another deputy of Virginia, proposed the declaration of independence. It was he, who, supported principally by John Adams, pressed the deliberation on the subject, and carried it, bearing down the wary prudence of some of his colleagues, possessed of an equal share of patriotism, but less courage. It was he, who was charged with drawing up this master-piece of dignified wisdom, and patriotic pride. It was he, who being afterwards appointed governor of Virginia at the period of the invasion of Arnold and Cornwallis, acquired a peculiar claim on the gratitude of his fellow-citizens. It was he, who, as the first ambassador of the United States to France, filled at that momentous epocha that distinguished post to the satisfaction of both nations. In fine, it was he, who as Secretary of State in 1792, when the ridiculous and disorganizing pretensions of Mr. Genêt, and the lofty arrogance of the * * * minister, endeavoured alternately to abuse the political weakness of the United States, induced his government to speak a noble and independent language, which would have done credit to the most formidable power. The long correspondence carried on with these two designing agents would, from its just, profound, and able reasoning, be alone sufficient to confer on its author the reputation of an accomplished statesman.

Since the beginning of 1794, Mr. Jefferson has withdrawn from public affairs. This was the time when the malevolent sentiments of * * * * * * were displayed against the United States in the strongest manner, and when her unjust proceedings were resented with the utmost indignation from one end of America to the other. This was the most important epocha of the policy of the United States, because they proposed to act with energy and vigour. The preference which under those circumstances the President was accustomed to give to the advice of Mr. Hamilton, which continually carried along with it the opinion not only of General Knox, but also of Mr. Randolph, then attorney-general of the Union, over that of Mr. Jefferson, caused him to embrace this resolution. Immediately after this step, Mr. Jefferson was considered by the ruling party as the leader of Opposition; he was suspected of revolutionary views; he was accused of an intention to overturn the constitution of the United States, of being the enemy of his country, and of a wish to become a tribune of the people. It is sufficient to know that Mr. Jefferson is a man of sense, to feel the absurdity of these scandalous imputations; and whoever is acquainted with his virtue, must be astonished at their having ever been preferred against him. His speeches are those of a man firmly attached to the maintenance of the Union, of the present constitution, and of the independence of the United States. He is the declared enemy of every new system the introduction of which might be attempted, but he is a greater enemy of a kingly form of government than of any other. He is clearly of opinion, that the present constitution should be carefully preserved, and defended against all infringements arising from an extension of the prerogatives of the executive power. It was framed and accepted on republican principles, and it is his wish that it should remain a republican constitution. On several occasions I have heard him speak with great respect of the virtues of the President, and in terms of esteem of his sound and unerring judgement.

But the spirit of party is carried to excess in America; men who embrace the opinion of Mr. Jefferson, attack their opponents with imputations, no doubt, equally unfounded. In all party-proceedings neither reason nor justice can be expected from either side, and very seldom strict morality with respect to the means employed to serve the favourite cause; one cause alone appears good; every thing besides is deemed bad, nay criminal, and probity itself serves to mislead probity. Personal resentments assume the colour of public spirit, and frequently, when the most odious acts of injustice have been committed, and the most atrocious calumnies spread, but few members of the party are in the secret, and know that they are the effusions of injustice and false representation. The truth of these observations being evident to all men who have lived amidst parties, should lead to mutual toleration and forbearance.

In private life Mr. Jefferson displays a mild, easy and obliging temper, though he is somewhat cold and reserved. His conversation is of the most agreeable kind, and he possesses a stock of information not inferior to that of any other man. In Europe he would hold a distinguished rank among men of letters, and as such he has already appeared there; at present he is employed with activity and perseverance in the management of his farms and buildings; and he orders, directs, and pursues in the minutest detail every branch of business relative to them. I found him in the midst of the harvest, from which the scorching heat of the sun does not prevent his attendance. His negroes are nourished, clothed, and treated as well as white servants could be. As he cannot expect any assistance from the two small neighbouring towns, every article is made on his farm; his negroes are cabinet-makers, carpenters, masons, bricklayers, smiths, &c. The children he employs in a nail-manufactory, which yields already a considerable profit. The young and old negresses spin for the clothing of the rest. He animates them by rewards and distinctions; in fine, his superior mind directs the management of his domestic concerns with the same abilities, activity, and regularity, which he evinced in the conduct of public affairs, and which he is calculated to display in every situation of life. In the superintendence of his household he is assisted by his two daughters, Mrs. *Randolph* and Miss *Mary*, who are handsome, modest, and amiable women. They have been educated in France. Their father went often with them to the house of Madame *d'Enville*, my dear and respectable aunt, where they became acquainted with my family, and as the names of many of my friends are not unknown to them, we were able to converse of them together. It will be easily conceived, that this could not but excite in my mind strong sensations, and recollections, sometimes painful, yet generally sweet. Fifteen hundred leagues from our native country, in another world, and frequently given up to melancholy, we fancy ourselves restored to existence, and not utter strangers to happiness, when we hear our family and our friends mentioned by persons who have known them, who repeat their names, describe their persons, and express themselves on so interesting a subject in terms of kindness and benevolence.

Mr. Randolph is proprietor of a considerable plantation, contiguous to that of Mr. Jefferson's; he constantly spends the summer with him, and, from the affection he bears him, he seems to be his son rather than his son-in-law. Miss Maria constantly resides with her father; but as she is seventeen years old, and is remarkably handsome, she will, doubtless, soon find, that there are duties which it is still sweeter to perform than those of a daughter. Mr. Jefferson's philosophic turn of mind, his love of study, his excellent library, which supplies him with the means of satisfying it, and his friends, will undoubtedly help him to endure this loss, which moreover is not likely to become an absolute privation, as the second son-in-law of Mr. Jefferson may, like Mr. Randolph, reside in the vicinity of Monticello, and, if he be worthy of Miss Maria, will not be able to find any company more desirable than that of Mr. Jefferson.

The situation of Monticello exempts this place from the pestilential effluvia which produces so many diseases in the lower countries. From its great elevation it enjoys the purest air; and the sea-breeze, which is felt on shore about eight or nine o'clock in the morning, reaches Monticello at one or two in the afternoon, and somewhat refreshes the atmosphere, but the sun is intolerable from its scorching heat; as indeed it is in all the southern States. The places that enjoy some advantage over others are those which, like Monticello, are exposed to its direct rays, without experiencing their reflection from more elevated mountains, or neighbouring buildings.

Mr. Jefferson, in common with all landholders in America, imagines that his habitation is more healthy than any other; that it is as healthful as any in the finest parts of France; and that neither the ague, nor any other bilious distempers are ever observed at Monticello. This is undoubtedly true, because he asserts it in regard to himself, to his family, and his negroes, none of whom is attacked by these maladies; but I am, nevertheless, of opinion, that an European, who during this season should expose himself too much to the air from nine in the morning until six at night, would not long enjoy a good state of health. During the seven days I continued there, not one passed without some moments of rain, and yet the intensity of the heat was not in the least abated by it.

In Virginia mongrel negroes are found in greater number than in Carolina and Georgia; and I have even seen, especially at Mr. Jefferson's, slaves, who, neither in point of colour nor features, shewed the least trace of their original descent; but their mothers being slaves, they retain, of consequence, the same condition. This superior number of people of colour is owing to the superior antiquity of the settlement of Virginia, and to the class of stewards or baliffs, who are accused of producing this mongrel breed. They are liable to temptation, because they are young, and constantly amidst their slaves; and they enjoy the power of gratifying their passions, because they are despots. But the public opinion is so much against this intercourse between the white people and the black, that it is always by stealth, and transiently, the former satisfy their desires, as no white man is known to live regularly with a black woman.

Before I close this article I must say, that during my residence at Monticello I witnessed the indignation excited in all the planters of the neighbourhood by the cruel conduct of a master to his slave, whom he had flogged to such a degree as to leave him almost dead on the spot. Justice pursues this barbarous master, and all the other planters declared loudly their wish, that he may be severely punished, which seems not to admit of any doubt.

But it is time to take leave of Mr. Jefferson, whose kind reception has perfectly answered what I had a right to expect from his civility, from our former acquaintance in France, and from his particular connection with my relations and friends. Mr. Jefferson is invited by the republican party, named anti-federalists, to succeed George Washington in the President's chair of the United States, the latter having publicly declared, that he will not continue in this place, although he should be re-elected by the majority of the people of the United States. The other party is desirous of raising John Adams to that station, whose past services, and distinguished conduct in the cause of liberty, together with his place of Vice-President, give him also, no doubt, very powerful claims. In the present situation of the United States, divided as they are between two parties, which mutually accuse each other of perfidy and treason, and involved in political measures which it is equally difficult to retract and to pursue, this exalted station is surrounded with dangerous rocks; probity, a zealous attachment to the public cause, and the most eminent abilities, will not be sufficient to steer clear of them all. There exists no more in the United States a man in a situation similar to that of George Washington. On his first election, the confidence and gratitude of all America were concentrated in him. Such a man cannot exist in the present conjunction of circumstances, and the next president of the United States will be only the president of a party. Without being the enemy of one of the pretenders, one cannot, therefore, concur in the wish which he may entertain of being elevated to that eminent post. The fleeting enjoyment of the vanity of him, who shall be elected president, may, perhaps, be followed by the keenest pangs of grief in his remaining days. The two small towns of Charlotte-Ville and Milford trade in the produce of the country situated between them and the mountains. They also form a sort of depôt for the commodities of more distant parts of the country; especially Milford, where the navigation begins, and does not experience any further interruption from this point to Richmond. The water-carriage of merchandise and commodities costs one third of a dollar per hundred weight. The trade, which in a small degree is also carried on with money, is chiefly managed by barter, because money is scarce, and notes are not readily received. The price of land is from four to five dollars per acre, and the quantity of land to be sold is very considerable. Meat, that is, mutton, veal and lamb, fetches four pence a pound; beef cannot be had but in winter. The wages of white workmen, such as masons, carpenters, cabinet-makers, and smiths, amount to from one and a half dollar to two dollars a day, according as they are scarce in the country. During the present season masons obtain the highest pay; there are not four stone-masons in the whole county of Albemarle, where Monticello is situated, which I left on the 29th of June.

A VISIT TO MONTICELLO IN 1796

ISAAC WELD

The salubrity of the climate is equal also to that of any part of the United States; and the inhabitants have in consequence a healthy ruddy appearance. The female part of the peasantry, in particular, is totally different from that in the low country. Instead of the pale, sickly, debilitated beings, whom you meet with there, you find amongst these mountains many a one who would be a fit subject to be painted for a Lavinia. It is really delightful to behold the groups of females, assembled here, at times, to gather the cherries and other fruits, which grow in the greatest abundance in the neighbourhood of almost every habitation. Their shapes and complexions are charming; and the carelessness of their dresses, which consist of little more, in common, than a simple bodice and petticoat, makes them appear still more engaging.

The common people in this neighbourhood appeared to me to be of a more frank and open disposition, more inclined to hospitality, and to live more contentedly on what they possessed, than the people of the same class in any other part of the United States I passed through. From being able, however, to procure the necessaries of life upon very easy terms, they are rather of an indolent habit, and inclined to dissipation. Intoxication is very prevalent, and it is scarcely possible to meet with a man who does not begin the day with taking one, two, or more drams as soon as he rises. Brandy is the liquor which they principally use, and having the greatest abundance of peaches, they make it at a very trifling expence. There is hardly a house to be found with two rooms in it, but where the inhabitants have a still. The females do not fall into the habit of intoxication like the men, but in other respects they are equally disposed to pleasure, and their morals are in like manner relaxed.

From *Travels through the States of North America, and the Provinces of Upper and Lower Canada, during the years 1795, 1796, and 1797*, by Isaac Weld, Junior. Fourth Edition. London, 1800.

Along these mountains live several gentlemen of large landed property, who farm their own estates, as in the lower parts of Virginia; among the number is Mr. Jefferson, from whose seat I date this letter. His house is about three miles distant from Charlottesville, and two from Milton, which is on the head waters of Rivanna River. It is most singularly situated, being built upon the top of a small mountain, the apex of which has been cut off, so as to leave an area of about an acre and a half. At present it is in an unfinished state; but if carried on according to the plan laid down, it will be one of the most elegant private habitations in the United States. A large apartment is laid out for a library and museum, meant to extend the entire breadth of the house, the windows of which are to open into an extensive greenhouse and aviary. In the centre is another very spacious apartment, of an octagon form, reaching from the front to the rear of the house, the large folding glass doors of which, at each end, open under a portico. An apartment like this, extending from front to back, is very common in a Virginian house; it is called the saloon, and during summer is the one generally preferred by the family, on account of its being more airy and spacious than any other. The house commands a magnificent prospect on one side of the blue ridge of mountains for nearly forty miles, and on the opposite one, of the low country, in appearance like an extended heath covered with trees, the tops of which alone are visible. The mists and vapours arising from the low grounds give a continual variety to the scene. The mountain whereon the house stands is thickly wooded on one side, and walks are carried round it, with different degrees of obliquity, running into each other. On the south side is the garden and a large vineyard, that produces abundance of fine fruit.

Several attempts have been made in this neighbourhood to bring the manufacture of wine to perfection; none of them, however, have succeeded to the wish of the parties. A set of gentlemen once went to the expence even of bringing six Italians over for the purpose; but the vines which the Italians found growing here were different, as well as the soil, from what they had been in the habit of cultivating, and they were not much more successful in the business than the people of the country. We must not, however, from hence conclude, that good wine can never be manufactured upon these mountains. It is well known that the vines, and the mode of cultivating them, vary as much in different parts of Europe as the soil in one country differs from that in another. It will require some time, therefore, and different experiments, to ascertain the particular kind of vine, and the mode of cultivating it, best adapted to the soil of these mountains. This, however, having been once ascertained, there is every reason to suppose that the grape may be cultivated to the greatest perfection, as the climate is as favourable for the purpose as that of any country in Europe. By experiments also it is by no means improbable, that they will in process of time learn the best method of converting the juice of the fruit into wine.

REMINISCENCES OF PRESIDENT JEFFERSON

Margaret Bayard Smith

"And is this," said I, after my first interview with Mr. Jefferson, "the violent democrat, the vulgar demagogue, the bold atheist and profligate man I have so often heard denounced by the federalists? Can this man so meek and mild, yet dignified in his manners, with a voice so soft and low, with a countenance so benignant and intelligent, can he be that daring leader of a faction, that disturber of the peace, that enemy of all rank and order?" Mr. Smith, indeed, (himself a democrat) had given me a very different description of this celebrated individual; but his favourable opinion I attributed in a great measure to his political feelings, which led him zealously to support and exalt the party to which he belonged, especially its popular and almost idolized leader. Thus the virulence of party-spirit was somewhat neutralized, nay, I even entertained towards him the most kindly dispositions, knowing him to be not only politically but personally friendly to my husband; yet I did believe that he was an ambitious and violent demagogue, coarse and vulgar in his manners, awkward and rude in his appearance, for such had the public journals and private conversations of the federal party represented him to be.[1]

In December, 1800, a few days after Congress had for the first time met in our new Metropolis, I was one morning sitting alone in the parlour, when the servant opened the door and showed in a gentleman who wished to see my husband. The usual frankness and care with which I met strangers, were somewhat checked by the dignified and reserved air of the present visitor; but the chilled feeling was only momentary, for after taking the chair I offered him in a free and easy manner, and carelessly throwing his arm on the table near which he sat, he turned towards me a countenance beaming with an expression of benevolence and with a manner and voice

From *The First Forty Years of Washington Society*, by Margaret Bayard Smith. Edited by Gaillard Hunt. New York, 1906.

[1] Col. John Bayard, Mrs. Smith's father, was a federalist.

almost femininely soft and gentle, entered into conversation on the commonplace topics of the day, from which, before I was conscious of it, he had drawn me into observations of a more personal and interesting nature. I know not how it was, but there was something in his manner, his countenance and voice that at once unlocked my heart, and in answer to his casual enquiries concerning our situation in our *new home,* as he called it, I found myself frankly telling him what I liked or disliked in our present circumstances and abode. I knew not who he was, but the interest with which he listened to my artless details, induced the idea he was some intimate acquaintance or friend of Mr. Smith's and put me perfectly at my ease; in truth so kind and conciliating were his looks and manners that I forgot he was not a friend of my own, until on the opening of the door, Mr. Smith entered and introduced the stranger to me as *Mr. Jefferson.*

I felt my cheeks burn and my heart throb, and not a word more could I speak while he remained. Nay, such was my embarrassment I could scarcely listen to the conversation carried on between him and my husband. For several years he had been to me an object of peculiar interest. In fact my destiny, for on his success in the pending presidential election, or rather the success of the democratic party, (their interests were identical) my condition in life, my union with the man I loved, depended. In addition to this personal interest, I had long participated in my husband's political sentiments and anxieties, and looked upon Mr. Jefferson as the corner stone on which the edifice of republican liberty was to rest, looked upon him as the champion of human rights, the reformer of abuses, the head of the republican party, which must rise or fall with him, and on the triumph of the republican party I devoutly believed the security and welfare of my country depended. Notwithstanding those exalted views of Mr. Jefferson as a political character; and ardently eager as I was for his success, I retained my previously conceived ideas of the coarseness and vulgarity of his appearance and manners and was therefore equally awed and surprised, on discovering the stranger whose deportment was so dignified and gentlemanly, whose language was so refined, whose voice was so gentle, whose countenance was so benignant, to be no other than Thomas Jefferson. How instantaneously were all these preconceived prejudices dissipated, and in proportion to their strength, was the reaction that took place in my opinions and sentiments. I felt that I had been the victim of prejudice, that I had been unjust. The revolution of feeling was complete and from that moment my heart warmed to him with the most affectionate interest and I implicitly believed all that his friends and my husband believed and which the after experience of many years confirmed. Yes, not only was he great, but a truly good man!

The occasion of his present visit, was to make arrangements with Mr. Smith for the publication of his *Manual* for *Congress*, now called *Jefferson's manual*. The original was in his own neat, plain, but elegant handwriting. The manuscript was as legible as printing and its unadorned simplicity was emblematical of his character. It is still preserved by Mr. Smith and valued as a precious relique.

After the affair of business was settled, the conversation became general and Mr. Jefferson several times addressed himself to me; but although his manner was unchanged, my feelings were, and I could not recover sufficient ease to join in the conversation. He shook hands cordially with us both when he departed, and in a manner which said as plain as words could do, "I am your friend."

During part of the time that Mr. Jefferson was President of the Philosophical Society (in Philadelphia) Mr. Smith was its secretary. A prize offered by the society for the best system of national education, was gained by Mr. Smith. The merit of this essay, first attracted the notice of Mr. J. to its author; the personal acquaintance which then took place, led to a friendly intercourse which influenced the future destiny of my husband, as it was by Mr. Jefferson's advice, that he moved to Washington and established the *National Intelligencer*. Esteem for the talents and character of the editor first won Mr. Jefferson's regard, a regard which lasted to the end of his life and was a thousand times evinced by acts of personal kindness and confidence.

DINNER WITH PRESIDENT JEFFERSON

JOHN QUINCY ADAMS

November 3d. [1807] Nothing done in Senate. I am tired of this continued state of nihility at the commencement of a session, and will attempt something further to rescue the Senate from it. It will, however, be necessary to proceed with caution. I went into the House, where they were doing as little as nothing, and soon adjourned. Dined at the President's, with a company consisting chiefly of members of Congress—Messrs. Mitchell, Van Cortlandt, Verplanck, Van Allen, Johnson, Key, Magruder, Taylor, Calhoun, Butler, Thompson, and Eppes. I mentioned to Mr. Jefferson that the publishing committee had a letter from him to the Earl of Buchan, sent by him to the Massachusetts Historical Society with a view to its publication. But the committee thought it most consistent at least with delicacy to ascertain whether the publication would be not disagreeable to him. He asked whether it did not contain some free sentiments respecting the British Government. I told him it did. He then desired that it might not be published, *at least while he remained in public office;* and said he could not conceive why Lord Buchan could have sent it for publication, unless it were because it contained some compliments to himself. At dinner there was much amusing conversation between him and Dr. Mitchell [Samuel Latham Mitchell], though altogether desultory. There was, as usual, a dissertation upon wines; not very edifying. Mr. Jefferson said that the *Epicurean* philosophy came nearest to the truth, in his opinion, of any ancient system of philosophy, but that it had been misunderstood and misrepresented. He wished the work of Gassendi concerning it had been translated. It was the only accurate account of it extant. I mentioned Lucretius. He said that was only a part—only the *natural* philosophy. But the *moral* philosophy was only to be found in Gassendi. Dr. Mit-

From *Memoirs of John Quincy Adams, Comprising Portions of his Diary from 1795 to 1848,* edited by Charles Francis Adams. Philadelphia, 1874.

chell mentioned Mr. Fulton's steamboat as an invention of great importance. To which Mr. Jefferson, assenting, added, "and I think his torpedoes a valuable invention too." He then enlarged upon the certainty of their effect, and adverted to some of the obvious objections against them, which he contended were not conclusive. Dr. Mitchell's conversation was very various, of chemistry, of geography, and of natural philosophy; of oils, grasses, beasts, birds, petrifactions, and incrustations; Pike and Humboldt, Lewis and Barlow, and a long train of et cetera—for the Doctor knows a little of every thing, and is communicative of what he knows—which makes me delight in his company. Mr. Jefferson said that he had always been extremely fond of agriculture, and knew nothing about it, but the person who united with other sciences the greatest agricultural knowledge of any man he knew was Mr. Madison. He was the best farmer in the world. On the whole, it was one of the *agreeable* dinners I have had at Mr. Jefferson's.

MY GRANDFATHER, MR. JEFFERSON

Thomas Jefferson Randolph

In compliance with your request, I have committed to paper my reminiscences of Mr. Jefferson, as they, still green and fresh in my memory, have occurred to me. I was thirty-four years old when he died. . . .

His manner was dignified, reserved with strangers, but frank and cordial with his friends; his conversation cheerful, often sportive, and illustrated by anecdotes. He spoke only of the good qualities of men, which induced the belief that he knew little of them, but no one knew them better. I had formed this opinion, and on hearing him speak very favorably of men with defects known to myself, stated them to him, when he asked if I supposed he had not observed them, adding others not noted by me, and evincing much more accurate knowledge of the individual character than I possessed, observing, "My habit is to speak only of men's good qualities." When he believed that either men or measures were adverse to Republican institutions, he spoke of them with open and unqualified condemnation.

Standing himself on an elevated position, from his talents, education, fortune and political station, he was emphatically the friend of the working-man. On passing the home of a neighbor (Mr. Jesse Lewis), a blacksmith, remarkable for his probity, his integrity and his industry, and too wise, when past the meridian of life, to be ashamed to work at the trade that had made his fortune, he often remarked of him, "it is such men as that who constitute the wealth of a nation, not millionaires."

He never indulged in controversial conversation, because it often excited unpleasant feeling, and illustrated its inutility by the anecdote of two men who sat down candidly to discuss a subject, and each converted the other. His maxim was, that every man had a right to his own opinion on all subjects, and others were bound to respect

From a letter to Henry S. Randall, Appendix No. xxxvi, Volume iii, *The Life of Thomas Jefferson*, by Henry S. Randall. New York, 1858.

that right; hence, in conversation, if any one expressed a decided opinion differing from his own, he made no reply, but changed the subject; he believed men could always find subjects enough to converse on, which they agreed in opinion, omitting those upon which they differed; unreserved and candid himself, he was a listener, encouraging others to converse. His tact in the management of men was great; he inquiringly followed out adverse opinions to their results, leaving it to their friends to note the error into which it led them, taking up their doubts as important suggestions, never permitting a person to place himself upon the defensive, or if he did, changing the subject, so as not to fix him in a wrong opinion by controverting it. With men of fertile and ingenious minds, fond of suggesting objections to propositions stated, he would sometimes suggest the opposite of the conclusion to which he desired them to come, then assent to the force of their objections, and thus lead them to convert themselves. If information was sought, he gave it freely; if doubts were suggested, he explained them without reserve, never objecting to the scrutiny or canvass of his own opinion. As a public man, his friends complained that he spoke too freely, communicating more than they thought prudent. His powers of conversation were great, yet he always turned it to subjects most familiar to those with whom he conversed, whether laborer, mechanic or other; and if they displayed sound judgment and a knowledge of the subject, entered the information they gave, under appropriate heads, for reference, embodying thus a mass of facts upon the practical details of every-day life. His capacity to acquire knowledge was of the highest order; his application intense and untiring—his system and arrangement for the preservation of, and reference to the sources of his acquirements, most methodical and exact. The Hon. Littleton Waller Tazewell told me, that when a young man, his father being in the Senate, and Mr. Jefferson Vice-President, some case of impeachment coming on, he was sent with a note to Mr. Jefferson, asking some references to authorities on the subject. On the delivery of the note, he took a notebook from a drawer and instantly copied the references. On delivering them to his father, the latter observed he believed he had sent him chapter and verse for everything written on the subject. Of his voluminous correspondence, embracing upwards of forty thousand letters, written and received, and the private and public accounts of his whole life, he could in a moment lay his hand on any letter or receipt.

Shortly after his death, Mr. Madison expressed to me the opinion, that Mr. Jefferson would be found to be the most learned man that had ever devoted so much time to public life. He was economical, exact, and methodical in his expenses and accounts. The account books, now in my possession, of his Maître d'Hotel, at Paris and Washington, show the minutest details of household expenditures, and notes and figures in his own hand-writing, exhibit the closest personal inspection by himself, and a monthly analysis in a tabularized form of the expenditures in each item. His own numerous account books show the entry at the time, in his own hand, of each expenditure, however minute.

His manners were of that polished school of the Colonial Government, so remarkable in its day—under no circumstances violating any of those minor conventional observances which constitute the well-bred gentleman, courteous and considerate to all persons. On riding out with him, when a lad, we met a negro who bowed to us; he returned his bow, I did not; turning to me he asked, "do you permit a negro to be more of a gentleman than yourself?"

There was a little emulation endeavored to be excited among the older gentlemen of the neighborhood, in their gardening; and he who had peas first, announced his success by an invitation to the others to dine with him. A wealthy neighbor, without children, and fond of horticulture, generally triumphed. Mr. Jefferson, on one occasion had them first, and when his family reminded him that it was his right to invite the company, he replied "No, say nothing about it, it will be more agreeable to our friend to think that he never fails." In his person he was neat in the extreme. In early life, his dress, equipage, and appointments were fastidiously appropriate to his rank. As he grew old, although preserving his extreme neatness, his dress was plainer, and he was more indifferent to the appearance of his equipage. When at Paris, Philadelphia, and Washington, his furniture, table, servants, equipage and the *tout ensemble* of his establishment, were deemed highly appropriate to the position he held. He was a gentleman everywhere. On entering the Presidency, he determined not to have weekly levees, like his predecessors, and so announced. His political opponents determined that he should continue the custom. On the first levee day, he rode out at his usual hour of one o'clock, returning at three, and on entering the President's house, booted, whip in hand, soiled with his ride, found himself in a

Jefferson at 44.

OIL MINIATURE BY JOHN TRUMBULL

(Replica painted by Trumbull in London in 1788 for Angelica Church.)

Courtesy of the Metropolitan Museum of Art, New York

Jefferson at 46.

PLASTER BUST BY JEAN ANTOINE HOUDON, PARIS, 1789

Courtesy of The New-York Historical Society, New York City

crowd of ladies and gentlemen, fashionably dressed for the occasion. He greeted them with all the ease and courtesy of expected guests that he had been prepared to receive, exhibiting not the slightest indication of annoyance. They never again tried the experiment. At home, he desired to live like his neighbors, in the plain hospitality of a Virginia gentleman. It was a source of continued and deep regret to him, that the number of strangers who visited him, kept his neighbors from him; he said, "he had to exchange the society of his friends and neighbors for those whom he had never seen before, and never expected to see again."

Mr. Jefferson's hair, when young, was of a reddish cast, sandy as he advanced in years—his eye, hazel—dying in his 84th year, he had not lost a tooth, or had one defective; his skin, thin, peeling from his face on exposure to the sun, and giving it a tettered appearance; the superficial veins so weak, as upon the slightest blow, to cause extensive suffusions of blood, in early life, upon standing to write for any length of time, bursting beneath the skin: it, however, gave him no inconvenience. His countenance was mild and benignant, and attractive to strangers. While President, returning on horseback from court, with company whom he had invited to dinner, and who were, all but one or two, riding ahead of him, on reaching a stream over which there was no bridge, a man asked him to take him up behind and carry him over. The gentlemen in the rear coming up just as Mr. Jefferson had put him down and rode on, asked the man how it happened that he had permitted the others to pass without asking them? He replied, "From their looks I did not like to ask them—the old gentleman looked as if he would do it, and I asked him." He was very much surprised to hear that he had ridden behind the President of the United States. Mr. Jefferson's stature was commanding, six feet two and a half inches in height, well formed, indicating strength, activity, and robust health; his carriage, erect; step firm and elastic, which he preserved to his death; his temper, naturally strong, under perfect control—his courage, cool and impassive—no one ever knew him exhibit trepidation—his moral courage of the highest order—his will, firm and inflexible—it was remarked of him that he never abandoned a plan, a principle, or a friend. A bold and fearless rider, you saw at a glance, from his easy and confident seat, that he was master of his horse, which was usually the fine blood horse of Virginia. The only impatience of temper he ever exhibited, was with his horse, which he subdued to his will by a fearless application of the whip, on the slightest manifestation of restiveness. He retained to the last his fondness for riding on horseback; he rode within three weeks of his death, when from disease, debility and age, he mounted with difficulty. He rode with confidence, and never permitted a servant to accompany him; he was fond of solitary rides and musing, and said that the presence of a servant annoyed him. He held in little esteem the education that made men ignorant and helpless as to the common necessities of life; and he exemplified it by an incident which occurred to a young gentleman returned from Europe, where he had been educated. On riding out with his companions, the strap of his girth broke, at the hole of the buckle; and they, perceiving it an accident easily remedied, rode on and left him. A plain man coming up and seeing that his horse had made a circular path in the road in his impatience to get on, asked if he could aid him? "Oh, sir," replied the young man, "if you could only assist me to get it up to the next hole." "Suppose you let it out a hole or two on the other side," said the man.

His habits were regular and systematic. He was a miser of his time, rose always at dawn, wrote and read until breakfast, breakfasted early, and dined from three to four—after breakfast read for half an hour in his public rooms or portico, in summer—visited his garden and workshops—returned to his writing and reading till one, when he rode on horseback to three or half past—dined, and gave the evening to his family and company—retired at nine, and to bed from ten to eleven. He said in his last illness, that the sun had not caught him in bed for fifty years. He always made his own fire. He drank water but once a day, a single glass, when he returned from his ride. He ate heartily, and much vegetable food, preferring French cookery, because it made the meats more tender. He never drank ardent spirits or strong wines—such was his aversion to ardent spirits that when, in his last illness, his physician desired him to use brandy as an astringent, he could not induce him to take it strong enough.

RECOLLECTIONS OF JEFFERSON'S OVERSEER
AT MONTICELLO

EDMUND BACON

Chief Overseer at Monticello

as told to

HAMILTON W. PIERSON

"Mr. Jefferson was six feet two and a half inches high, well proportioned, and straight as a gun-barrel. He was like a fine horse—he had no surplus flesh. He had an iron constitution, and was very strong. He had a machine for measuring strength. There were very few men that I have seen try it, that were as strong in the arms as his son-in-law, Col. Thomas Mann Randolph; but Mr. Jefferson was stronger than he. He always enjoyed the best of health. I don't think he was ever really sick, until his last sickness. His skin was very clear and pure—just like he was in principle. He had blue eyes. His countenance was always mild and pleasant. You never saw it ruffled. No odds what happened, it always maintained the same expression. When I was sometimes very much fretted and disturbed, his countenance was perfectly unmoved. I remember one case in particular. We had about eleven thousand bushels of wheat in the mill, and coopers and every thing else employed. There was a big freshet—the first after the dam was finished. It was raining powerfully. I got up early in the morning, and went up to the dam. While I stood there, it began to break, and I stood and saw the freshet sweep it all away. I never felt worse. I did not know what we should do. I went up to see Mr. Jefferson. He had just come from breakfast. 'Well, sir,' said he, 'have you heard from the river?' I said, 'Yes, sir; I have just come from there with very bad news. The milldam is all swept away.' 'Well, sir,' said he, just as calm and quiet as though nothing had happened, 'we can't make a new dam this summer, but we will get Lewis' ferry-boat, with our own, and get the hands from all the quarters, and boat in rock enough in place of the dam, to answer for the present and next summer. I will send to Baltimore and get ship-bolts, and we will make a dam that the freshet can't wash away.' He then went on and explained to me in

From *Jefferson At Monticello. The Private Life of Thomas Jefferson. From entirely new Materials.* By Rev. Hamilton W. Pierson. New York, 1862.

detail just how he would have the dam built. We repaired the dam as he suggested, and the next summer we made a new dam, that I reckon must be there yet.

"Mr. Jefferson was always an early riser—arose at daybreak, or before. The sun never found him in bed. I used sometimes to think, when I went up there *very* early in the morning, that I would find him in bed; but there he would be before me, walking on the terrace.

"He never had a servant make a fire in his room in the morning, or at any other time, when he was at home. He always had a box filled with nice dry wood in his room, and when he wanted fire he would open it and put on the wood. He would always have a good many ashes in his fireplace, and when he went out he would cover up his fire very carefully, and when he came back he would uncover the coals and make on a fire for himself.

"He did not use tobacco in any form. He never used a profane word or any thing like it. He never played cards. I never saw a card in the house at Monticello, and I had particular orders from him to suppress card-playing among the negroes, who, you know, are generally very fond of it. I never saw any dancing in his house, and if there had been any there during the twenty years I was with him I should certainly have known it. He was never a great eater, but what he did eat he wanted to be very choice. He never eat much hog-meat. He often told me, as I was giving out meat for the servants, that what I gave one of them for a week would be more than he would use in six months. When he was coming home from Washington I generally knew it, and got ready for him, and waited at the house to give him the keys. After saying 'How are all?' and talking awhile, he would say, 'What have you got that is good?' I knew mighty well what suited him. He was especially fond of Guinea fowls; and for meat he preferred good beef, mutton, and lambs. Those broad-tailed sheep I told you about made the finest mutton I ever saw. Merriweather Lewis' mother made very nice hams, and every year I used to get a few from her for his special use. He was very fond of vegetables and fruit, and raised every variety of them. He was very ingenious. He invented a plough that was considered a great improvement on any that had ever been used. He got a great many premiums and medals for it. He planned his own carriage, buildings, garden, fences, and a good many other things. He was nearly always busy upon some plan or model.

"Every day, just as regularly as the day came, unless the weather was very bad, he would have his horse brought out and take his ride. The boy who took care of his horse knew what time he started, and would bring him out for him, and hitch him in his place. He generally started about nine o'clock. He was an uncommonly fine rider—sat easily upon his horse, and always had him in the most perfect control. After he returned from Washington he generally rode Brimmer or Tecumseh until I bought Eagle for him of Capt. John Graves, of Louisa Co., just before I left him.

"He was always very neat in his dress, wore short breeches and bright shoe buckles. When he rode on horseback he had a pair of overalls that he always put on.

"Mr. Jefferson never debarred himself from hearing any preacher that came along. There was a Mr. Hiter, a Baptist preacher, that used to preach occasionally at the Charlottesville Court House. He had no regular church, but was a kind of missionary — rode all over the country and preached. He wasn't much of a preacher, was uneducated, but he was a good man. Everybody had confidence in him, and they went to hear him on that account. Mr. Jefferson's nephews Peter Carr, Sam. Carr, and Dabney Carr thought a great deal of him. I have often heard them talk about him. Mr. Jefferson nearly always went to hear him when he came around. I remember his being there one day in particular. His servant came with him and brought a seat—a kind of camp stool, upon which he sat. After Mr. Jefferson got old and feeble, a servant used to go with him over the plantation, and carry that stool, so that he could sit down while he was waiting and attending to any kind of work that was going on. After the sermon there was a proposition to pass round the hat and raise money to buy the preacher a horse. Mr. Jefferson did not wait for the hat. I saw him unbutton his overalls, and get his hand into his pocket, and take out a handful of silver, I don't know how much. He then walked across the Court House to Mr. Hiter, and gave it into his hand. He bowed very politely to Mr. Jefferson, and seemed to be very much pleased.

"Mr. Jefferson was very liberal and kind to the poor. When he would come from Washington, the poor people all about the country would find it out immediately, and would come in crowds to Monticello to beg him. He would give them notes to me, directing me what to give them. I knew them all a great deal better than he did.

Many of them I knew were not worthy—were just lazy, good-for-nothing people, and I would not give them any thing. When I saw Mr. Jefferson I told him who they were, and that he ought not to encourage them in their laziness. He told me that when they came to him and told him their pitiful tales, he could not refuse them, and he did not know what to do. I told him to send them to me. He did so, but they never would come. They knew what to expect.

"In, I think, the year 1816, there was a very severe frost, and the corn was almost destroyed. It was so badly injured that it would hardly make bread, and it was thought that the stock was injured by eating it. There was a neighborhood at the base of the Blue Ridge where the frost did not injure the corn. They had a good crop, and the people were obliged to give them just what they were disposed to ask for it. I went up there and bought thirty barrels for Mr. Jefferson of a Mr. Massey—gave him ten dollars a barrel for it. That spring the poor trifling people came in crowds for corn. I sent the wagon after what I had bought, and by the time it would get back, Mr. Jefferson had given out so many of his little orders that it would pretty much take the load. I could hardly get it hauled as fast as he would give it away. I went to Mr. Jefferson and told him it never would do; we could not give ten dollars a barrel for corn, and haul it thirty miles, and give it away after that fashion. He said, What can I do? These people tell me they have no corn, and it will not do to let them suffer. I told him again, I could tell him what to do. Just send them all to me. I knew them all a great deal better than he did, and would give to all that were really deserving.

"There was an old woman named * * * * who used to trouble us a great deal. She had three daughters that were bad girls—large, strapping, lazy things—and the old woman would beg for them. One day she went to Mr. Jefferson in a mean old dress, and told him some pitiful story, and he gave her a note to me directing me to give her two bushels of meal. I did so. The same day she went to Mrs. Randolph and got three sides of bacon—middling meat. There was more than she could carry, and she had two of her daughters' illegitimate children to help her carry it home. When she got to the river, the old negro who attended the ferry was so mad to see her carrying off the meat that he would not ferry her over. So she laid the meat on the edge of the boat, and they ferried themselves across. When the boat struck the bank it jarred the meat off, and it went to the bottom of the river, and she had a great deal of trouble to get it.

"Afterwards she went to Mr. Jefferson and told him the meal I gave her was not good—would not make bread, and he sent her to me again. I told her the meal in the mill was all alike, and she could only get better by going to the Blue Ridge for the corn. She said she had no horse, it was too far to walk, and she could not go. I told her I would furnish her a mule. Mr. Jefferson had an old mule that must have been thirty or forty years old, called Dolphin. He was too old to work and we did not like to kill him. His hair grew very long, and he was a sight to look at. He was too old to jump much, but he would tear down the fence with his nose and go over the plantation pretty much as he pleased. I was very anxious to get rid of the mule and of the old woman too, and I thought that may be if I loaned her the mule she would not come back. So I told her she could have the old mule and go and get her corn. She came and stayed over night, so as to get an early start. My wife gave her a coffee sack, and I gave her an order on Massey, and she started off on old Dolphin. When she got up there the people knew nothing about her, and she could do so much better begging that, sure enough, she never came back at all. Mr. Jefferson used to enjoy telling people how I got rid of the old woman and Dolphin. She soon sent for her daughters. Two of them went up there; but a man named * * * * had taken up with one of them, and he moved her off into another neighborhood. He was a well-educated man, and much of a gentleman. His poor old mother was a mighty good woman, and she was so distressed about it that it almost made her crazy.

"Some six weeks or two months after the old woman had gone, I saw something moving about in the wheat-field, and, sure enough, there was Dolphin home again. After this there was a couple of Kentucky drovers named Scott and Dudley, from whom we used to buy a good many mules for the plantation, came along with a drove. I told them about the trouble we had with Dolphin. They said they would take him away so that he would trouble us no more, and I gave him to them. They sheared off his long hair and trimmed him up so that he looked quite well. They found one in the drove that matched him very well, and went on a few miles, and sold the pair to Hon. Hugh Nelson. He was a Congressman. He and Wm. C. Rives married sisters, daughters of Frank Walker. He was very wealthy and popular. I knew his father, too, Col. Walker. He used to wear short breeches and shoebuckles. It wasn't long before Dolphin was back, and I told Mr. Jefferson. He laughed and said, 'You treat him so much better than anybody else will, that he will come back and see you.' When Mr. Nelson's overseer came over for him I asked him how old he supposed he was. He said he could not tell. I then told him his history. He took him off, and we never saw any more of Dolphin.

"Mr. Jefferson was very particular in the transaction of all his business. He kept an account of every thing. Nothing was too small for him to keep an account of. He knew exactly how much of every thing was raised at each plantation, and what became of it; how much was sold, and how much fed out. Here is one of his little crop accounts. [Estimate of grain for forty weeks omitted.] All the overseers had such. Some of them used to grumble over them mightily. But I told them we were paid by Mr. Jefferson to attend to his business, and we ought to do it exactly as he wanted it done. One of them to whom I gave one of these little papers one day, after fretting a good deal about it, said, 'Well, I believe if Mr. Jefferson told you to go into the fire, you would follow his instructions.'

"I reported to Mr. Jefferson every dollar that I received and just what I paid it out for. The first day of every January I gave him a full list of all the servants, stock, and every thing on the place, so that he could see exactly what had been the gain or loss. In all his business transactions with people, he had every thing put down in writing, so that there was no chance for any misunderstanding. There was quite a village at Milton. It was the head of navigation for bateaux. A great deal of flour, grain, and other produce was brought from the western part of the State and shipped there, the wagons carrying back groceries and other things that the bateaux had brought from Richmond. This and other business employed a good many families. Nearly all the families in Milton were supplied with firewood from Mr. Jefferson's estate. They paid him five dollars a year for what wood they would burn in a fireplace. Mr. Jefferson wrote a blank form for me, and I made a written contract with all the people who got their firewood from his place, and once a year I went around and made collections. Here is the blank form that he wrote for me that I filled out, and from which I copied all these contracts for wood:

" 'These presents witness that the subscriber, Thomas Jefferson, has leased to the subscriber, James Marr, of the town of Milton, a right, in common with other lessees, to cut and take away suf-

ficient firewood for one fireplace from the lands of the said
Thomas Jefferson, on the south side of the road leading through
from Milton towards Colle, for the year which began on the 1st
day of October last past, and ending the 1st day of October of
the present year, 1813; the said James Marr yielding and paying
to the said Thomas Jefferson five dollars on the 1st day of October
closing the year, which he covenants to do, and it is further
agreed that this lease, and on the same conditions, shall continue
from year to year until notice to the contrary be given by either
party to the other. Witness their hands this 6th day of February,
1813.   Th. Jefferson.
                                                      James Marr.

    " 'Witness,
      " 'E. Bacon.'

"He was just as particular as this with all his business. Whenever I
engaged an overseer for him, or any kind of a mechanic, I always
made a written contract with him, that stated just what he was to do,
and just what pay he was to receive. In this way he avoided all difficulties with the men he employed. I used to write Mr. Jefferson's
name so often to contracts that I made for him, that I could imitate
his signature almost exactly. A good many people could not tell
whether he or I had written his name. Here is one of my contracts
with a carpenter, written and signed by myself for Mr. Jefferson:

    " 'It is agreed between Thomas Jefferson and Richard Durrett
    both of the county of Albemarle, that the said Durrett shall serve
    the said Jefferson one year as a carpenter. And the said Durrett
    does by these presents oblige himself to do whatever work the
    said Jefferson shall require in the business of carpenter work;
    and the said Durrett obliges himself to faithfully do his duty.
    The year commences on the day that the said Durrett shall take
    charge of the said Jefferson's employ; for which year's service
    the said Jefferson agrees to pay the said Durrett forty pounds,
    and to find him four hundred and fifty pounds of pork, and a
    peck of corn meal a week; or, in case the said Durrett should
    have three in the family, the said Jefferson agrees to find him
    three pecks a week, and to find him a cow to give milk from 15th
    April to 15th November. As witness our hands this 28th of
    October, 1812.   " 'Richard Durrett.
                       " 'E. Bacon, for
                         " 'Th. Jefferson.' "

RECOLLECTIONS OF A MONTICELLO SLAVE

Isaac Jefferson

I

Mr Jefferson was a tall strait-bodied man as ever you see, right square-shouldered: nary man in this town walked so straight as my old master: neat a built man as ever was seen in Vaginny, I reckon or any place—a straight-up man: long face, high nose.

Jefferson Randolph (Mr. Jefferson's grandson) nothing like him, except in height—tall, like him: not built like him: old master was a Straight-up man. Jefferson Randolph pretty much like his mother. Old master wore Vaginny cloth & a red waistcoat, (all the gentlemen wore red waistcoats in dem days) & small clothes: arter dat he used to wear red breeches too. Governor Page used to come up there to Monticello, wife & daughter wid him: drove four-in-hand: servants John, Molly & a postilion. Patrick Henry visited old master: coach & two: his face for all the world like the images of Bonaparte: would stay a week or more. Mann Page used to be at Monticello—a plain mild-looking man: his wife & daughter along with him. Dr Thomas Walker lived about ten miles from Monticello—a thin-faced man. John Walker (of Belvoir), his brother, owned a great many black people.

II

Old master was never seen to come out before breakfast—about 8 o'clock. If it was warm weather he would'nt ride out till evening: studied upstars till bell ring for dinner. When writing he had a copyin

From *Memoirs of a Monticello Slave: As Dictated to Charles Campbell in the 1840's by Isaac, one of Thomas Jefferson's Slaves*, edited by Rayford W. Logan. Charlottesville: The Tracy W. McGregor Library. Copyright 1951 by the University of Virginia. Reprinted by permission.

The work is divided into twenty brief chapters; the excerpts here are chapters eight, nine, and ten in their entirety. Footnotes omitted.

machine: while he was a-writin he would'nt suffer nobody to come in his room: had a dumb-waiter: When he wanted anything he had nothing to do but turn a crank & the dumb-waiter would bring him water or fruit on a plate or anything he wanted. Old master had abundance of books: sometimes would have twenty of 'em down on the floor at once: read fust one, then tother. Isaac has often wondered how old master came to have such a mighty head: read so many of them books: & when they go to him to ax him anything, he go right straight to the book & tell you all about it. He talked French & Italian. Madzay [Philip Mazzei] talked with him: his place was called Colle. General Redhazel [Riedesel] stayed there. He (Mazzei) lived at Monticello with old master some time: Didiot a Frenchman married his daughter Peggy: a heavy chunky looking woman — mighty handsome: She had a daughter Frances & a son Francis: called the daughter Franky. Mazzei brought to Monticello Antonine, Jovanini, Francis, Modena & Belligrini, all gardiners. My old master's garden was monstrous large: two rows of pailings, all round ten feet high.

III

Mr Jefferson had a clock in his kitchen at Monticello; never went into the kitchen except to wind up the clock. He never would have less than eight covers at dinner—if nobody at table but himself: had from eight to thirty two covers for dinner: plenty of wine, best old Antigua rum & cider: very fond of wine & water. Isaac never heard of his being disguised in drink. He kept three fiddles: played in the arternoons & sometimes arter supper. This was in his early time: When he begin to git so old he did'nt play: kept a spinnet made mostly in shape of a harpsichord: his daughter played on it. Mr Fauble a Frenchman that lived at Mr Walker's—a music-man used to come to Monticello & tune it. There was a forte piano & a guitar there: never seed anybody play on them but the French people. Isaac never could git acquainted with them: could hardly larn their names. Mr Jefferson always singing when ridin or walkin: hardly see him anywhar out doors but what he was a-singin: had a fine clear voice, sung minnits (minuets) & sich: fiddled in the parlor. Old master very kind to servants.

TWO PROPER YOUNG BOSTONIANS VISIT JEFFERSON IN 1815

I. Francis Calley Gray

On Thursday the 2nd of February, Mr. Ticknor and myself at half after three o'clock A.M. with each a small bundle left Richmond in the stage coach for Charlottesville in the County of Albemarle, in order to pay a visit to Mr. Jefferson, to whom we both had letters from Mr. Adams. At twelve miles from town we passed Tuckahoe Creek and soon after reached our breakfasting house, where, for the first time in my life, I sat down to table with the landlord and his wife, and we continued to do so during the whole ride to Charlotte. We were here told that all the people east of the mountains call those on the west [side] cohees, and are called by them Tuckahoes. The first is Irish, from which nation the valley was first settled, and the latter the Indian name of a vegetable growing in the southern and eastern parts of Virginia eaten by the hogs and perhaps formerly by the inhabitants. (This vegetable I once supposed to be the truffle, but find from Mr. Jefferson that it certainly is not so).

On leaving our breakfasting house we rode for sixteen miles through a fine country along the northern bank of [the] James River, soon quitting the country of coal in the centre of which is situated the inn at which we had breakfasted fourteen miles from Richmond. In several of the houses at which we stopped the whiskey drunk by the passengers did not form an item in the bill as they were private not public houses, i.e. they had no license.

At forty-five miles from Richmond according to the regular course of the stage we slept the first night. On the next day we passed through a miserable barren country covered with pines and found a ford at Junk Creek half frozen over and in quite as bad a state as the Matawoman. But our white driver with a spirit of industry far superior to that of the Maryland black, broke the ice before his horses and carried them through without difficulty. (A dead horse was lying

From *Thomas Jefferson in 1814: Being an account of a visit to Monticello, Virginia, by Francis Calley Gray*. With notes and introduction by Henry S. Rowe and T. Jefferson Coolidge, Jr. Boston, 1924. Copyright 1924 by the Club of Odd Volumes. Reprinted by permission.

The visit was in fact made in February 1815.

on the farther bank, who had been drowned in attempting to pass).
We overtook, particularly on the first day, many soldiers of the militia
who had been in the service of the United States six months at Norfolk without winter clothing, exposed to three epidemics which desolated their camp, the ague and fever, the typhus, and the throat dis-
temper, and were now discharged without pay. Many of them had
not sufficient money to procure food and some, as we were told, had
eaten nothing for thirty hours. The country constantly ascended as
we proceeded west and on Friday soon after noon, we crossed the
North River at the Ford near Milton and soon reached Monticello,
between which and another mountain belonging to Mr. Jefferson,
passed our road to Charlottesville, at which town we dined. It contains a few brick houses, a court house very large and a stone gaol,
the basement story of which is occupied as shops by a couple of
saddlers. This town, though the largest in this part of the country,
contains no meeting-house, nor is there any within seven miles, but
divine service is performed here in the court house every other Sunday. On Saturday it rained and at twelve o'clock we went from our
tavern in a hack to Monticello, three miles east of Charlottesville on
the same road we had passed the day before. Our road passed between Monticello and the S. W. mountain which is much higher and
along whose side runs the narrow path which led us between these
hills to the gate on the S. E. side of Monticello. The sides of both
these hills and the valley between them are covered with a noble
forest of oaks in all stages of growth and of decay. Their trunks
straight and tall put forth no branches till they reach a height almost
equal to the summits of our loftiest trees in New England. Those
which were rooted in the valley, in the richest soil overtopped many
which sprung from spots far above them on the side of the mountain.
The forest had evidently been abandoned to nature; some of the
trees were decaying from age, some were blasted, some were uprooted by the wind and some appeared even to have been twisted
from their trunks by the violence of a hurricane. They rendered the
approach to the house even at this season of the year extremely grand
and imposing. On reaching the house we found no bell nor knocker
and, entering through the hall in the parlour, saw a gentleman (Col.
Randolph), who took our letters to Mr. Jefferson.

Mr. Jefferson soon made his appearance. [In the margin: Mr. J.
72 yrs. old.] He is quite tall, six feet, one or two inches, face streaked

and speckled with red, light gray eyes, white hair, dressed in shoes of very thin soft leather with pointed toes and heels ascending in a peak behind, with very short quarters, grey worsted stockings, corduroy small clothes, blue waistcoat and coat, of stiff thick cloth made of the wool of his own merinos and badly manufactured, the buttons of his coat and small clothes of horn, and an under waistcoat flannel bound with red velvet. His figure bony, long and with broad shoulders, a true Virginian. He begged he might put up our carriage, send for our baggage and keep us with him some time. We assented and he left the room to give the necessary directions, sending as we requested the carriage back to Charlottesville. On looking round the room in which we sat the first thing which attracted our attention was the state of the chairs. They had leather bottoms stuffed with hair, but the bottoms were completely worn through and the hair sticking out in all directions; on the mantle-piece which was large and of marble were many books of all kinds, Livy, Orosius, Edinburg Review, 1 vol. of Edgeworth's Moral Tales, etc., etc. There were many miserable prints and some fine pictures hung round the room, among them two plans for the completion of the Capitol at Washington, one of them very elegant. A harpsichord stood in one corner of the room. There were four double windows from the wall to the floor of fine large glass and a recess in one side of the apartment. This was the breakfasting room. After half an hour's conversation with Mr. Jefferson and Col. Randolph, we were invited into the parlour where a fire was just kindled and a servant occupied in substituting a wooden pannel for a square of glass, which had been broken in one of the folding doors opening on the lawn. Mr. Jefferson had procured the glass for his house in Bohemia, where the price is so much the square foot whatever be the size of the glass purchased, and these panes were so large that, unable to replace the square in this part of the country, he had been obliged to send to Boston to have some glass made of sufficient size to replace that broken, and this had not yet been received.

We passed the whole forenoon, which was rainy, in conversation with Mr. Jefferson and Mr. Randolph and at four o'clock toddy was brought us, which neither of us took, and which was never after handed again, and we were ushered back into the breakfast room to dinner, where we were introduced to Mrs. Randolph, Miss Randolph, and Mr. T. J. Randolph. The rest of the family at table were Mrs.

Marks, a sister of Mr. Jefferson and two other daughters of Col. Randolph.

The drinking cups were of silver marked G. W. to T. J., the table liquors were beer and cider and after dinner wine. In the same room we took tea and at ten in the evening retired. Fires were lighted in our bedrooms and again in the morning before we rose and the beds were all in recesses.

At fifteen minutes after eight we heard the first breakfast bell and at nine, the second, whose sound assembled us in the breakfast room. We sat an hour after breakfast chatting with the ladies and then adjourned to the parlour. Mr. Jefferson gave us the catalogue of his books to examine and soon after conducted us to his library, and passed an hour there in pointing out to us its principal treasures. His collection of ancient classics was complete as to the authors, but very careless in the editions. They were generally interleaved with the best English Translations. The Ancient English authors were also all here and some very rare editions of them. A black letter Chaucer and the first of Milton's Paradise Lost, divided into ten books, were the most remarkable. A considerable number of books valuable to the Biblical critic were here, and various ancient editions of all the genuine and apocryphal books, Erasmus' edition, etc. Many of the most valuable works on the civil and maritime law and on diplomacy, together with a complete collection of the laws of the different states, those of Virginia in manuscript, and all the old elementary writers and reporters of England formed the legal library. The ancient and most distinguished modern historians render this department nearly complete, and the histories and descriptions of the Kingdoms of Asia were remarkably numerous. Rapin was here in French, though very rare in that language. Mr. Jefferson said that after all it was still the best history of England, for Hume's tory principles are to him insupportable. The best mode of counteracting their effect is, he thinks, to publish an edition of Hume expunging all those reflections and reasonings whose influence is so injurious. This has been attempted by Baxter, but he has injured the work by making other material abridgements. D'Avila was there in Italian, in Mr. Jefferson's opinion, one of the most entertaining books he ever read. I was surprised to find here two little volumes on Chronology by Count Potocki of St. Petersburg. Mr. Jefferson has also a fine collection of Saxon and Moeso Gothic books, among them Alfred's translations of Orosius and Boethius, and shewed us some attempts he had made at facilitating the study of this language. He thought the singularity of the letters one of the greatest difficulties and proposed publishing the Saxon books in four columns, the first to contain the Saxon, the second the same in Roman characters, the third a strictly verbal translation and the fourth a free one. Mr. Jefferson said the French dictionary of Trévoux was better than that of the Academy, thought Charron's "de la Sagesse" an excellent work and brought us a commentary and review on Montesquieu published by Duane the translator from the French manuscript [by Destutt de Tracy], which he called the best book on politics which had been published for a century and agreed with its author in his opinion of Montesquieu.

Of all branches of learning, however, that relating to the history of North and South America is the most perfectly displayed in this library. The collection on this subject is without a question the most valuable in the world. Here are the works of all the Spanish travellers in America and the great work of De Brie in which he has collected latin translations of the smaller works published by the earliest visitors of America whose original publications are now lost. It is finely printed and adorned with many plates. Here also is a copy of the letters of Fernando Cortes in Spanish, one of a small edition, and the copy retained by the Editor the Cardinal Archbishop of Toledo for himself, but given by him to the American Consul for Mr. Jefferson. This work contains the official letters of Cortes to his court, his maps of the country and plates representing the dresses, armour and other contents of the treasury of the Mexican Sovereigns. We saw here also some beautiful modern manuscripts, one of a work which had been suppressed in France, most of the Greek Romances.

Mr. Jefferson took us from his library into his bed chamber where, on a table before the fire, stood a polygraph with which he said he always wrote.

Mr. Jefferson took his accustomed ride before dinner and on his return told us that the ice was crowded and thick on the banks of the Rivanna and had carried away thirty feet of his mill-dam. This was all he said on the subject and from his manner I supposed his loss was probably about one or two hundred dollars, but on our ride back to Richmond we heard it everywhere spoken of as a serious loss and the countrymen, some of them, even estimated it at $30,000. This to be sure must have been a most wonderful miscalculation, but no doubt the loss was serious.

TWO PROPER YOUNG BOSTONIANS VISIT
JEFFERSON IN 1815

II. George Ticknor

A LETTER TO MR. E. TICKNOR

Charlottesville, February 7, 1815

We left Charlottesville on Saturday morning, the 4th of February, for Mr. Jefferson's. He lives, you know, on a mountain, which he has named Monticello, and which, perhaps you do not know, is a synonyme for Carter's mountain. The ascent of this steep, savage hill, was as pensive and slow as Satan's ascent to Paradise. We were obliged to wind two thirds round its sides before we reached the artificial lawn on which the house stands; and when we had arrived there, we were about six hundred feet, I understand, above the stream which flows at its foot. It is an abrupt mountain. The fine growth of ancient forest-trees conceals its sides and shades part of its summit. The prospect is admirable. . . . The lawn on the top, as I hinted, was artificially formed by cutting down the peak of the height. In its centre, and facing the southeast, Mr. Jefferson has placed his house, which is of brick, two stories high in the wings, with a piazza in front of a receding centre. It is built, I suppose, in the French style. You enter, by a glass folding-door, into a hall which reminds you of Fielding's "Man of the Mountain," by the strange furniture of its walls. On one side hang the head and horns of an elk, a deer, and a buffalo; another is covered with curiosities which Lewis and Clarke found in their wild and perilous expedition. On the third, among many other striking matters, was the head of a mammoth, or, as Cuvier calls it, a mastodon, containing the only *os frontis*, Mr. Jefferson tells me, that has yet been found. On the fourth side, in odd union with a fine painting of the Repentance of Saint Peter, is an Indian map on leather, of the southern waters of the Missouri, and an Indian representation of a bloody battle, handed down in their traditions.

From *Life, Letters, and Journals of George Ticknor*. Boston, 1876.

Through this hall—or rather museum—we passed to the dining-room, and sent our letters to Mr. Jefferson, who was of course in his study. Here again we found ourselves surrounded with paintings that seemed good.

We had hardly time to glance at the pictures before Mr. Jefferson entered; and if I was astonished to find Mr. Madison short and somewhat awkward, I was doubly astonished to find Mr. Jefferson, whom I had always supposed to be a small man, more than six feet high, with dignity in his appearance, and ease and graciousness in his manners. . . . He rang, and sent to Charlottesville for our baggage, and, as dinner approached, took us to the drawing-room,—a large and rather elegant room, twenty or thirty feet high,—which, with the hall I have described, composed the whole centre of the house, from top to bottom. The floor of this room is tessellated. It is formed of alternate diamonds of cherry and beech, and kept polished as highly as if it were of fine mahogany.

Here are the best pictures of the collection. Over the fireplace is the Laughing and Weeping Philosophers, dividing the world between them; on its right, the earliest navigators to America,—Columbus, Americus Vespuccius, Magellan, etc.,—copied, Mr. Jefferson said, from originals in the Florence Gallery. Farther round, Mr. Madison in the plain, Quaker-like dress of his youth, Lafayette in his Revolutionary uniform, and Franklin in the dress in which we always see him. There were other pictures, and a copy of Raphael's Transfiguration.

We conversed on various subjects until dinner-time, and at dinner were introduced to the grown members of his family. These are his only remaining child, Mrs. Randolph, her husband, Colonel Randolph, and the two oldest of their unmarried children, Thomas Jefferson and Ellen; and I assure you I have seldom met a pleasanter party.

The evening passed away pleasantly in general conversation, of which Mr. Jefferson was necessarily the leader. I shall probably surprise you by saying that, in conversation, he reminded me of Dr. Freeman. He has the same discursive manner and love of paradox, with the same appearance of sobriety and cool reason. He seems equally fond of American antiquities, and especially the antiquities of his native State, and talks of them with freedom and, I suppose, accuracy. He has, too, the appearance of that fairness and simplicity which Dr. Freeman has; and, if the parallel holds no further here, they will again meet on the ground of their love of old books and young society.

On Sunday morning, after breakfast, Mr. Jefferson asked me into his library, and there I spent the forenoon of that day as I had that of yesterday. This collection of books, now so much talked about, consists of about seven thousand volumes, contained in a suite of fine rooms, and is arranged in the catalogue, and on the shelves, according to the divisions and subdivisions of human learning by Lord Bacon. In so short a time I could not, of course, estimate its value, even if I had been competent to do so.

Perhaps the most curious single specimen—or, at least, the most characteristic of the man and expressive of his hatred of royalty— was a collection which he had bound up in six volumes, and lettered "The Book of Kings," consisting of the "Memoires de la Princesse de Bareith," two volumes; "Les Memoires de la Comtesse de la Motte," two volumes; the "Trial of the Duke of York," one volume; and *"The Book,"* one volume. These documents of regal scandal seemed to be favorites with the philosopher, who pointed them out to me with a satisfaction somewhat inconsistent with the measured gravity he claims in relation to such subjects generally.

On Monday morning I spent a couple of hours with him in his study. He gave me there an account of the manner in which he passed the portion of his time in Europe which he could rescue from public business; told me that while he was in France he had formed a plan of going to Italy, Sicily, and Greece, and that he should have executed it, if he had not left Europe in the full conviction that he should immediately return there, and find a better opportunity. He spoke of my intention to go, and, without my even hinting any purpose to ask him for letters, told me that he was now seventy-two years old, and that most of his friends and correspondents in Europe had died in the course of the twenty-seven years since he left France, but that he would gladly furnish me with the means of becoming acquainted with some of the remainder, if I would give him a month's notice, and regretted that their number was so reduced.

The afternoon and evening passed as on the two days previous; for everything is done with such regularity, that when you know how one day is filled, I suppose you know how it is with the others. At eight o'clock the first bell is rung in the great hall, and at nine the

second summons you to the breakfast-room, where you find everything ready. After breakfast everyone goes, as inclination leads him,
to his chamber, the drawing room, or the library. The children retire
to their school-room with their mother, Mr. Jefferson rides to his
mills on the Rivanna, and returns at about twelve. At half past three
the great bell rings, and those who are disposed resort to the drawing-
room, and the rest go to the dining-room at the second call of the
bell, which is at four o'clock. The dinner was always choice, and
served in the French style; but no wine was set on the table till the
cloth was removed. The ladies sat until about six, then retired, but
returned with the tea-tray a little before seven, and spent the evening with the gentlemen; which was always pleasant, for they are
obviously accustomed to join in the conversation, however high the
topic may be. At about half past ten, which seemed to be their usual
hour of retiring, I went to my chamber, found there a fire, candle,
and a servant in waiting to receive my orders for the morning, and
in the morning was waked by his return to build the fire.

To-day, Tuesday, we told Mr. Jefferson that we should leave Monticello in the afternoon. He seemed much surprised, and said as much
as politeness would permit on the badness of the roads and the prospect of bad weather, to induce us to remain longer. It was evident, I
thought, that they had calculated on our staying a week. At dinner,
Mr. Jefferson again urged us to stay, not in an oppressive way, but
with kind politeness; and when the horses were at the door, asked
if he should not send them away; but, as he found us resolved on
going, he bade us farewell in the heartiest style of Southern hospitality, after thrice reminding me that I must write to him for letters
to his friends in Europe. I came away almost regretting that the
coach returned so soon, and thinking, with General Hamilton, that
he was a perfect gentleman in his own house.

Two little incidents which occurred while we were at Monticello
should not be passed by. The night before we left, young Randolph
came up late from Charlottesville, and brought the astounding news
that the English had been defeated before New Orleans by General
Jackson. Mr. Jefferson had made up his mind that the city would fall,
and told me that the English would hold it permanently— or for some
time—by a force of Sepoys from the East Indies. He had gone to bed,
like the rest of us; but of course his grandson went to his chamber
with the paper containing the news. But the old philosopher refused

to open his door, saying he could wait till the morning; and when we met at breakfast I found he had not yet seen it.

One morning, when he came back from his ride, he told Mr. Randolph, very quietly, that the dam had been carried away the night before. From his manner, I supposed it an affair of small consequence, but at Charlottesville, on my way to Richmond, I found the country ringing with it. Mr. Jefferson's great dam was gone, and it would cost $30,000 to rebuild it.

There is a breathing of notional philosophy in Mr. Jefferson,—in his dress, his house, his conversation. His setness, for instance, in wearing very sharp toed shoes, corduroy small-clothes, and red plush waistcoat, which have been laughed at till he might perhaps wisely have dismissed them.

So, though he told me he thought Charron, "De la Sagesse," the best treatise on moral philosophy ever written, and an obscure Review of Montesquieu, by Dupont de Nemours, the best political work that had been printed for fifty years,—though he talked very freely of the natural impossibility that one generation should bind another to pay a public debt, and of the expediency of vesting all the legislative authority of a State in one branch, and the executive authority in another, and leaving them to govern it by joint discretion,—I considered such opinions simply as curious *indicia* of an extraordinary character.

A VISIT TO MONTICELLO IN 1817

Francis Hall

Having an introduction to Mr. Jefferson, I ascended his *little mountain* on a fine morning, which gave the situation its due effect. The whole of the sides and base are covered with forest, through which roads have been cut circularly, so that the winding may be shortened or prolonged at pleasure: the summit is an open lawn, near to the south side of which, the house is built, with its garden just descending the brow: the saloon, or central hall, is ornamented with several pieces of antique sculpture, Indian arms, Mammoth bones, and other curiosities collected from various parts of the Union. I found Mr. Jefferson tall in person, but stooping and lean with old age; thus exhibiting that fortunate mode of bodily decay, which strips the frame of its most cumbersome parts, leaving it still strength of muscle and activity of limb: his deportment was exactly such as the Marquis de Chastellux describes it, above thirty years ago: "At first serious, nay even cold," but in a very short time relaxing into a most agreeable amenity; with an unabated flow of conversation on the most interesting topics, discust in the most gentlemanly, and philosophical manner. I walked with him round his grounds, to visit his pet trees, and improvements of various kinds; during the walk, he pointed out to my observation a conical mountain, rising singly at the edge of the southern horizon of the landscape: its distance he said, was 40 miles, and its dimensions those of the greater Egyptian pyramid; so that it accurately represents the appearance of the pyramid at the same distance; there is a small cleft visible on its summit, through which, the true meridian of Monticello exactly passes: its most singular property, however, is, that on different occasions it *looms*, or alters its appearance, becoming sometimes cylindrical, sometimes square, and sometimes assuming the form of an inverted cone. Mr. Jefferson

From *Travels in Canada, and the United States, in 1816 and 1817*, by Lieut. Francis Hall, 14th Light Dragoons, H. P. Second Edition. London, 1819.

had not been able to connect this phenomenon with any particular season, or state of the atmosphere, except, that it most commonly occurred in the forenoon; he observed, that it was not only wholly unaccounted for by the laws of vision, but that it had not as yet engaged the attention of philosophers so far as to acquire a name; that of *looming*, being in fact, a term applied by sailors, to appearances of a similar kind at sea. The Blue Mountains are also observed to loom, though not in so remarkable a degree.

It must be interesting to recall and preserve the political sentiments of a man who has held so distinguished a station in public life as Mr. Jefferson. He seemed to consider much of the freedom and happiness of America, to arise from local circumstances: "Our population," he observed, "has an elasticity, by which it would fly off from oppressive taxation." He instanced the beneficial effects of a free government, in the case of New Orleans, where many proprietors who were in a state of indigence under the dominion of Spain, have risen to sudden wealth, solely by the rise in the value of land, which followed a change of government. Their ingenuity in mechanical inventions, agricultural improvements, and that mass of general information to be found among Americans of all ranks and conditions, he ascribed to that ease of circumstances, which afforded them leisure to cultivate their minds, after the cultivation of their lands was completed. —In fact, I have frequently been surprised to find mathematical and other useful works in houses which seemed to have little pretension to the luxury of learning. Another cause, Mr. Jefferson observed, might be discovered in the many court and county meetings, which brought men frequently together on public business, and thus gave them habits, both of thinking and of expressing their thoughts on subjects, which in other countries are confined to the consideration of the privileged few. Mr. Jefferson has not the reputation of being very friendly to England: we should, however, be aware, that a partiality in this respect, is not absolutely the duty of an American citizen; neither is it to be expected that the policy of our government should be regarded in foreign countries, with the same complacency with which it is looked upon by ourselves: but whatever may be his sentiments in this respect, politeness naturally represt any offensive expression of them: he talked of our affairs with candour, and apparent good-will, though leaning, perhaps, to the gloomier side of the picture. He did not perceive by what means we could be extricated from our present financial embarrassments, without some kind of revolution in our government: on my replying, that our habits were remarkably steady, and that great sacrifices would be made to prevent a violent catastrophe, he acceded to the observation, but demanded, if those who made the sacrifices, would not require some political reformation in return. His repugnance was strongly marked to the despotic principles of Bonaparte, and he seemed to consider France under Louis XVI. as scarcely capable of a republican form of government; but added, that the present generation of Frenchmen had grown up with sounder notions, which would probably lead to their emancipation. . . .

I slept a night at Monticello, and left it in the morning, with such a feeling as the traveller quits the mouldering remains of a Grecian temple, or the pilgrim a fountain in the desert. It would indeed argue great torpor, both of understanding and heart, to have looked without veneration and interest, on the man who drew up the declaration of American independence; who shared in the councils by which her freedom was established; whom the unbought voice of his fellow-citizens called to the exercise of a dignity, from which his own moderation impelled him, when such example was most salutary, to withdraw; and who, while he dedicates the evening of his glorious days to the pursuits of science and literature, shuns none of the humbler duties of private life; but, having filled a seat higher than that of kings, succeeds with graceful dignity to that of the good neighbour, and becomes the friendly adviser, lawyer, physician, and even gardener of his vicinity. This is the "still small voice" of philosophy, deeper and holier than the lightnings and earthquakes which have preceded it. What monarch would venture thus to exhibit himself in the nakedness of his humanity? On what royal brow would the laurel replace the diadem? But they who are born and educated to be kings, are not expected to be philosophers. —That is a just answer, though no great compliment either to the governors or the governed.

My travels had nearly terminated at the Rivannah, which flows at the foot of Monticello: in trying to ford it, my horse and waggon were carried down the stream: I escaped with my servant, and by the aid of Mr. Jefferson's domestics, we finally succeeded in extricating my equipage from a watery grave. The road to Richmond follows the James River, and has few features to attract notice. There are no towns, and very few villages. . . .

A VISIT TO MONTICELLO IN 1824

DANIEL WEBSTER

Mr. Jefferson is now between eighty-one and eighty-two, above six feet high, of an ample long frame, rather thin and spare. His head, which is not peculiar in its shape, is set rather forward on his shoulders; and his neck being long, there is, when he is walking or conversing, an habitual protrusion of it. It is still well covered with hair, which having been once red, and now turning gray, is of an indistinct sandy color.

His eyes are small, very light, and now neither brilliant nor striking. His chin is rather long, but not pointed. His nose small, regular in its outline, and the nostrils a little elevated. His mouth is well formed and still filled with teeth; it is strongly compressed, bearing an expression of contentment and bears the marks of age and cutaneous affection. His limbs are uncommonly long; his hands and feet very large, and his wrists of an extraordinary size. His walk is not precise and military, but easy and swinging. He stoops a little, not so much from age as from a natural formation. When sitting, he appears short, partly from a rather lounging habit of sitting, and partly from the disproportionate length of his limbs.

His dress, when in the house, is a gray surtout coat, kerseymere stuff waistcoat, with an under one faced with some material of a dingy red. His pantaloons are very long and loose, and of the same color as his coat. His stockings are woollen either white or gray; and his shoes of the kind that bear his name. His whole dress is very much neglected, but not slovenly. He wears a common round hat. His dress, when on horseback, is a gray straight-bodied coat and a spencer of the same material, both fastened with large pearl buttons. When we first saw him, he was riding; and, in addition to the above articles of apparel, wore round his throat a knit white woollen tippet,

From *The Writings and Speeches of Daniel Webster*, edited by Fletcher Webster. Boston, 1903. Volume 17.

in the place of a cravat, and black velvet gaiters under his pantaloons. His general appearance indicates an extraordinary degree of health, vivacity, and spirit. His sight is still good, for he needs glasses only in the evening. His hearing is generally good, but a number of voices in animated conversation confuses it.

Mr. Jefferson rises in the morning as soon as he can see the hands of his clock, which is directly opposite his bed, and examines his thermometer immediately, as he keeps a regular meteorological diary. He employs himself chiefly in writing till breakfast, which is at nine. From that time, till dinner, he is in his library, excepting that in fair weather he rides on horseback from seven to fourteen miles. Dines at four, returns to the drawing-room at six, when coffee is brought in, and passes the evening till nine in conversation. His habit of retiring at that hour is so strong, that it has become essential to his health and comfort. His diet is simple, but he seems restrained only by his taste. His breakfast is tea and coffee, bread always fresh from the oven, of which he does not seem afraid, with sometimes a slight accompaniment of cold meat. He enjoys his dinner well, taking with his meat a large portion of vegetables. He has a strong preference for the wines of the continent, of which he has many sorts of excellent quality, having been more than commonly successful in his mode of importing and preserving them. Among others, we found the following, which are very rare in this country, and apparently not at all injured by transportation: L'Ednau, Muscat, Samian, and Blanchette de Limoux. Dinner is served in half Virginian, half French style, in good taste and abundance. No wine is put on the table till the cloth is removed.

In conversation, Mr. Jefferson is easy and natural, and apparently not ambitious; it is not loud, as challenging general attention, but usually addressed to the person next him. The topics, when not selected to suit the character and feelings of his auditor, are those subjects with which his mind seems particularly occupied; and these, at present, may be said to be science and letters, and especially the University of Virginia, which is coming into existence almost entirely from his exertions, and will rise, it is to be hoped, to usefulness and credit under his continued care. When we were with him, his favorite subjects were Greek and Anglo-Saxon, historical recollections of the times and events of the Revolution, and of his residence in France from 1783-4 to 1789.

A VISIT TO MONTICELLO IN 1825

BERNHARD, DUKE OF SAXE-WEIMAR EISENACH

On the 25th of November, we set out for Charlotteville, thirty-two miles distant, passing over the Blue Ridge. The road is through a country little cultivated, and without a single village; and the number of separate houses could scarcely be more than a dozen. After we had gone about five miles, we arrived at the western base of the Blue Ridge, which affords an agreeable view, being overgrown with wood up to the top. Then we entered a narrow valley, and when the road began to ascend, we alighted and walked over the mountains. I was surprised to find the road less steep than I expected, and it was also pretty good. From elevated places, the day being not so foggy as the preceding ones, we had many fine views of the mountains. The wood consisted of oak trees, and different kinds of nut trees; here and there were colossal fir, larch, Weymouth's pine and acacia trees. Evergreen rhododendrons, for which some amateurs in Europe spend a great deal of money, are growing here in abundance, also wild vines, which wind themselves round the trees. The prospect on the mountains would have been more pleasant, had there been some marks of human dwellings, but we saw only two miserable log houses, inhabited by dirty and ragged negro families, on the whole tract for eight miles over the mountains; and we met but a few carts loaded with flour.

Having crossed the Blue Ridge, we arrived at a good-looking country house, and a mill called Brown's Farm, situated at the base of the mountains, and took our dinner there. This house is surrounded by fields belonging to it, and from its piazza there is a very fine view of the mountains. From this place we had yet twenty miles to Charlotteville. The road became less hilly, at least we had no more mountains to cross; however, the road continued very rough, and we were

From *Travels Through North America. During the Years 1825 and 1826*, by His Highness, Bernhard, Duke of Saxe-Weimar Eisenach. Philadelphia, 1828.

rudely jolted. About eight o'clock in the evening we reached Charlotteville, in which the houses appeared to be scattered. In its vicinity is a new establishment for education, called University of Virginia. The next morning we went to see the university, which is one
mile distant from the town.

This establishment has been open since March, 1824, and it is said
to have already one hundred and thirty students; but a spirit of insub-
ordination has caused many of the pupils to be sent away. The
buildings are all new, and yet some of them seem to threaten to fall
in, which may be the case with several others also, being chiefly built
of wood. The interior of the library was not yet finished, but according to its plan it will be a beautiful one. The dome is made after the
model of the Pantheon in Rome, reduced on half. This place is intended for public meetings of the academy: but it is said that an echo
is heard in case of loud speaking, which renders the voice of the
speaker unintelligible.

Under the rotunda are three elliptical halls, the destination of
which is not yet entirely determined. The set of columns on the outside of this building, I was told is to be a very fine one; the capitals
were made in Italy.

As for the rest, the ten buildings on the right and left are not at
all regularly built, but each of them in a different manner, so that
there is no harmony in the whole, which prevents it from having a
beautiful and majestic appearance.

The garden walls of the lateral building are also in crooked lines,
which gives them a singular but handsome appearance. The buildings have been executed according to Mr. Jefferson's plan, and are
his hobby; he is rector of the University, in the construction of which
the state of Virginia is said to have laid out considerable sums of
money.

We addressed a gentleman whom we met by chance, in order to
get some information, and we had every reason to be satisfied with
his politeness. It was Dr. Dunglison, professor of medicine. He is an
Englishman, and came last year with three other professors from
Europe. He showed us the library, which was still inconsiderable,
and has been provisionally arranged in a lecture room; it contained
some German belles lettres works, among others a series of Kotze-
bue's calendar of dramatic works. It was said a great quantity of
books was coming from Europe.

The university is situated on a hill in a very healthy situation, and there is a very fine view of the Blue Ridge. President Jefferson invited us to a family dinner; but as in Charlotteville there is but a single hackney-coach, and this being absent, we were obliged to go the three miles to Monticello on foot.

We went by a pathway, through well cultivated and enclosed fields, crossed a creek named Rivanna, passing on a trunk of a tree cut in a rough shape, and without rails; then ascended a steep hill overgrown with wood, and came on its top to Mr. Jefferson's house, which is in an open space, walled round with bricks, forming an oblong, whose shorter sides are rounded; on each of the longer sides are portals of four columns.

The unsuccessful waiting for a carriage, and our long walk, caused such a delay, that we found the company at table when we entered; but Mr. Jefferson came very kindly to meet us, forced us to take our seats, and ordered dinner to be served up anew. He was an old man of eighty-six years of age, of tall stature, plain appearance, and long white hair.

In conversation he was very lively, and his spirits, as also his hearing and sight, seemed not to have decreased at all with his advancing age. I found in him a man who retained his faculties remarkably well in his old age, and one would have taken him for a man of sixty. He asked me what I had seen in Virginia. I eulogized all the places, that I was certain would meet with his approbation, and he seemed very much pleased. The company at the table, consisted of the family of his daughter, Mrs. Randolph, and of that of the professor of mathematics at the university, an Englishman, and of his wife. I turned the conversation to the subject of the university, and observed, that this was the favourite topic with Mr. Jefferson; he entertained very sanguine hopes as to the flourishing state of the university in future, and believed that it, and the Harvard University near Boston, would in a very short time be the only institutions, where the youth of the United States would receive a truly classical and solid education. After dinner we intended to take our leave, in order to return to Charlotteville; but Mr. Jefferson would not consent to it. He pressed us to remain for the night at his house. The evening was spent by the fire; a great deal was said about travels, and objects of natural history; the fine arts were also introduced, of which Mr. Jefferson was a great admirer. He spoke also of his travels in France, and the country on the Rhine, where he was very much pleased. His description of Virginia is the best proof what an admirer he is of beauties of nature. He told us that it was only eight months since he could not ride on horseback; otherwise, he rode every day to visit the surrounding country; he entertained, however, hopes of being able to re-commence the next spring his favourite exercise. Between nine and ten o'clock in the evening, the company broke up, and a handsome room was assigned to me.

The next morning I took a walk round the house, and admired the beautiful panorama, which this spot presents. On the left, I saw the Blue Ridge, and between them and Monticello are smaller hills. Charlotteville and the University lay at my feet; before me, the valley of the Rivanna river, which farther on, makes its junction with the James river, and on my right was the flat part of Virginia, the extent of which is lost in distance; behind me was a towering hill, which limited the sight. The interior of the house was plain, and the furniture somewhat of an old fashion. In the entrance was a marble stove with Mr. Jefferson's bust, by Ceracchi. In the rooms hung several copies of the celebrated pictures of the Italian school, views of Monticello, Mount-Vernon, the principal buildings in Washington and Harper's Ferry; there were also an oil painting, and an engraving of the Natural Bridge, views of Niagara by Vanderlin, a sketch of the large picture by Trumbull, representing the surrender at Yorktown, and a pen drawing of Hector's departure, by Benjamin West, presented by him to General Kosciuszko; finally, several portraits of Mr. Jefferson, among which the best was that in profile by Stuart. In the saloon there were two busts, one of Napoleon as first consul, and another of the Emperor Alexander. Mr. Jefferson admired Napoleon's military talents, but did not love him. After breakfast, which we took with the family, we bid the respectable old man farewell, and set out upon our return on foot to Charlotteville.

Mr. Jefferson tendered us the use of his carriage, but I declined, as I preferred walking in a fine and cool morning. In the afternoon we left Charlotteville, in a tolerably good stage, in order to go to Richmond, the chief town of Virginia, distant eighty miles. . . .

◇◇

THREE CONTEMPORARY POEMS
AND A SATIRE

Jefferson at 46.

PROFILE DRAWING BY EDME QUENEDEY, PARIS, 1789

(Engraving from a physiognotrace portrait.)

Courtesy of the Bibliothèque Nationale, Paris, and Mr. Howard C. Rice, Jr.

Jefferson at 48.

BUST BY GIUSEPPE CERACCHI, 1790 OR 1791

(Plaster from the lost original which belonged to Jefferson.)

Courtesy of Mr. Fiske Kimball, Philadelphia Museum of Art

THE PEOPLE'S FRIEND

Attributed to
REMBRANDT PEALE

No more to subtle arts a prey,
Which fearful of the eye of day;
    A nation's ruin plann'd:
Now entering on th' auspicious morn,
In which a people's hopes are born,
    What joy o'erspreads the land!

While past events portended harm,
And rais'd the spirit of alarm,
    Uncertain of the end:
Ere all was lost, the prospect clear'd,
And a bright star of hope appear'd,
    The People's chosen friend.

Devoted to his country's cause,
The rights of Man and equal Laws,
    His hallow'd pen was given:
And now those Rights and Laws to save
From sinking to an early grave
    He comes, employ'd by Heav'n.

What joyful prospects rise before!
Peace, Arts and Science hail our shore,
    And through the country spread:
Long may these blessings be preserv'd
And by a virtuous land deserv'd,
    With JEFFERSON our head.

From The Thomas Jefferson Scrapbook, Alderman Library, University of Virginia. Courtesy Francis L. Berkeley, Jr., Curator of Manuscripts.

Chorus

Rejoice, ye States, rejoice,
    And spread the patriot flame;
Call'd by a nation's voice;
    To save his country's fame;
And dissipate increasing fears,
Our favorite Jefferson appears.

Let every heart unite,
    Th' eventful day to hail;
When from the Freemen's Right,
    The people's hopes prevail;
That hence may horrid faction cease,
And honor be maintain'd with peace.

JEFFERSON AND LIBERTY

Attributed to

ROBERT TREAT PAINE

The gloomy night before us flies:
The reign of terror now is o'er,
Its gags, inquisitors and spies,
Its hordes of harpies are no more.

> *Rejoice! Columbia's sons, rejoice!*
> *To tyrants never bend the knee,*
> *But join with heart, and soul, and voice,*
> *For* JEFFERSON *and* LIBERTY.

O'er vast Columbia's varied clime,
Her cities, forests, shores and dales,
In rising majesty sublime,
Immortal Liberty prevails.

> *Rejoice! Columbia's Sons, &c.*

Hail! long expected glorious day!
Illustrious, memorable morn;
That freedom's fabric from decay
Secures—for millions yet unborn.

> *Rejoice! Columbia's sons, &c.*

From The Thomas Jefferson Scrapbook, Alderman Library, University of Virginia. Courtesy Francis L. Berkeley, Jr., Curator of Manuscripts.

In a note to an 1874 printing, Jared Potter Kirtland wrote: "The Foregoing Song was composed by Robert Treat Payne of Boston, and was first sung in public at the Great Festival, held at Wallingford, Ct., March 11, 1801, in commemoration of the election of Thomas Jefferson to the Presidency of the United States. For the tune, Asahael Benham, Sen., selected the air of an old Irish Song, and composed for it a sublime and beautiful bass, adapted to the measure of the words. He led the numerous and well-drilled Choir in singing the piece at that Festival. . . .

56661

His country's glory, hope and stay,
In virtue and in talents tri'd,
Now rises to assume the sway,
O'er freedom's temple to preside.

    Rejoice! Columbia's sons, &c.

Within its hallow'd walls immense,
No hireling band shall e'er arise,
Array'd in tyranny's defence,
To hear an injur'd people's cries.

    Rejoice! Columbia's sons, &c.

No lordling here with gorging jaws,
Shall wring from industry its food,
No fiery bigot's holy laws,
Lay waste our fields and streets in blood.

    Rejoice! Columbia's sons, &c.

Here strangers from a thousand shores,
Compell'd by tyranny to roam,
Shall find amidst abundant stores,
A nobler and a happier home.

    Rejoice! Columbia's sons, &c.

Here art shall lift her laurel'd head,
Wealth, industry and peace divine,
And where dark pathless forests spread,
Rich fields and lofty cities shine.

    Rejoice! Columbia's sons, &c.

From Europe's wants and woes remote,
A dreary waste of waves between,
Here plenty cheers the humble cot,
And smiles on every village green.

    Rejoice! Columbia's sons, &c.

Here free as air's expanded space,
To every soul and sect shall be,
The sacred priv'lege of our race,
The worship of the Deity.

    Rejoice! Columbia's sons, &c.

These gifts, great Liberty, are thine;
Ten thousand more we owe to thee!
Immortal may their mem'ries shine,
Who fought and died for liberty.

    Rejoice! Columbia's sons, &c.

What heart but hails a scene so bright,
What soul but inspiration draws,
Who would not guard so dear a right,
Or die in such a glorious cause.

    Rejoice! Columbia's sons, &c.

Let foes to freedom dread the name,
But should they touch the sacred tree,
Twice fifty thousand swords shall flame
For JEFFERSON and LIBERTY.

    Rejoice! Columbia's sons, &c.

From Georgia up to Lake Champlain,
From seas to Mississippi's shore,
Ye sons of freedom loud proclaim,
THE REIGN OF TERROR IS NO MORE.

    Rejoice! Columbia's sons, rejoice!
    To tyrants never bend the knee,
    But join with heart, and soul, and voice,
    For JEFFERSON *and* LIBERTY.

From THE EMBARGO

William Cullen Bryant

(Written when the poet was thirteen)

When shall this land, some courteous angel say,
Throw off a weak, and erring ruler's sway?
Rise, injured people, vindicate your cause!
And prove your love of liberty and laws;
Oh wrest, sole refuge of a sinking land,
The sceptre from the slave's imbecile hand!
Oh ne'er consent, obsequious, to advance,
The willing vassal of imperious France!
Correct that suffrage you misus'd before
And lift your voice above a congress roar.

And thou, the scorn of every patriot name,
Thy country's ruin, and her council's shame!
Poor servile thing! derision of the brave!
Who erst from Tarleton fled to Carter's cave;
Thou, who, when menac'd by perfidious Gaul,
Didst prostrate to her whisker'd minion fall;
And when our cash her empty bags supply'd
Didst meanly strive the foul disgrace to hide;
Go, wretch, resign the presidential chair,
Disclose thy secret measures, foul or fair.
Go, search with curious eye, for hornéd frogs,
Mid the wild wastes of Louisianian bogs;
Or, where Ohio rolls his turbid stream,
Dig for huge bones, thy glory and thy theme.
Go, scan, Philosophist, thy ****** charms
And sink supinely in her sable arms;
But quit to abler hands the helm of state,
Nor image ruin on thy country's fate!

From *The Embargo; or Sketches of the Times*, by William Cullen Bryant. Second edition, corrected and enlarged. Boston, 1809.

A SATIRE ON MR. JEFFERSON'S DAY

The Port Folio

Monday, 8 o'clock, 20th February, 1804

Left Sally—damn'd bore, to rise early—but must seem industrious, though nothing to do. Met Madison at breakfast—don't much like him—talked of virtue and conscience—thought he looked hard at me— Gallatin's the man—never hear such stuff from him—no danger too of his pushing me out—good fellow! pay him well, and he'll do any thing—'point d'argent, point de suisse.'

10 o'clock. Wrote half a page of my dissertation on cock-roaches— servant came in to say, people below wanted to see me on public business—cursed their impertinence—sent word, I was out. Why don't they go to Gallatin or Madison—office of President must be sinecure— trouble enough to sign bills and messages—returned to my cock-roaches, in a fret, and couldn't write. Received note from Gallatin, inclosing bill I told him to read yesterday—says, it's all right—signed it, and sent it to the senate. Mem. to ask Gallatin, what's its purport.

Took up Port Folio—saw the name of *Gabriel Jones*—found myself in a cold sweat; and threw it into the fire. Wonder folks will talk of old stories—better mind their own business—troublesome fellow that Editor—worries me cursedly—lets nothing escape him. Beau Dawson lounged in—had on pair of new breeches—devilish proud of 'em— thought more of them than of me—mentioned pretty mulatto girl at ——'s — made my mouth water — take a peep at her — Sally's grow-ing stale — told him to bring her in the back way. Beau talked of manufactures of France, famous hair-powder, and almond-paste—

From *The Port Folio*, Philadelphia, August 18, 1804, Volume 4, Number 33.
    Title supplied. Published with the caption "Levity" and the note "The follow-ing fragment of a journal was picked up by a traveller, while *tantioying* along the banks of the Potomac."

stock he brought with him almost out. Mem. must make another errand for him.

12 *o'clock*. Randolph came in—looked rather queer—found he'd been trying to answer that damn'd fellow Griswold—desperate case— made many bold assertions, but was detected in all—got into a cursed scrape, and was obliged to sit down—damn'd provoking, can't find any one to cope with Griswold—Jack's flippant enough, but quite on the surface, better than any of our side—though—tried Giles, found he wouldn't do—been looking out some time to buy over a Fed of talents—can't meet with one who'd take a bribe—very strange that.

Ordered my horse—never ride with a servant—looks proud—mob doesn't like it—must gull the boobies. Adams wouldn't bend so—had rather lose his place—knew nothing of the world. Pass'd Merry and his wife—saw her whisper and smile—look'd foolish—thought she was laughing at me—Why do women of fashion come to this coun- try?—wish she had staid in England—heard her jest once about my dirty stockings—must cringe to 'em now though!—hope he hasn't written home about my first reception of them—only did so to please our party, and to shew the world, that republicans affect not to con- duct themselves by the rules of gallantry and politeness.

Stopp'd at Judge K——'s, to be qualified to a deposition—swore on a volume of 'Devil on two Sticks,' by mistake—pretended to make a fuss about it—afraid I overacted my part—K. was seized with a cough- ing fit—believe him to be a sneering son of a bitch. Found Paine wait- ing to dine with me—sorry I invited him from France—nothing gained by him—people despise him—all owing to his impudence—gave him some hints—a man may be an atheist without proclaiming it to the world—pleasant fellow tho'—several good jokes on the new testa- ment—talked of the vision of Machiavel—outrageous about the res- toration of the clergy in France. To put him in good humour, drank success to the invaders of England—plied him well with brandy, and, as usual, left the stay-maker under the table.

Received letter from Lewis, giving account of the Osage Indians— wonderfully curious terrapins—dare say it's a fine country—must have a breed—send commissioners to make a treaty with 'em. Dr. Mitchell came to tea—spoke of his new method of drying frogs—his new chemi- cal nomenclature—folks cursed obstinate—will stick to Lavoisier's— all of a piece with preferring America to *Fredonia*—Read me a part of his letter to king of Naples—wonder who he got *to do it into Latin*—good thing his signature of *Centumvir*—a prig of a fellow—glad to get rid of him—no bad plan tho' of drying the frogs.

10 *o'clock.* Went to bed—could not sleep—took up *National Intelligencer*—found myself getting drowsy—began one of Caesar Rodney's speeches, and soon fell into a slumber.

SOME CONTEMPORARY CALUMNY
AND A COMMENT IN VERSE

AN UNTRUE AND VICIOUS ATTACK
ON THE PRESIDENT'S CHARACTER

JAMES THOMSON CALLENDER

It is well known that the man, *whom it delighteth the people to honor,* keeps, and for many years has kept, as his concubine, one of his own slaves. Her name is Sally. The name of her eldest son is Tom. His features are said to bear a striking although sable resemblance to those of the president himself. The boy is ten or twelve years of age. His mother went to France in the same vessel with Mr. Jefferson and his two daughters. The delicacy of this arrangement must strike every person of common sensibility. What a sublime pattern for an American ambassador to place before the eyes of two young ladies!

If the reader does not feel himself *disposed to pause* we beg leave to proceed. Some years ago this story had once or twice been hinted at in *Rind's Federalist.* At that time, we believed the surmise to be an absolute calumny. One reason for thinking so was this. A vast body of people wished to debar Mr. Jefferson from the presidency. *The establishment of this* SINGLE FACT would have rendered his election impossible. We reasoned thus: that if the allegation had been true, it was sure to have been ascertained and advertised by his enemies, in every corner of the continent.

We do not wish to give wanton offence to many very good kind of people. Concerning a certain sort of connection, we have already stated that, "of boys and bachelors, we have said nothing, and *we have nothing to say."* They will be pleased, therefore, to stand out of the way. When the king of Prussia was upon the point of fighting the great and decisive battle of Lissa, he assembled his principal officers,

From the *Richmond Recorder,* as reprinted in the *New-York Evening Post,* September 10, 1802.

and, under the penalty of his utmost contempt, exhorted them to bravery. In the midst of this address, an old veteran dissolved into tears. "My dear general," said Frederic, "*I did not refer to* YOU." Some of our acquaintances are, upon the same principle, requested to believe that we do not, in this allusion, refer to *them*. We have formerly stated that *supereminent pretensions to chastity are always suspicious*. This hint was sufficiently plain to shew that the Recorder does not desire to set up a manufacture of wry faces. The writer of this article does not bear the stamp of a Scots presbyterian parson of the last century. But still, we all know that some things may be overlooked, which can hardly be excused, and which it is impracticable either to praise, or even to vindicate. Such is human nature, and such is human life. One of our correspondents very justly observes that "there is nobody, of whom something disagreeable may not be said."

By this wench Sally, our President has had several children. There is not an individual in the neighbourhood of Charlottesville who does not believe the story; and not a few who *know it*.

If Duane sees this account, he will not prate any more about the treaty between Mr. Adams and Toussaint. Behold the favorite! the first born of republicanism! the pinnacle of all that is good and great! in the open consummation of an act which tends to subvert the policy, the happiness, and even the existence of this country!

'Tis supposed that, at the time when Mr. Jefferson wrote so smartly concerning negroes, when he endeavored so much to *belittle* the African race, he had no expectation that the chief magistrate of the United States was to be the ringleader in shewing that his opinion was erroneous; or, that he should chuse an African stock whereupon he was to engraft his own descendants.

Duane and Cheetham are not worth asking whether this is a lie or not? But censor Smith is requested to declare whether the statement is a FEDERAL MISREPRESENTATION? Mute! Mute! Mute! Yes, very mute will all those republican printers of political biographical information be upon this point. Whether they stir, or not, they must feel themselves like a horse in a quick-sand. They will plunge deeper and deeper, until no assistance can save them.

The writer of this piece has been arraigned as capable of *selling himself* to the British ambassador. The impeachment was made by a printer, who is in the confidence of Mr. Jefferson. The president had the utmost reason to believe that the charge was an utter fiction. This charge was met in a decisive stile. We at once, selected and appealed to the testimony, or belief, of *five persons,* who were intimately acquainted with the situation of Callender, at the period of the pretended project of sale. These were Mr. Israel Israel, Dr. James Reynolds, Mr. John Beckley, Mr. John Smith, federal marshal of Pennsylvania, and Mr. Mathew Carey, bookseller, whose name has been heard of in every county and corner of the United States. This appeal harmonised with the feelings of innocence and defiance. If the friends of Mr. Jefferson are convinced of *his* innocence, *they* will make an appeal of the same sort. If they rest in silence, or if they content themselves with resting upon a *general denial,* they cannot hope for credit. The allegation is of a nature too *black* to be suffered to remain in suspence. We should be glad to hear of its refutation. We give it to the world under the firmest belief that such a refutation *never can be made.* The African Venus is said to officiate as housekeeper at Monticello. When Mr. Jefferson has read this article, he will find leisure to estimate how much has been lost or gained by so many unprovoked attacks upon

J. T. Callender

"WHAT THE NAME OF NERO WAS TO ROME, WILL THINE BE TO THY COUNTRY . . ."

New-York Evening Post

. . . Let it be asked, who, in the most Infamous manner endeavored to defame the American character in Europe? The answer will be JEFFERSON. If it be inquired who, with the hand of a base assassin, attempted to stab the reputation of the great Father of his country, the immortal Washington? The name of JEFFERSON again occurs. —And if it be demanded, who hired the most profligate outlaws of foreign countries to plunge the political poniard into the well earned fame of John Adams? Still the name of JEFFERSON presents itself.

But supposing Mr. Burr does hold a competition with the runaway governor of 1780, — where was the harm, nay, the impropriety of it? Had he not as many of the suffrages of the electors as Jefferson? This even Duane, Denniston, or Cheetham dare not deny. If facts come properly to light, however, it will soon rise in judgement against him, that he is himself the director behind the scenes, of these political automatons.

Nero affected humanity, and *thou*, even thou, Jefferson affectest *virtue*—but what the name of Nero was to Rome, will thine be to thy Country, when once the unerring hand of time shall place thy actions, in the proper point of view, and that your country may be speedily and happily relieved from the evils of your public agency is the ardent wish, and fervent prayer of every friend to the fame and principles of WASHINGTON.

From the *New-York Evening Post,* November 10, 1802.

ON DEFAMATION

THE JEFFERSON SCRAPBOOK

My soul, what pen can draw, what tongue explain
The baseness of that mind—prone to defame,
The baseness of that tongue, which loves to dwell
On characters—and blow the fire of hell;
With breath malign—fair reputation spot,
And throw at purest innocence a blot.

From The Thomas Jefferson Scrapbook, Alderman Library, University of Virginia. Courtesy Francis L. Berkeley, Jr., Curator of Manuscripts.

SOME ASPECTS OF THE
MANY-SIDED MR. JEFFERSON

THOMAS JEFFERSON, ATTORNEY AT LAW

John W. Davis

... The year [1926] is the one hundredth anniversary of the death of that Virginia lawyer who penned the Declaration of Independence. As a statesman he has been called not unjustly by a recent English reviewer the greatest liberal of the modern world. By common consent he has influenced, living and dead, the daily thought of his fellow countrymen more than any other man in all their history; for he it was who formulated, defended and made victorious that social and political philosophy of individualism and equality by which America has lived and to which all American statesmen of whatever party since his day have given their allegiance. Without Washington America could not have won through the trials that beset her birth, without Hamilton she might have perished in the quagmire of false finance, without Marshall the Constitution might have proved itself a rope of sand; but the social life of Americans, meaning thereby the feelings they entertain one toward another and the hopes they cherish for themselves, could not be what it is today without the teachings of Thomas Jefferson. In speaking of him at this time, however, I wish to turn aside from a consideration of his career as author, or diplomat or statesman and submit to you some reflections gathered from the less familiar portion of his life which he spent as a devotee

From an address delivered before the Virginia State Bar Association, August 4, 1926, and published in the Association's *Proceedings*, Volume 38. Reprinted by permission of Hon. John W. Davis.

of the legal profession. My topic is Thomas Jefferson, Attorney at Law.

It is the fate of great men to devour themselves; the earlier man is swallowed up in the later, or perhaps it would be fairer to say that the greater obscures the less. Washington, the boy surveyor of the unsubdued frontier, is lost in Washington the general and president; the young artillerist at the siege of Toulon is forgotten in the romance of Napoleon, Emperor of the French and dictator of thrones and nationalities; or if you will have a later illustration, history will have little to say of a certain college professor at Princeton, but will write many pages of Woodrow Wilson, war president and founder of the League of Nations. So the lawyer Jefferson; and yet I make for him this claim—that if he had not been called away to public life, if the times had not opened to him broader avenues of public service, he would still have won his place in the history of Virginia as one of the brightest ornaments of an illustrious bar. I base this confident statement upon a consideration of his training, his success as a practitioner and his later contributions to the ordered progress of the law. Will you follow me in a hurried review of these three phases of his legal career?

His education was truly unusual. At the early age of seventeen he entered an advanced class at William and Mary College and left it two years later a "profound and accomplished scholar for one so young," but at the mere threshold of a course of study that endured until his death. It was in 1775 that John Adams quoted Duane's remark that "Jefferson is the greatest rubber-off of dust that I have met with; he has learned French, Italian and Spanish and wants to learn German." Before he left college he had studied deeply and read widely in mathematics, languages, the sciences, the classics and belles lettres; and if the requirements for entry upon the study of the law had been as exacting as those of our most advanced law schools of today he would have easily fulfilled them all.

No such schools were open to the American colonial, however. He had but two avenues of approach to the gateway of the bar. The first, by enrollment at one of the Inns of Court in London, was available only to those of substantial means. Residence there was an expensive business. A long ocean journey and several years' attendance as a student of the Inn lay between the aspirant and his call to the bar; years in which such learning as he acquired was gained by lectures, disputations and attendance upon the courts of Westminster and the Guildhall with little guidance on the way. The rigor of study was further softened no doubt by many social interludes, which added to the expense; although it was perhaps no longer true of the Inns as Sir John Fortescue had written three centuries earlier that "There they learn to sing and exercise themselves in all kinds of harmony. There also they practice dansing and other noblemen's pastimes, as they used to do that are brought up in the king's house."

The other road was that which so long prevailed in America—the reading of law in some practitioner's office. The law school was to come later on the initiative of Jefferson himself. Of his immediate predecessors and colleagues, the Inner Temple trained St. George Tucker—he of the Blackstone—and Thomas Nelson; while to the Middle Temple had gone John Blair, Carter Harrison, Thomas Mason (whom St. George Tucker said was "esteemed the first lawyer at the bar"), Arthur Lee, Joseph Jones, Peyton and John Randolph, and William Byrd, of Westover—the latter bearing a name distinguished in his day and which in the present generation has won new lustre in Virginia and the world. Such men as George Wythe, Robert Carter Nicholas, John Tyler, Dabney Carr, Patrick Henry and Gabriel Jones, of the Valley, on the other hand, were trained at home. No other course was open to Jefferson as the son of a widowed mother with eight children by her side. He counted himself fortunate therefore when the kindly Dr. Small, who he says "fixed the destinies of my life," procured him entrance in 1762 to the office of George Wythe.

One wonders what it was that turned his ambition toward the law. Perhaps, mere love for the mental exercise, of what we are fond of calling the most intellectual of the professions; perhaps attendance during his college days on the forensic battles in the General Court; perhaps the tradition of his maternal great-uncle, Sir John Randolph, attorney general under the Crown, and at his early death in 1737 regarded as one of the great practitioners in America. Or it may have been the contemplation of his cousins, Peyton and John Randolph, then in practice at Williamsburg, both attorneys general in their turn and the latter of whom has the distinction of having been the last attorney general of the colony under the Crown and father of the first attorney general of the United States under the Constitution. Peyton Randolph we know as the president of the Constitutional Congress; but John, feeling his allegiance to the Crown too strong

to be broken, bowed to the storm and went to London at the outbreak
of the Revolution to remain until his death. Mr. Wirt describes him as

> in person and manners among the most elegant gentlemen in the
> colony, and in his profession one of the most splendid ornaments
> of the bar. He was a polite scholar, as well as a profound lawyer
> and his eloquence was of a high order. His voice, action, style
> were stately and uncommonly impressive.

How could the boy Jefferson have remained unimpressed by such
examples?

What did he study during his five years under Wythe? That he
was industrious we know, for he rose in the grey of the summer
morning and in winter when the hands of his bedroom clock reached
five. He tells us little himself of his studies, passing over this period
of his life in his autobiography with scant words. No doubt he followed the advice which he later gave to another, and carefully
abstracted in his commonplace books all that he read, striving ever
to attain what he declared to be "the most valuable of all talents,
that of never using two words where one will do." There were thorns
along the way, we may be sure, if one may judge by his remark to
his friend Page that "I do wish the devil had old Coke, for I am sure
I was never so tired of an old dull scoundrel in my life."

Law books were few in America in those blissful days, and such
as there were were of English origin. Indeed but thirty-three law
books in all had been printed in America prior to 1776, and in this
tally are included eight editions of the same work. Virginia's sole
contribution to the list, outside of Purvis' "complete collection"
(1661-1687), Beverly's (1642-1720) and Mercer's (1661-1736) abridgements of her statutes was Webb's "The Office and Authority of a
Justice of the Peace." The flood gates of American Reports were still
to be opened and even a collection of the existing statutes was not
easy to come by. Prior to 1733 they were not even printed as they
were delivered from the legislative mill, but were preserved solely
in manuscript, leaving him to discover their contents who could.
Thereafter, although printed as passed, little effort had been made
to assemble them in complete collective form. Few, wrote St. George
Tucker in 1803, had ever been able to boast of possessing a complete
collection of the laws of Virginia. Jefferson's own laborious collection, the fruit of many years, was known in 1795 to be more all-

embracing than any other extant, and when he turned it over to Wythe for the use of the Committee on Publication he wrote that he had spared neither time nor trouble nor expense in gathering the manuscripts and printed copies of which it was composed. Lord Coke's Institutes was the stern meat upon which legal infants were nourished until the first volume of Blackstone came into the field in 1765; and with them the student was invited to consider Bracton, Britton, Fleta, Glanville and such like, Bacon's Abridgement, Comyn's Digest, Lord Kames and Fonblanque on Equity and the reports of Salkeld, Modern, Vernon, Ventries and such others as were then extant. Nor were the civilians, Domat, Puffendorf, Justinian and the rest overlooked. If Jefferson's reading pursued the course which he outlined for his young friend Bernard Moore it was truly prodigious. (See Randall, Vol. 1, page 53.) In this letter he commends to the student the following division of time: from rising until eight in the morning, physical studies; from eight to twelve, read law; from twelve to one, read politics; in the afternoon read history; from dark to bedtime, belles lettres, criticism, rhetoric and oratory.

Of Blackstone his views seem to have been variable. In the letter to Moore he speaks of Blackstone's "inimitable commentaries—the best perfect digest to both branches of the law." Later in a letter to Judge Tyler, penned in 1812, he writes:

> Blackstone, whose book although the most elegant and best digested in our catalogue, has been perverted more than all others, to the degeneracy of legal science. A student finds there a smattering of everything and his indolence persuades him that if he understands that book he is a master of the whole body of the law. The distinction between these and those who have drawn their stores from the deep mines of Coke and Littleton, seem well understood, even by the appellation of Blackstone lawyers to the ephemeral insects of the law.

If any remain in this generation to share his reverence for Lord Coke and his *magnum opus*, they would find interest in Coke's own copy of Littleton's Tenures, which still survives in the private library of his kinsman, the present Earl of Leicester. It is a small black-bound volume "annotated in the margent," as Coke said in the careful catalogue which he annexed to his will, and every page is covered with the crabbed and minute handwriting of the great annotator. Those students who, like Jefferson, were at his mercy, had a similar course to follow, for commonplace books, the annotation of texts and notes on the cases that came to their attention were the sure but laborious steps by which they climbed to legal proficiency. This was supplemented no doubt by attendance upon any courts that were open to them; a practice which in my judgment can still be usefully commended to the law students of to-day.

The American bar at long last is exerting itself with vigor to raise the standard of legal education in the United States. It is insisting that three years of legal study preceded by at least two years of collegiate training is little enough of preparation for the labors of the lawyer. Every effort of the sort, however, provokes an invocation of those high spirits of the past who, like Patrick Henry or like Lincoln, came to fame, if not fortune, by a shorter route; Lincoln, who called himself a "mast-fed lawyer," and Henry, with his six weeks spent on Coke and the Virginia Statutes and a certificate for license signed by John and Peyton Randolph, who "perceived him to be a young man of genius, very ignorant of law, but did not doubt he would soon qualify himself." In this Wythe, the third examiner, inflexibly just as always, refused to join, believing him not qualified. There is no record of any trial of strength between Henry and Jefferson, yet fancy if you can a court room contest between the two: Henry, all fire and flame, more advocate than lawyer, seeking to carry the day solely by the storm of his passionate oratory; Jefferson, cool, unemotional, prepared, more lawyer than advocate, stating the issues as he stated everything he touched with a clarity born both of industry and genius. Madison, who had heard him in the court room, says that he spoke "fluently and well." We all have seen at one time or another both types in action. They have each their functions; and yet in the long run those who wish entertainment will take Henry, but those who want to win their cases will retain Jefferson.

Five years under Wythe and then Jefferson at the age of twenty-four was introduced to the bar of the General Court of Virginia by that "faithful and beloved mentor in youth and most affectionate friend through life." Who composed the Committee of Councillors of the General Court that examined him for license we do not know; quite probably the same persons who had passed on Henry seven years before. There is in his case, however, no record of any dissent.

It was an odd tribunal, that old General Court, tested by modern standards. It was composed of the governor and his council, drawn from the most prominent and wealthy men of the colony, few of whom were lawyers, and was commanded by statute to sit semi-yearly for twenty-four days in April and October at Williamsburg. Five made a quorum. Its jurisdiction was all-embracing, civil, criminal and appellate, and except for the evil days under Governor Berkeley it seems to have dealt out justice with a pretty even hand in the sort of cases that would naturally arise in a purely agricultural community—ejectments and boundaries and wills and partitions and contracts and torts and crimes, and not a few of the problems that arose from the institution of slavery and the effort to deal with human beings as something less than men and something more than cattle.

Reports it had none, wisely choosing perhaps not to imperil sound decisions by unsound reasoning. Some manuscript notes of decided cases were prepared for their own private use by Sir John Randolph (1728-1732), Edward Barradall (1733-1741), and Hopkins (1730-1740). These manuscripts Jefferson received from John Randolph in 1768 and abstracted from them all the cases they contained of a domestic character as distinguished from those governed by English law. He took four from Randolph, twenty-six from Barradall, and one from Hopkins; and continued to add to them like cases "arising under our peculiar laws" until "the Revolution dissolved our courts of justice and called those attached to them to far other occupations." It is interesting to note that the large majority of the cases so included dealt with some phase of property in slaves. The posthumous publication of these assembled cases in 1829 as Jefferson's Reports of Decisions in the General Court of Virginia enrolls him in the list of Virginia court reporters.

Little save his own notes remains to tell the story of Jefferson's seven years of practice, but his success was striking and immediate. He makes record of sixty-eight cases in the General Court in 1767, 115 in 1768, 198 in 1769, 121 in 1770, 137 in 1771, 154 in 1772, 127 in 1773, and 29 in 1774, up to the time when he gave up his business to his cousin, Edmund Randolph, and wound up his career at the bar. In addition he had many cases before the inferior courts, such as the county courts of Albemarle and Augusta and the Court of Oyer and Terminer at Williamsburg. He records that he was retained in a total of 430 cases in all courts in the year of 1771 and 347 in

1772. Measuring the future by the progress that he made, we may be sure that the highest place at the bar was his had fate permitted him to reach for it. Indeed, when Robert Cary Nicholas, the acknowledged leader of the bar, wished to retire in 1771, he put his unfinished business in the hands of the youthful Jefferson, and only after his declination was it turned over to Patrick Henry.

His average annual profits of $3,000.00 may not seem a dazzling figure in this auriferous age, but it bulked large in that day and time. It was not all beer and skittles either in matters of compensation. Fees were fixed by law: five pounds in the General Court; for an opinion, one pound, one shilling and six pence; in the inferior courts, thirty shillings where the suit concerned landed property, and seven and six pence if for small debts. Quite contrary, of course, to the happy customs of today, even these were not always promptly paid. So it was that an advertisement appeared in the Virginia Gazette of May 20, 1773, signed by Edmund Pendleton, John Randolph, James Mercer, Thomas Jefferson, Patrick Henry, Jr., and Gustavus Scott, which after reciting that

> The fees allowed by Law if regularly paid, would barely compensate our incessant Labors, reimburse our expenses and the losses incurred by Neglect of our private Affairs; yet even these Rewards, confessedly moderate, are withheld from us in a great Proportion, by the unworthy Part of our Clients,

goes on to advise the public that

> we have come to the following Resolution for the invariable Observance of which we mutually plight our Honor to each other: That after the 10th day of *October* next we will not give an Opinion on any Case stated to us but on Payment of the whole Fee, nor prosecute or defend any Suit or Motion unless the Tax and one-half of the Fee be previously advanced, excepting those Cases only where we choose to act *gratis;* and we hope no persons whatever may think of applying to us in any other Way. To prevent Disappointment, however, in Case this should be done, we think it proper to give this Warning, that no such Application, either verbal or by Way of Letter, will be answered to in the smallest Degree.

Then fearing lest they might give offense where offense was not intended, they hasten to add:

> We would feel much Concern if a thought could be entertained that the worthy Part of our Clients could disapprove this Measure. Their Conduct has been such as calls for our Acknowledgments and might merit exemption from this Strictness, were such Exemption practicable, but they will readily perceive this would defeat the Purpose, and that no distinction of Persons can by any means be attempted. We hope, therefore, from their Friendship, a cheerful concurrence in this plan, since the requisition is such only as their Punctuality would of itself prevent.

Of his arguments before the General Court those in *Howell* v. *Netherland* in April, 1770, and *Godwin* v. *Lunan* in October, 1771, are alone preserved to us through his small volume of reports. In the first he appeared to resist the detention in servitude of the grandchild of a person begotten of a white woman by a negro man. Along with a consideration of the statutes he took occasion to declare that

> Under the law of nature all men are born free, every one comes into the world with a right to his own person which includes the liberty of moving and using it at his own will. This is what is called personal liberty, and is given him by the author of nature, because necessary for his own sustenance. The reducing of the mother to servitude was a violation of the law of nature; surely then the same law cannot prescribe a continuance of the violation to her issue, and that, too, without end, for if it extends to any it must to every degree of descendants.

and he concludes,

> So that the position at first laid down is now proven, that the act of 1705 makes servants of the first mulatto, that of 1723 extends it to her children, but that it remains for some future legislature, if any shall be found wicked enough, to extend it to the grandchildren and other issue more remote, to the *nati natorum et qui nascentur ab illis.*

Alas, however, for the uncertainty of the lawyer's life; the argument failed, as many other good arguments have done before and since, and the court decided against him without even hearing from his opponent, Mr. Wythe. In the second case he was more fortunate. With a wealth of historical research running back to the days of Ethelwolf, he classifies churches as collatives, presentatives and donatives (terms which this learned audience will doubtless understand); and having placed those of Virginia in the last class, he successfully sustained the visitatorial right of the General Court at the suit of the church wardens and vestry to oust from his living a most disreputable and dissolute country parson who said that he "cared not of what religion he was so he got the tobacco, nor what became of the flock so that he could get the fleece."

But if Jefferson the practitioner had run his race by 1774, Jefferson the lawyer had still the greater part of his work to do. In the heart of every lawyer worthy of the name there burns a deep ambition so to bear himself that the profession may be stronger by reason of his passage through its ranks and that he may leave the law itself a better instrument of human justice than he found it. To many a man fate denies the opportunity to realize this desire, but it came to Jefferson in fullest measure. He grasped it with furious energy. It is true that the Revolution itself had stirred the foundations of the great deep and opened the way for many things that otherwise would have had long to wait. But I question whether the legislative history of any State can match the proceedings in Virginia during the years when Jefferson set the pace. Under his leadership a new and complete judiciary was established, the importation of slaves was prohibited, entails were abolished, expatriation recognized, naturalization provided for, and a committee on the general revision of the laws erected, the work of which fell to Wythe, Pendleton and himself.

In language which should be kept before all subsequent revisors he gives his views of the manner in which such work should be done.

> "In the execution of my part," said he, "I thought it material not to vary the diction of the ancient statutes by modernizing it, nor to give rise to new questions by new expressions. The text of these statutes had been so fully explained and defined by numerous adjudications as scarcely ever now to produce a question in our courts. I thought it would be useful also, in all new drafts, to reform the style of the later British statutes and of our own Acts of Assembly; which from their verbosity, their endless tautologies, their involutions of case within case and parenthesis within parenthesis, and their multiplied efforts at certainty, by

saids and *aforesaids*, by *ors* and by *ands*, to make them more
plain, are really rendered more perplexed and incomprehensible,
not only to common readers, but to the lawyers themselves."

All of which is most humbly and respectfully commended to Con-
gresses, legislatures and law-makers, whosoever, not omitting the
framers of the United States Revenue Act of 1926.

A remarkable thing it was, the work of those revisors, with their
126 bills rewriting the laws of the State; bills abolishing primogeni-
ture, proportioning crimes and punishments, confining the death
penalty to murder and treason, raising money for all public expenses
by assessments in proportion to property, outlining a free school
system for the State, granting full freedom of religion, and fore-
shadowing what they knew it would be useless then to insist upon—
the gradual and certain abolition of human slavery. To discuss these
bills or any of them would go beyond my purpose, which is only to
show in what measure Jefferson paid his debt to his profession. But
stay a moment and contemplate that statute of religious freedom as
Jefferson wrote it; how trumpet-like its words ring out across the
years. Listen to some of the sentences:

> Well aware that the opinions and beliefs of men depend not
> on their own will, but follow involuntarily the evidence pro-
> posed to their minds; that Almighty God hath created the mind
> free, and manifested his will that free it shall remain by making
> it altogether insusceptible of restraint; * * *
> —that our civil rights have no dependence on our religious
> opinions any more than our opinions in physics or geometry;
> that therefore the proscribing any citizens as unworthy the public
> confidence by laying upon him an incapacity of being called to
> offices of trust and emolument unless he profess or renounce this
> or that religious opinion is depriving him injuriously of those
> privileges and advantages to which, in common with his fellow-
> citizens, he has a natural right; * * *
> —that the opinions of men are not the subject of civil govern-
> ment nor under its jurisdiction; * * *
> —and finally that truth is great and will prevail if she is left to
> herself; that she is the proper and sufficient antagonist to error,
> and has nothing to fear from the conflict unless by human inter-
> position disarmed of her natural weapons, free argument and

debate; errors ceasing to be dangerous when it is permitted freely to contradict them.

We, the General Assembly, do enact, That no man shall be compelled to frequent or support any religious worship, place or ministry whatsoever, nor shall be enforced, restrained, molested or burdened in his body or goods, nor shall otherwise suffer, on account of his religious opinions or beliefs; but that all men shall be free to profess and by argument to maintain their opinions in matters of religion, and that the same shall in no wise diminish, enlarge or affect their civil capacities. * * *

What a message that was for Virginia to send resounding through the world! And yet how hard it dies, that spirit of religious intolerance. Surely it is one of the least flattering reflections upon human nature and human intelligence that men throughout the centuries have hated one another, oppressed one another, and wound up by slitting one another's throats, because they could not agree as to what would happen after the throat was slit. And though we in America have traveled far in the wake of Jefferson, and have wiped our statute books clear of religious discrimination, some recent manifestations warn us against too much vainglory over our liberality of thought. We have no monopoly of that virtue. Those who think otherwise may find a needed lesson in the fact that this generation has seen a Jew, Disraeli, the prime minister of gentile England, and another, Reading, her Lord Chief Justice and Viceroy of her greatest Dominion; a Catholic, Laurier, premier of Protestant Canada; and a Protestant, Doumergue, president of Catholic France.

Still another opportunity to serve his profession opened itself to Jefferson. In 1779 he became Governor of Virginia and was elected one of the visitors o ' William and Mary College. Busy as always, he turned to the reforı ation of her curriculum and succeeded in establishing as one of ' ıc six professorships allowed under her charter, a professorship of] aw and Police. It was the first law professorship set upon American soil and the second in any English-speaking country. George Wythe, the "incarnation of justice," was taken from the bench of the Court of Chancery to fill it, at the munificent salary of £80 in tobacco per year. John Marshall was among the first of his students, and under his careful tending the tree bore fruit before the turn of the century in such men and lawyers as Spencer Roane, Benjamin Watkins Leigh, John J. Crittenden, William A. Rives, John Breckenridge, John Wickham, H. St. George Tucker, W. H. Cabell, Littleton Waller Tazewell, William Munford and George Nicholas. No grapes from thorns or figs from thistles here! And when Wythe's work was done, St. George Tucker came to fill the chair and carry on the traditions he had established.

So we have Jefferson, the student, the practitioner, the court reporter, the revisor of the laws, the father of American law schools. In the light of all he did for the legal fraternity we can forgive some of the things he said about it, not always of the gentlest character. For instance, he writes to Madison in February of 1812:

> I have much doubted whether, in case of a war, Congress would find it practicable to do their part of the business. That a body containing one hundred lawyers in it should direct the measures of a war is, I fear, impossible; and that thus that member of our Constitution which is its bulwark will prove to be an impracticable one from its *cacoethes loquendi*.

Not flattering, surely; yet faithful are the wounds of a friend.

To say so much concerning Jefferson and not say more is difficult, and yet I have chosen to direct your attention to but one aspect of his varied life, and I must stick to my text. But I cannot close without stopping to inquire what was the secret of the influence he exerted over the men of his own generation, what the basis of his sway over the thought of those who have come after. I think it can be stated in short compass, for the mainspring of his power was and is an abiding faith in the worth and dignity of the individual man. It is the keynote of everything he said or did. The worth and dignity of the individual man; always imperfect, yet made in the image of Him by whom he was created; mistaken often, but entitled to correct his mistakes in his own way and time; misled not infrequently, but with the right to pass judgment upon those who mislead him; gifted by nature with unequal parts and faculties, but vested with the inalienable right to stand erect before a just and equal law; too feeble, as Lieber finely puts it, to wield unlimited power, but too noble to submit to it. For such a man and by him governments are made, and these are good or bad in the exact proportion in which they protect or restrict his God-given liberties. In the language of Jefferson himself, "The true foundation of Republican government is the equal right of every citizen in his person, his property and in their management." It is not a new doctrine, it was not new in the days of Jefferson. Indeed it has been the creed of all those lofty souls who have aspired throughout the ages to be leaders and teachers of mankind, finding its supreme exponent in the Man of Galilee. Yet new or old, it has never been without opponents, and, thank God, has never lacked defenders ready to die if need be in its behalf. Around the world today the combat rages, and everywhere the clarions of the battle call.

Lawyers of Virginia, heirs in body and in spirit of the mighty dead, I repeat to you the Laconian admonition—worthy, said Erasmus, to be written on the insignia of every prince—"You have been given Sparta. Adorn her!"

THOMAS JEFFERSON AS A WRITER:
AN INTRODUCTION TO
THE PAPERS OF JEFFERSON

*"The Richest Treasure House of Historical Information
Ever Left by a Single Man"*

JULIAN P. BOYD

The purpose of this work [*The Papers of Thomas Jefferson*, Princeton University Press, projected in some 50 volumes] is to present the writing and recorded actions of Thomas Jefferson as accurately and as completely as possible. Completeness in such a task, even for one who transmitted to posterity so full a record as Jefferson did, is only theoretically possible. "A great deal of the knolege of things," Jefferson once wrote Joel Barlow in an effort to persuade him to write a history of the American Revolution, "is not on paper but only within ourselves, for verbal communication."[1] He might have added that, so far as posterity was concerned, much was not communicable at all, verbally or otherwise. But few if any of Jefferson's contemporaries recognized an obligation to history so clearly as he did, and none exceeded him in his effort to discharge the debt. His aid to historians such as Girardin, Hazard, Ramsay, Wirt, and others; his indefatigable labors as a young lawyer in transcribing the ancient manuscript laws of Virginia; his answers to the queries of Marbois which resulted in one of the notable books of the eighteenth century; his compilation of vocabularies of Indian dialects; his meticulous care in recording the fullest and most exact account of the debates on the Declaration of Independence; his making available the best private library in America as the foundation of our national library; his copying, indexing, and organizing the vast number of letters, memoranda, accounts,

From the introductory essay, "A General View of the Work," in Volume I of *The Papers of Thomas Jefferson*. Julian P. Boyd, Editor. Lyman H. Butterfield and Mina R. Bryan, Associate Editors. Copyright 1950 by Princeton University Press. Reprinted by permission.

[1] To Joel Barlow, 3 May 1802.

131

and records in his personal files—these and countless other acts, performed throughout his career and at the cost of an untold amount of time and energy, reveal the consciousness of his effort to preserve for posterity a full account of the major events through which the country passed in its formative years and of his own part in those events.

Because of his conscious effort and because of his complete identity with the national purpose as it was pursued during his day, this and succeeding volumes take on significant meaning. They are, first of all, the record of a man's career—a record which, in the accepted opinion of a competent scholar, constitutes "the richest treasure house of historical information ever left by a single man."[2] But also, since the achievements of Jefferson's long career were extraordinarily fruitful, these volumes may be regarded as being, in part, a record of the origin, formation, and early growth of the Republic. More, they may be taken as being the best single gateway to the eighteenth century in America and to the manifold hopes then stirring the minds of men that reason and justice could be substituted for authority and superstition in guiding human affairs.

Yet, above all, these volumes should be regarded as the embodiment of an idea. They need to be viewed so if only because Jefferson's remarkable versatility and the very mass of evidence tend to obscure the nature of the idea. The generally accepted opinion of Jefferson as a versatile genius whose all-embracing mind explored every avenue of science and culture, much of which he enriched and all of which he gathered within the orbit of his lofty purpose, is indubitably correct and is amply set forth in these volumes. Parton's description of him as "a gentleman of thirty-two who could calculate an eclipse, survey an estate, tie an artery, plan an edifice, try a cause, break a horse, dance a minuet, and play the violin" is, for all its incongruity, only a partial picture. Among all Jefferson's contemporaries in America, if not among all who preceded and followed him, only Franklin could be said to approach him in the extent and variety of his inquiry. To catalogue the areas of his explorations is to list most of the principal categories of knowledge—law, government, history, mathematics, architecture, medicine, agriculture, languages and literature, education, music, philosophy, religion, and almost every

---

[2] Chinard, *Thomas Jefferson*, Boston, 1929, p. xvi.

branch of the natural sciences from astronomy through meteorology
to zoology. Yet, in the twentieth century when the vast accumulation
of knowledge has made universal inquiry impossible and specialization inevitable, versatility is too likely to be regarded either as an
accomplishment reserved to the geniuses of the earth, and therefore
inaccessible to the generality of human beings, or as a fruitless dis-
persal of energy through meaningless inquiry, and therefore not to
be emulated.

To view Jefferson's versatile and endless inquiries from either point
of view would be to run the risk of unduly magnifying his genius or,
worse, to miss its central meaning. That he possessed many of the
qualities of a genius is plain; the drafting of the Declaration of
Independence and the invention of a cryptographic device more than
a century in advance of his time[3]—to take two wholly unrelated
examples—are surely evidences of an elevated and even inspired
intellect. But his natural genius was supported by indefatigable
industry, an industry exhibited with such unremitting application as
to be almost without parallel. In this varied and ceaseless pursuit of
knowledge, ramifying in all directions, Jefferson nevertheless rarely
if ever revealed the defects of his virtues. Omnivorous of knowledge,
he was the least pedantic of men and scornful of ostentatious learning; a prodigious transcriber of statutes, he was never an unimagina-
tive drudge; a zealous traveler who delighted in new scenes and took
countless notes on his journeys, he was far removed from the mere
gazers at new sights; an unrivaled collector of books about his own
country and about every subject of human thought, he never descended to bibliolatry; a legislator and therefore a politician, he was
recognized and respected as one who consistently acted upon principle. The inescapable conclusion—a conclusion that has forced itself
insistently upon those who are editing these volumes—is that Jefferson's compulsion to investigate all avenues of human knowledge was
purposeful.

This purpose aimed beyond his own time or his own country.
"Jefferson aspired beyond the ambition of a nationality and embraced

---

[3] "Jefferson's invention of the *Wheel Cypher* represents a contribution to
cryptographic science so far in advance of his time that at least a century had
to elapse before a similar invention was independently made by a second inventor
in the field" (extracted from a communication to the editors, 17 Nov. 1949, from
William F. Friedman, Chief of the Technical Division, Armed Forces Security
Agency).

in his view the whole future of man," wrote Henry Adams. This, to Jefferson, was the meaning of the American Revolution. "A just and solid republican government maintained here," he wrote to John Dickinson, "will be a standing monument and example for the aim and imitation of the people of other countries; and I join with you in the hope and belief that they will see from our example that a free government is of all others the most energetic; that the enquiry which has been excited among the mass of mankind by our revolution and it's consequences, will ameliorate the condition of man over a great portion of the globe. What a satisfaction have we in the contemplation of the benevolent effects of our efforts, compared with those of the leaders on the other side, who have discountenanced all advances in science as dangerous innovations, have endeavored to render philosophy and republicanism terms of reproach, to persuade us that man cannot be governed but by the rod, &c. I shall have the happiness of living and dying in the contrary hope."[4] But this hope and this satisfaction would disappear if the standing monument fell. Its strength and virtue lay in its character as an example to be emulated, a beacon to be followed. Its force would be a moral force, and this meant that all of the citizens of the free government—every citizen—faced a responsibility to sustain the example and to keep it from failure. The urgency that permeated all of Jefferson's versatile activity betrayed, perhaps, a fear that the great experiment might fail; that the mass of the people here might not be, as he knew they were not in some parts of the world, ready for the trial; and if he exhibited a missionary zeal in what he called the "holy republican gospel," it was no doubt because he felt it necessary to set an example to his fellow citizens as they in turn were obligated to set it for other peoples. When, therefore, as ambassador, he sat in an Italian dairy from dawn until dusk to learn the process by which Parmesan cheese was made, or when, in the same capacity, he smuggled a few grains of rice from the valley of the Po to send to South Carolina; when, as traveler, he jotted down data about "designs for machines and furniture and landscape details; recipes for macaroni and other dishes; . . . and notes and memoranda on an incredible variety of subjects, from the use of Archimedes' screw at Kew to snuff, Sophocles, and specific

[4] To John Dickinson, 6 Mch. 1801.

gravity";[5] when, as governor, he interrupted his activities in behalf of the defense of the commonwealth to answer questions about ancient records; when, as president, he investigated the possibilities of vaccination against smallpox and, against the preponderance of conservative medical opinion, successfully carried out the first mass vaccination in America; when, in retirement, he studied new methods of improving agriculture or projected an institution of higher learning or explored the languages of the Anglo-Saxons and of the American Indians—when he engaged in these and countless other activities, his investigations were guided by a central and controlling purpose, unifying all and elevating the lowliest to a majestic dignity.

That purpose is to be found stated and restated, explicitly and implicitly, in this and in the volumes that are to follow. It was far from being a new concept. But what caused it to seize upon Jefferson with the power of religious conviction and to dominate his entire life was the fact that here in America, for the first time in history, the philosophical concept seemed ready to march hand in hand with actuality. Here was to be tried the grand experiment of self-government, on whose success or failure would hang the future course of human improvement. It was reserved to Jefferson to join actuality with philosophy for himself, for his countrymen, and for all humanity when he wrote: "We hold these truths to be self-evident; that all men are created equal, that they are endowed by their creator with certain inalienable rights; that among these are life, liberty, & the pursuit of happiness; that to secure these rights, governments are instituted among men, deriving their just powers from the consent of the governed; that whenever any form of government becomes destructive of these ends, it is the right of the people to alter or to abolish it, & to institute new government, laying it's foundation on such principles & organising it's powers in such form, as to them shall seem most likely to effect their safety & happiness."[6]

This, perhaps the most potent idea of modern history, as valid for the twentieth century as for the eighteenth, was the idea that gave meaning to Jefferson's versatile inquiry and selfless industry. It is the idea that dominated and guided his entire life, the idea to which he

[5] Lyman H. Butterfield, "The Papers of Thomas Jefferson: Progress and Procedures in the Enterprise at Princeton," *American Archivist*, XII (1949), 132-3.

[6] Quoted from Jefferson's "original Rough draught" of the Declaration of Independence.

yielded an allegiance warmed by a passionate faith, clarified by a brilliant intellect, and expressed by an eloquent and felicitous pen. These volumes, like his own public life, will begin and end with the same affirmation; the principles set forth in the Declaration of Independence were reaffirmed half a century later in a final testament of faith: "May it be to the world what I believe it will be (to some parts sooner, to others later, but finally to all) the Signal of arousing men to burst the chains, under which Monkish ignorance and superstition had persuaded them to bind themselves, and to assume the blessings and security of self-government. The form which we have substituted restores the free right to the unbounded exercise of reason and freedom of opinion. All eyes are opened, or opening to the rights of man. The general spread of the light of science has already laid open to every view the palpable truth that the mass of mankind has not been born, with saddles on their backs, nor a favored few booted and spurred, ready to ride them legitimately, by the grace of god." [7]

"The letters of a person, especially of one whose business has been chiefly transacted by letters," wrote Jefferson late in life, "forms the only full and genuine journal of his life." [8] The observation is as sound as it is comprehensive, for it views "the letters of a person" not merely as those written by him but also as embracing letters received and other correspondence involved in the transaction of business. It is an observation particularly applicable to the man who made it. For Thomas Jefferson ranks high among the great letter writers of his own or of any other age, and the Jefferson canon, though it includes also public addresses, statutes, state papers, pamphlets, and many other types of documents, is to be found primarily in his voluminous correspondence. The extent of this correspondence is as remarkable as its content. Beginning in 1760 when its author was a youthful subject of the monarch of Great Britain and ending in 1826 when he was already revered as one of the great citizens of the vigorous young Republic, this correspondence, carried on with thousands of persons of every station of life—scientists, statesmen, explorers, merchants, scholars, philosophers, planters, overseers, soldiers, family, and friends, at home and abroad—is estimated to number upwards of fifty thousand separate items.

[7] To Roger C. Weightman, 24 June 1826.
[8] To Robert Walsh, 5 Apr. 1823.

Though the special quality which makes this correspondence still significant was the lofty purpose and the felicitous style which characterized even its most trivial part, its sheer volume and the energy required to produce it were as impressive to Jefferson's contemporaries as they are to us. "I wonder how Mr. Jefferson made out to answer everybody who wrote to him even while the labours of the Department of State and then of the Presidency were on his hands?" wrote William Wirt in 1827.[9] Knowing that Jefferson's lifelong habit was to spend several hours daily at his desk, Wirt placed a discerning finger on one of the chief means by which Jefferson accomplished so much when he exclaimed, in answer to his own question, "O! System!" As none of Jefferson's contemporaries equaled him in the volume and richness of his correspondence, so none equaled him in the systematic organization of his personal archives. Though he was felicitous in phrasing, Jefferson was not facile in composition, and it was not merely his interest in technical improvements that drove him to the use of the letterpress, the polygraph, the stylograph, and other devices for making multiple copies of letters and documents. These devices were means by which his hours at the desk were employed creatively rather than in the drudgery of copying. Among the prodigious letter writers of his generation, for example Washington and Franklin, Jefferson was alone also in the production of an exact, laboriously compiled, and precisely indexed record of his correspondence—the so-called "Epistolary Record," extending from 1783 to 1826, in which he recorded in parallel columns virtually every letter that he wrote or received. Important as this remarkable 656-page document may have been in enabling its compiler to transact his extensive business and in what it reveals to us of his love of system and order, it became equally important as a legacy to his editors, providing as it does an almost complete census of his letters and also an authoritative device for establishing the dates of undated or mutilated letters, for ascertaining the author's whereabouts, and for unlocking some of the mysteries of postal communication during his time. Nor was this all. Dispersed and confused as Jefferson's personal archives have become since 1826, they must have presented at his death an exemplary picture of systematic arrangement. A single fragment of what was probably a comprehensive catalogue of his records

[9] William Wirt to Dabney Carr, 27 Oct. 1827, MS, Virginia State Library.

shows in part what that arrangement was. This fragment includes such rubrics as "Law cases, opinions and tracts"; "State Revolutionary proceedings"; "Draughts, Notes &c. relating to Revised Code"; "documents for Notes on Virginia"; "Rough draughts, notes &c. while Member of Congress & Minister Plenipo. at Paris."; "Bank Accounts"; "Acct books, to wit. P. Jefferson. J. Harvey. N. Lewis. Th: J's"; and "family letters, plantation papers," &c.[10]

❖   ❖   ❖   ❖   ❖

It was only five months after Jefferson had retired as President that the first proposal was brought forth to publish "a complete edition" of his writings. To this Jefferson gave a depreciative response: the *Notes on the State of Virginia*, he wrote, was to be revised and enlarged; messages to Congress, interesting at the moment, would scarcely be read a second time, "and answers to addresses are hardly read a first time." In short, only those who were in the habit of preserving state papers would be interested in such a publication and, Jefferson added, they "are not many." [11]

Historians and the general public have differed with this overmodest appraisal. Aside from numerous publications of Jefferson documents in newspapers, periodicals, biographies, monographs, and selected volumes, there have been four collected editions of his letters and writings. The first was that edited by his grandson, Thomas Jefferson Randolph, *Memoirs, Correspondence, and Miscellanies from the Papers of Thomas Jefferson*, in four volumes, which first appeared at Charlottesville in 1829 and was promptly brought out in other editions printed in London (1829), Boston (1830), and Paris (1833). The second was edited by Henry A. Washington, *The Writings of Thomas Jefferson*, published in nine volumes at Washington in 1853-1854. The third was *The Writings of Thomas Jefferson*, edited by Paul Leicester Ford and published at New York in ten volumes between the years 1892 and 1899; it was reissued in twelve volumes as the "Federal Edition," 1904-1905. The fourth, with the same title, was edited by A. A. Lipscomb and A. E. Bergh in twenty volumes, Washington, 1903-1904, and was several times reissued.

[10] Memorandum in Jefferson's hand, in the possession of Roger W. Barrett, Chicago.
[11] To John W. Campbell, 3 Sep. 1809.

The first of these four collected editions was issued in 6,000 copies, all of which were subscribed for within the year in which they were published.[12] Each succeeding edition, exerting an incalculable influence in establishing Jefferson as one of the great figures of world history, brought about an increasing demand for a complete and more dependable text of his utterances. The reason for this demand lay not alone in the quality of Jefferson's mind and in the warmth of his faith, but also in the character of the editions themselves, all of which are long since out of print. The most accurate and useful edition—that edited by Ford—suffered from a severe limitation of space and from a disproportionate emphasis upon the purely political aspects of Jefferson's career. The most recent, the most extensive, and the most widely used edition—that edited by Lipscomb and Bergh and usually referred to as the Memorial Edition—was in large part a mere reprinting of the text of the Henry A. Washington edition of 1853-1854. Though Washington's edition of *The Writings of Thomas Jefferson* was a noteworthy accomplishment in its day and added greatly to the public knowledge of Jefferson in the mid-nineteenth century, it was characterized by the sort of editorial liberties with the text which reflected the inexact scholarly standards of that day. Thus the only edition originating in the twentieth century and the one most widely used is one that includes such distortions as the willful suppression of names, the silent omission of passages, and the substitution of the editors' choice of words for Jefferson's.

The inaccuracies, incompleteness, and unavailability of all previous editions led to an increasing demand on the part of historians for an edition of Jefferson's writings so comprehensive in scope and so accurate in presentation that the work would never need to be done again. . . .

---

[12] *The Virginia Literary Museum,* I (1829), 432.

THOMAS JEFFERSON AS A
CLASSICAL SCHOLAR

GILBERT CHINARD

... In our day of public libraries, circulating libraries, book of the month clubs, and literary mass production, we can hardly realize the power exerted by the classics at a time and in a land where only a few books were available. In those days a young man did not take a course in intensive reading but he had time for the slow assimilation of the best books, for meditation and reflection. We, on the contrary, are willy nilly stuffed with unwelcome and unpalatable information and facts; indeed, according to an advertisement which I recently clipped from a newspaper: "Every minute, every hour of the day, the world's greatest artists are saturating the very air you breathe, the atmosphere around and through your home, with musical entertainments, information, amusement, and educational features." No such intrusion upon the mind's privacy, and no such "saturation" were to be feared by the banks of the Rivanna when Thomas Jefferson was introduced through Homer to the beauties of the Ancient World. Reading the old poet, in a canoe which he had built himself, the boy dreamed of ancient navigators who sailed the wine-colored sea from island to island, of fierce battles, of feasts of warriors, and magic vistas of the Greece of old were opened to him. Or, stretched out in the shade of the great oak tree which he and his friend Page loved so much, he read Virgil, Horace, and Catullus. Strange to say it was not an entirely new world, for between these ancient Greeks and Romans and the early Americans existed more than one resemblance. From the coast of Maine to Georgia the shore of the Atlantic was settled with colonies bearing somewhat the same relation to their mother country as did the Greek colonies to their metropolis; and Stanyan was in a way, and in anticipation, a sort of epitome of American chronicles.

An address delivered before the Johns Hopkins Chapter of Phi Beta Kappa, April 12, 1930, printed in *The Johns Hopkins Alumni Magazine*, Volume 18, Number 4, June 1930, and in *The American Scholar*, Volume 1, Number 2, March 1932. Reprinted by permission of Gilbert Chinard.

The American settlements, like the ancient civilizations, were largely agricultural; and this was particularly true of Virginia. There was so little difference between the method used by the farmers to make a cart-wheel and the description of the same process in Homer that, as Jefferson himself pointed out, one might almost believe the American agriculturists had borrowed their knowledge from the Greek poet. A Virginia plantation presented a striking resemblance to the estate of a well-to-do Roman farmer, and, after Horace, Jefferson repeated: "Happy the man who, free from business worries, like the men of the old days, tills with his oxen his ancestral fields without being harassed by mortgages," *solutus omni foenore!* And again, "What a joy to see the sheep hurrying back to the farm after pasturing, to see the tired oxen dragging along the upturned ploughshare, and the young slaves, industrious swarm of an opulent house, gathered around the resplendent fireplace!"

This bucolic strain permeated Jefferson's life. Whenever his political duties keep him long from Monticello, be he detained in Philadelphia, Paris, or Washington, his private letters echo the longing of the Latin poet: *"O rus, quando te aspiciam!"* In the midst of political strife he yearned for his ancestral acres, the sweet coolness of the woods, and the swift running streams of the country of his boyhood. *In angello cum libello,* "to live in a nook of the woods, with a choice book"—if I may venture this homely translation—such was the ideal life and the limits of his ambition during adolescence. Proud as he was of his Anglo-Saxon ancestry, the Mediterranean world nevertheless exerted on him a strange fascination. Once during his trip to Italy, traveling a-foot from Louana to Alberga and from village to village along the coast, marveling at the incredible azure of the sea, he almost forgot his dear Monticello and exclaimed, "If any person wished to retire from his acquaintance, to live absolutely unknown and yet in the midst of physical enjoyments, it should be in some of the little villages of this coast, where air, water, and earth concur to offer what each has most precious!"

This constant commerce with the Ancients is largely responsible for that felicity of expression which made Jefferson famous even among his contemporaries and caused him to be designated to frame the Declaration of Independence. In certain respects he was an original thinker, but in matters politic the method of expression is far more important than the idea itself—for ideas are common property, at the disposal of all comers; the real discoverer is he who coins the felicitous formula enabling it to fly on the lips of men. Clear-cut definitions, political aphorisms, and striking formulas abound in the letters of Jefferson. Passed around and repeated by his friends they contributed more rapidly and permanently than long treatises, political disquisitions, or eloquent, harmonious, and easily forgotten speeches, to the diffusion of the Jeffersonian doctrine. Once for all he gave expression to the aspirations, the wishes, and ideals of his country. More than any other man in your national history he was the *vox populi,* and to such a degree, indeed, that even his opponents, when they wish to appeal to the fundamental principles which constitute true Americanism, must use not only his language but his very words. Such a quality cannot be entirely acquired—it can be strengthened and developed, however, by education; and the classical education which Jefferson gave himself largely accounts for it. Here an observation should be made. Jefferson was not blind in his admiration for the Ancients, hesitating to depart from conventional and traditional worship of everything Greek or Latin—on the contrary, he preserved a singular independence of judgment. At a time when Southern oratory was flourishing and American oratory in general was taking as a model the worst there is in Cicero he boldly declared: "The models for that oratory which is to produce the greatest effect by securing the attention of hearers and readers, are to be found in Livy, Tacitus, Sallust, and most assuredly not in Cicero." This statement explains Jefferson's abhorrence of rhetorical effects. His speech, in which metaphors and similes are rarely found, has the trim, stripped beauty of a Greek athlete, and for this reason, perhaps, is not always appreciated as it should be. Above all he was fond of the *imperatoria brevitas* of the Latin language which even monosyllabic Anglo-Saxon cannot emulate. He used Latin when writing in one of his memorandum books those maxims by which he intended to regulate his life: *bonum est quod honestum—ex recto decus—non votum nobis sed patriae—fiat justitia ruat coelum.*

The study of Latin has declined nowadays to such a degree that a Latin quotation is apt to bring an indulgent smile to the lips of the hearers. I can hardly conceive of an undergraduate, even a newly elected member of the Phi Beta Kappa Society, entering Latin quotations in his diary; yet less than a hundred and fifty years ago these old precepts formed the very substance of the moral life of the men, in Europe as well as in America, who played such important roles in the destinies of their countries.

In our estimate of American civilization we are apt to over-emphasize the influence of Puritanism. The fact that some of the men of the Revolution had a moral fiber stronger, as it seems, than ours, and possessed perhaps superior but sterner virtues than more recent generations, may be attributed to the Puritanical "climate" in which they lived; but for many of them, and particularly Jefferson, to the influence of the Bible was added the influence of the classics, for in spite of the apparent supremacy of Puritanism the insidious campaign of the Deists had reached the New World, undermining the faith and respect for the authority of its traditions. Even more than we, the men of the close of the eighteenth century put confidence in science and the power of reason. The mechanistic explanations of the universe were just as generally accepted then as they are now although they rested on foundations that seem to us unscientific. Early in life Jefferson had reflected upon the riddle of the universe and soon after his introduction, by Governor Fauquier, to the works of Bolingbroke he ceased to consider the Bible as containing an authentic account of creation and the word of God. In reading Cicero he had come to the conclusion that "if either the heart, or the blood, or the brain, is the soul, then certainly the soul, being corporeal, must perish with the rest of the body; if it is air, it will perhaps be dissolved; if it is fire, it will be extinguished."

At this point of his moral development, he appears to have been overwhelmed with despair. More than once in his anguish Jefferson, like Orestes in the beginning of Euripides' play, called for the "sovereign oblivion of suffering, supreme wisdom yearned for by the unhappy." He took a sort of bitter pleasure—a *delectatio morosa* not so different from the attitude of our new humanists—in recording in his *Commonplace Book* the most pessimistic utterances of the ancient poets, entering among others the sad conclusion from Anacreon:

> A scanty dust to feed the wind
> Is all the trace 't will leave behind.

At that time he could have put the query of his old friend, John Adams: "Watchman, what of the night? Is darkness that may be felt to prevail over the whole world? Or can you perceive any rays of re-

turning dawn?" The props of traditional faith once removed, his
moral structure had collapsed, and the young man was left apparently without a beacon to direct his course. He might have become a
cynic or a voluptuary; indeed there are indications in the *Commonplace Book* that he nearly succumbed to the temptation. After
Horace he repeated: "Since all earthly beings have received only
perishable lives and neither the great nor the poor can escape death,
so my dear friend, enjoy all the good things in life, and while you
live remember how short life is." But this was just a passing mood—
his aristocratic pride and the stern teachings of the Stoics saved him.
He was conscious that he was of good stock and he had read in
Euripides: "To be of the noble born gives a peculiar distinction
clearly marked among men, and the noble name increases in lustre
in those who are worthy."

Ever to be upright and worthy of one's good blood was the sim-
plest, the most obvious, the most imperious duty—yet some coherent
system, some working hypothesis must be found to justify one's existence. To dismiss from the mind all preoccupation regarding future
life, to attain the ataraxia of the ancient sages, was at best an opiate,
not a remedy; and to rebuild a whole theory of life on enlightened
self-interest, as had been proposed by several philosophers, seemed
to him unsatisfactory. Equally unsatisfactory were the theories which
"placed the foundation of morality in truth, the To Kalon, etc., as
fanciful writers have imagined." Taking his cue from Bolingbroke, he
consequently undertook to construct a system from the writings of
the "ancient heathen moralists, of Tully and Seneca, of Epictetus
and others," which would be "more full, more coherent, and more
clearly deduced from unquestionable principles of knowledge." Are
not the "new humanists" turning to Aristotle, Confucius, and Buddha
in a similar endeavor?

Whatever system might be adopted, it was evident that a man
could never justify his existence, even in his own eyes, unless he lived
for others as much as for himself, and thought beyond the narrow
span allotted to him. After Cicero he repeated: "Death which threat-
ens us daily from a thousand accidents, and which, by reason of the
shortness of life, can never be far off, does not deter a wise man from
making such provision for his country and his family as he hopes may
last forever, and from regarding posterity, of which he can never
have any real perception, as belonging to himself." To devote oneself

to some great task, to associate in some worthy undertaking, to survive in one's deeds—this is the most consoling substitute for the old faith in personal immortality. As Euripides said: "Nay for myself while living day by day, even if my lot were humble, it would be quite enough; but as for a tomb I should wish mine to be one that men honor when they see it; long enduring is that satisfaction." And Jefferson, had he not chosen to inscribe on his monument the simple enumeration of his three great contributions to the moral progress of his country, could have found no more fitting epitaph.

It was at this period of his development that the young man, with little practical experience, culled from Homer and Euripides the maxims by which he was to govern his life. In the moral works of Cicero and in the old writers who had crystallized the experiences of countless generations he found precious bits of worldly wisdom. And after all, in spite of the hypotheses of our modern psychologists, knowledge of the human heart has advanced very little; the basic facts regulating the relations between human beings living side by side in a given society have not changed much since the days of Homer. "Man," wrote Jefferson, "was destined for society. His morality, therefore, was to be formed on this object. He was endowed with a sense of right and wrong merely relative to this. This sense is as much part of his nature as the sense of hearing, seeing, feeling; it is the true foundation of morality."

Thus bit by bit, stone by stone, Thomas Jefferson in his student days reerected the moral structure which had been torn down by the philosophical storm of the eighteenth century; thus he determined to live "as if posterity belonged to him," and to work for the future without much hope of any immediate and personal reward, for he had learned that "the race of men is ungrateful," and "most cities are so constituted that a man who is noble and zealous wins no higher prize than baser men." This knowledge of the past preserved him from the blind optimism of so many reformers—for whatever one may aim to accomplish, he must realize that mankind does not advance by leaps and bounds, but "in a snail-gaited progress." Slow as this progress had been it was, however, real; and Jefferson was the first to acknowledge that the courageous, stoic, and disenchanted philosophy upon which he relied for a time had its limitations. Cicero had admitted that there is by nature something soft and tender in our souls—*est natura in animis tenerum quiddam atque molle*—and Seneca had coined the beautiful expression *caritas generis humani* to define the solidarity existing between all men, irrespective of creed or race; but later in life Jefferson realized that "in developing our duties to others [the ancient philosophers] were short and defective. They embraced indeed, the circles of kindred and friends, and inculcated patriotism or the love of our country in the aggregate, as a primary obligation; towards our neighbors and countrymen they taught justice, but scarcely viewed them as within the circle of benevolence. Still less have they inculcated peace, charity, and love of our fellow men, or embraced with benevolence the whole family of mankind."

This humanitarian mood would probably draw the fire of the humanists, and Professor Babbitt on this occasion might reiterate the accusations launched against Jefferson in his volume entitled *Leadership and Democracy*, but, old-fashioned, sentimental professor that I am, I confess that I would rather agree with Cicero and Jefferson than with my stern colleague from granite-clad New England, and with them hold that *non silice nati sumus*—we are not the offspring of flint.

In still another respect Jefferson would disagree with the new humanists. He saw no antinomy in his creed combining the teachings of the pagan philosophers with the morals of Jesus and material progress or scientific discoveries. With Bolingbroke he agreed that "there is a gradation of sense and intelligence here from animal beings imperceptible to us for their minuteness, without the help of microscopes, and even with them, up to man, in whom, though this be their highest stage, sense and intelligence stop short and remain very imperfect." He saw nothing distressing in the assumption that man was made for the planet, and not the planet for man: "The habitation is fit for him, and he is fitted to live in it. He could not exist in any other. But will it follow that the planet was made for him, not he for the planet? The ass would be scorched in Venus or Mercury and be frozen in Jupiter or Saturn. Will it follow that this temperate planet was made for him to bray and to eat thistles in it?"

Such a contemplation of the very unimportant place we occupy in the general scheme of the universe should not unduly depress us nor deter us from our immediate duties. After all, concluded Jefferson, the business of life is with life, that is to say, with matter; and our first preoccupation should be to know the world in which we live—

our most imperious task, to utilize and develop the resources at our disposal. He was too fond of new inventions to be afraid of machinism. The man who knew how to plan and construct all the ingenious contraptions with which he surrounded himself was not afraid of being crushed or annihilated by machines. His knowledge of the ploughs used by the ancients did not prevent him from inventing a new one, better in design and more effective; the man who had built for himself the curious pantograph, which enabled him to make four copies of a letter at one time, would not have hesitated to use a typewriter. Most certainly he would not have considered material progress an obstacle to moral advancement; and were he to come back today he would probably find that the problems so greatly agitating us do not differ essentially from those confronting him when he was a student at William and Mary and which he solved with the help of the old philosophers. If dragged into the controversy he would no doubt write a long letter to Professor Babbitt and Mr. Paul Elmer Moore. He would admit, with them, that some "inner check" is needed to control our moral life; he would call their attention to the fact that, in his youth, he too felt the greatest admiration for certain old philosophers "whose principles related chiefly to ourselves and the government of those passions which, unrestrained, would disturb our tranquillity of mind"; but he would add that he had clearly seen the necessity of completing those principles and theories with something less humanistic, perhaps, but certainly more human.

Thus, as he advanced in age, the classics ceased to be the sole staff upon which Jefferson leaned; but his love for the old masters who had taught him to look at life with courage remained undiminished. Now he read them for pleasure rather than with a practical object in mind. "I enjoyed Homer in his own language infinitely beyond Pope's translation of him," he wrote, in 1800, to Priestley, "and both beyond the dull narrative of the same event by Dares Phrygius; and it is an innocent enjoyment. I thank on my knees him who directed my early education, for having put into my possession this rich source of delight; and I would not exchange it for anything which I could then have acquired, and have not acquired."

Jefferson had commissioned Ticknor to send him from Europe the best and most recent editions of Greek and Latin classics, but I have a suspicion that more than once he preferred the thin scrap-book with yellow leaves and turned-up corners, kept by Mrs. Randolph "among her treasures," in which he had gathered the essence of ancient wisdom, and, thumbing its pages, he reviewed his life in the light of the old maxims he had copied when a student. Time and again his experience bore witness to the wisdom of the sages. At last, like the Roman farmer, he was back on his ancestral acres and, reading in his book the famous lines of Horace, *O rus, quando te aspiciam,* he could feel that having fulfilled one of his most cherished and constant desires, he might now be permitted "to read the books of ancient writers," or to give "to sleep drowsy hours to enjoy the sweet oblivion of a restless existence."

THOMAS JEFFERSON AND SCIENCE

Austin H. Clark

As a scientific man Jefferson was interested in all lines of science, but in all rather as an enthusiastic, highly appreciative, and intelligent amateur than as a professional. He had no time to make himself thoroughly proficient in any one line. The working out of the details he left to others, whom he assisted and encouraged to the best of his ability. His tremendous enthusiasm, which continued unabated, or perhaps even increased, during his term of office as President of the United States, was a most important factor in bringing before the people the value of science.

Tangible evidence of Jefferson's many and varied scientific interests is furnished by his contributions to the proceedings and collections of the American Philosophical Society in Philadelphia, of which he was elected a member, together with George Washington, in 1786, after the death of David Rittenhouse succeeding him as the third president of the Society on January 6, 1797. His contributions to the Society's program and collections were in the fields of meteorology, chemistry, economic entomology, archeology, vertebrate paleontology, and applied mechanics in reference to agricultural operations.

On December 17, 1779, there was recorded in the Society's proceedings a letter from Rev'd Wm. Maddison (sic), president of William and Mary College, containing "a series of Meteorological Observations by His Excellency Governor Jefferson and himself separately, for a year and a half; likewise a set of Experiments on what are called 'Sweet Springs'." On April 15, 1791, on motion of Jefferson, a select committee (consisting of Jefferson and four others) was appointed to collect materials for forming the natural history of the Hessian fly and determining the best means for its prevention or destruction "and whatever else relative to the same may be interesting to agriculture." On August 19, 1791, he presented to the Society

Excerpt from "Thomas Jefferson and Science," by Austin H. Clark in *Journal of the Washington Academy of Sciences*, Volume 33, Number 7, July 15, 1943. Reprinted by permission of Austin H. Clark.

"a curious piece of Indian sculpture, supposed to represent an Indian woman in labor, found near Cumberland River, Virginia." On August 19, 1796, his letter to Rittenhouse (deceased) describing bones of extraordinary size found beyond the Blue Mountains in Virginia [in a cave in Greenbrier County, W. Va.] "appearing to be of the Tyger-lion & Panther species" was read by Dr. Barton. Under date of March 10, 1797, we read: "Jefferson's memoire 'On the Discovery of certain Bones of a Quadruped of the [space of four lines left blank].' A resolution was passed ordering the memoir to be put in the hands of the Committee of Selection of Publications, drawings of the bones to be made by a proper person. Mr. Peale was requested to put the bones 'in the best order for the Society's use'." These were the bones of the famous *Megalonyx,* the first giant sloth found in North America, and formed the subject of the only scientific memoir ever published by Jefferson, which appeared in 1799. On January 19, 1798, he presented to the Society bones of a mammoth "some time ago found in Virginia." On April 20, 1798, he presented a hand threshing machine invented by T. C. Martin of Virginia, "which he had procured to be made." On May 4, 1798, a "Description of a Mould Board of the least resistance, &c.," by Mr. Jefferson was read and referred to Mr. Patterson. This is the first mention of his famous plow. On May 7, 1804, W. Lewis, of Campbell County, Va., donated a bone and some rocks through Jefferson. On April 27, 1805, William Bartram sent some bones to be forwarded to [Jefferson at] Monticello.

Much more detailed evidence of his extensive interests is furnished by his famous book on Virginia. In June, 1781, he was injured by a fall from his horse, and he occupied the leisure forced upon him by this accident in organizing the abundant and accurate memoranda that he had accumulated over a series of years. These memoranda were arranged in the order of a series of questions that had been submitted to him by M. Barbé de Marbois, Secretary of the French Legation. During the winter of 1782-83 he revised and expanded them and had them published in 1784 under the title of "Notes on the State of Virginia." The date of this work is given as 1782, which is probably the date of the completion of the manuscript, as he did not reach Paris until 1784. Two hundred copies were privately printed, as the work was not intended for general distribution. According to Sabin, a copy presented to M. Malherbe has the following note in Jefferson's handwriting: "Mr. Jefferson having had a few copies of these notes printed to present to some of his friends, and to some estimable characters beyond that line, takes the liberty of presenting a copy to M. de Malherbe, as a testimony to his respect to his character. Unwilling to expose them to the public eye, he begs the favour of M. de M. to put them into the hands of no person on whose care and fidelity he cannot rely, to guard them against publication."

This work, however, did not long remain confidential. A French translation, with a map, entitled "Observations sur la Virginie, par M. J***. Traduit de l'Anglais," was published in Paris in 1786, and an English reprint of the original was published in London in 1788. The first American edition was published in Philadelphia in 1788. In the *Virginia Independent Chronicle* (Richmond) for Wednesday, December 12, 1787, we read that "the work will be comprised in a handsome octavo volume, with an elegant type and good paper, and delivered to the subscribers neatly bound and lettered at the very moderate price of one dollar. The price to non-subscribers will be seven shillings and six pence Virginia currency ... Subscriptions are taken in at Mr. Davis's Printing-Office in Richmond, where a specimen of the work is left for inspection." A second edition was printed in Philadelphia in the same year. This was followed by many other American editions—Philadelphia, 1792, 1794, 1801, 1812, 1815, 1825; Baltimore, 1800 (two editions); New York, 1801, 1804; Newark, 1801; Boston, 1801, 1829, 1832; Trenton, 1803, 1812; and Richmond, 1853. There was also a German translation entitled "Beschreibung von Virginien," published at Leipzig in 1789.

This was the first comprehensive treatise to be published on any section of the United States. In it were discussed the boundaries of the State, the rivers, the seaports, the mountains, the cascades, the mineral, vegetable, and animal productions, climate, population, military force, marine force, aborigines, etc. It was the precursor of that great library of more or less similar reports that have been issued by the State and Federal Governments. Measured by its influence, it was the most important scientific work published in America up to this time. It laid the foundation for Jefferson's high contemporary reputation as a universal scholar, and for his enduring fame as a pioneer American scientific man.

Further evidence of his interests is given by various printed reports, such as his report of July 4, 1790, presented to Congress on July 13, in which he made suggestions regarding a plan for establishing uniformity in the coinage and in the weights and measures of the United States, the first suggestion of the idea that was subsequently expanded into the National Bureau of Standards, and his scholarly report on the history and economics of the cod and whale fisheries made to the House of Representatives on February 1, 1791, and published on January 8, 1872.

Then there are the manuscript notes left by him, among which are the extensive meteorological records kept at Monticello, his notices of the first appearance of the birds and flowers in spring, and his comparative notes on Indian languages.

But by far the greatest part of what we know regarding Jefferson's scientific interests is gathered from the great number of letters that he wrote to various friends and that were published after his death.

Applied science appealed to him quite as much as pure science. He was much interested in horticulture and in every form of agriculture. Botany was always a favorite subject with him, and he had one of the best botanical libraries in America, though on this he never published anything further than the lists of plants in his "Notes on the State of Virginia," which includes the first description of the pecan, written in 1781 or 1782.

Jefferson was an inventor of great ingenuity, as is made evident at once by a visit to his home at Monticello. He also had a keen interest in the inventions of others, especially those of practical application. When he was in France he wrote dozens of letters about inventions. When on a visit to England in 1786 he made careful notes on English domestic gardening and on mechanical appliances. He went to northern Italy in 1787 to inspect machines for cleaning rice, and in 1788 he made other observations in Germany. At the time of the creation of the Patent Office, Jefferson was Secretary of State. As such, he became *ex officio* the Keeper of the Records of the Patents, and according to Dr. Frederick E. Brasch was the most active examining member of the board, and therefore its first administrator. Dr. Brasch says that the scientific foresight that he exercised at this time must be considered the cornerstone of our patent system and patent laws.

Jefferson's keen interest in inventions more than anything else gives the key to his interest in science in general, which was the ultimate practical application of scientific discoveries for the good of man. No matter what line of scientific investigation he undertook, this idea of ultimate practical application seems always to have been in his mind. He seems never to have followed any line through mere pointless curiosity. Even in his study of fossils he appears to have had the idea that some time, somehow, a knowledge of them would prove of value.

Of his numerous and varied scientific interests, three deserve special mention. First and foremost was his interest in man in general, evidenced not only by his political philosophy but also by his detailed study of the native Indians and his efforts to improve their relations with the Europeans, and by his sympathetic study of the Negroes; second was his interest in the exploration and description of the country; and third was his interest in paleontology.

The French historian and philosopher Guillaume Thomas François Raynal, usually called the Abbé Raynal, a leader of the French freethinkers who was exiled from France in 1781, had maintained, among other things, that Europeans had degenerated in America, and that the American Indians were a degenerate race. Jefferson denied this, and he also denied that the American Indians are inferior to Europeans in the same state of culture. He also said he has supposed that the black man, in his present state, might not be equal to the European, "but it would be hazardous to affirm that, equally cultivated for a few generations, he would not become so." In his "Notes on the State of Virginia" he gave an excellent account of the Indians and described the "barrows of which many are to be found all over this country," listing the contents of one in the Rivanna River bottom. He also described the characteristics of the Negroes in dispassionate detail.

He was greatly interested in the multiplicity of radically different Indian languages and contrasted this with the lack of diversification among the red men of eastern Asia. He said that "the resemblance between the Indians of America and the eastern inhabitants of Asia, would induce us to conjecture, that the former are the descendants of the latter, or the latter of the former; excepting, indeed, the Eskimaux, who, from the same circumstances of resemblance, must be derived from the Greenlanders, and thus probably from some of the northern parts of the old continent."

In his "Notes on the State of Virginia" he wrote: "Were vocabularies formed of all the languages spoken in North and South America, preserving their appellations of the most common objects in nature, of those which must be present to every nation, barbarians or civilized, with the inflections of their names and verbs, their principles of regimen and concord, and these deposited in all the public libraries, it would furnish opportunities to those skilled in the languages of the old world to compare them with the new, now or at any future time, and hence to construct the best evidence of the derivation of this part of the human race." He compiled comparative vocabularies of various Indian tribes, which were unfortunately stolen; but some fragments of these are deposited in the American Philosophical Society's archives.

Dr. Clark Wissler has pointed out that at about the same time the Empress Catharine the Great of Russia had adopted the same approach to the study of languages and had written to President Washington for lists of Indian vocabularies.

Jefferson's practical and sympathetic interest in the Indians is perhaps best illustrated by the instructions given by him to Capt. Meriwether Lewis in 1803 when the Lewis and Clark Expedition was about to be organized. These were as follows: "The commerce which may be carried on with the people inhabiting the lines you will pursue renders a knowledge of these people important. You will therefore endeavour to make yourself acquainted, as far as a diligent pursuit of your journey shall admit, with the names of the natives and their numbers; the extent and limits of their possessions; their relations with other tribes or nations; their language, traditions, monuments; their ordinary occupations in agriculture, fishing, hunting, war, arts, and the implements for these; their food, clothing, and domestic accommodations; the diseases prevalent among them, and the remedies they use; moral and physical circumstances which distinguish them from the tribes we know; peculiarities in their laws, customs, and dispositions; and articles of commerce they may need or furnish, and to what extent. And considering the interest which every nation has in extending and strengthening the authority of reason and justice among the people around them, it will be useful to acquire what knowledge you can of the state of morality, religion, and information among them, as it may better enable those who may endeavour to civilize and instruct them to adapt their measures to the existing notions and practices of those on whom they are to operate ...

"In all your intercourse with the natives, treat them in the most friendly and conciliatory manner which their own conduct will admit;

allay all jealousies as to the object of your journey; satisfy them of its innocence; make them acquainted with the position, extent, character, peaceable and commercial dispositions of the United States, of our wish to be neighbourly, friendly and useful to them, and of our dispositions to a commercial intercourse with them; confer with them on the points most convenient as mutual emporiums, and the articles of most desirable interchange for them and us. If a few of their influential chiefs, within practicable distance, wish to visit us, arrange such a visit with them, and furnish them with authority to call on our officers on their entering the United States, to have them conveyed to this place at the public expense. If any of them should wish to have some of their young people brought up with us, and taught such arts as may be useful to them, we will receive, instruct, and take care of them. Such a mission, whether of influential chiefs or of young people, would give some security to your own party. Carry with you some matter of the kine-pox, inform those of them with whom you may be of its efficiency as a preservation from the small-pox and instruct and encourage them in the use of it. This may be especially done wherever you winter."

Dr. O. F. Cook wrote that the traditional sponsors of the repatriation and colonization of the Negroes in west Africa were Thomas Jefferson and George Washington. Jefferson studied the racial problem from many sides, including the need of educating the more capable Negroes so that they might furnish the necessary skill and leadership for the new communities in Africa. Washington instructed his executors to provide such education for some of his freedmen.

Almost immediately after his inauguration as the third President of the United States Jefferson began to make preparations for developing his long-cherished plans for the exploration of the great and unknown West and the discovery and description of its vast resources. His secretary, Capt. Meriwether Lewis, of Albemarle County, Va., who had long wished to go on an exploring expedition, was appointed leader of the first party to be sent out—partly at Jefferson's personal expense. Captain Lewis chose as his chief associate Capt. William Clark, also of Albemarle County, a younger brother of Gen. George Rogers Clark. The choice of these two leaders was a most fortunate one, and the expedition, which was in the field from 1803 (the year in which the territory extending from New Orleans to British America and westward to the Rocky Mountains known as

Louisiana was purchased from Napoleon) until 1806 was highly successful. This was the first of a long series of more or less similar expeditions by which a detailed knowledge of our great West and of its resources and products was gradually accumulated. These expeditions, at first individual enterprises, were later consolidated under the United States Geological Survey.

Jefferson's interest in exploration was not confined to the land areas. Dr. Brasch writes that in 1806 he made a recommendation for a Coast Survey to Congress, which took favorable action on February 10, 1807, and authorized the President to cause a survey to be made of the coasts of the United States, including islands, shoals, and all other physical features deemed proper for completing an accurate chart of every part of the coast. This project was later organized as the United States Coast (now Coast and Geodetic) Survey. Dr. Brasch adds that during Jefferson's second term the idea of establishing longitude 0° through Washington (77° 03′ 58″ west of Greenwich, England) was much discussed. Jefferson's thorough knowledge of astronomy and mathematics, together with navigation, enabled him to give much encouragement to members of Congress who wished to establish this standard American longitude. This discussion, according to Dr. Brasch, eventually led to the establishment of the Naval Observatory and the Hydrographic Office.

Enthusiasm for vertebrate paleontology seems to have been awakened in Jefferson before 1781, after which time he lost no opportunity for securing and examining bones. He was always especially interested in the mastodons, or "mammoths," and in the great sloth that he had called *Megalonyx*. As in other branches of science, his interest in paleontology was chiefly that of an enthusiastic amateur, and a stimulator of interest in others. Dr. Henry Fairfield Osborn has pointed out that in developing his scientific opinions in regard to paleontology he at first quoted the current tradition, later becoming a more serious and independent investigator.

The Lewis and Clark Expedition had brought back a few interesting fossils, which had whetted Jefferson's desire for more. In the summer of 1807 Captain Clark was sent on another expedition to Louisiana that took him through the region of Big Bone Lick, in Boone County, Ky. In obedience to President Jefferson's desires he stopped there and, employing ten laborers for several weeks, made a large collection of about 300 bones, which he shipped to Jefferson at the White House. Here they were laid out in the then unfinished East Room, the "mastodon room," where, at Jefferson's invitation, and later at Philadelphia, they were examined by Dr. Caspar Wistar.

Jefferson's interest in paleontology while President, as remarked by Dr. George Gaylord Simpson, helped to make it a respectable and honored pursuit, and he was largely responsible for bringing together the materials necessary for its advancement. He greatly encouraged the study of vertebrate paleontology by the American Philosophical Society while he was president of it. He also acted for a time as president of the board of trustees of Peale's Philadelphia Museum, which included the first public exhibition of fossil vertebrates, and the first mounted fossil skeleton in America. As the foremost citizen of the young nation, Jefferson's outspoken and excited interest in fossils conferred on their study the dignity and prestige inseparable from his personality and position. But it also brought down upon him the ridicule and wrath of many of his countrymen to whom scientific investigation meant wanton and deliberate neglect of one's proper duties, if not, indeed, atheism. This attitude is well illustrated by a poem written by William Cullen Bryant at the age of 13, which runs in part as follows:

> Go, wretch, resign thy presidential chair,
> Disclose thy secret measures, foul or fair,
> Go, search with curious eye, for hornéd frogs,
> Mid the wild wastes of Louisianian bogs;
> Or, where the Ohio rolls his turbid stream,
> Dig for huge bones, thy glory and thy theme.

It is only fair to Bryant to say that this poem, entitled "The Embargo," was published not by himself but by his father, Dr. Peter Bryant, and that he did his best to suppress it.

It must not be supposed that during his brilliant and eventful career Jefferson was neglectful of his scientific colleagues in his native state of Virginia. Before the American Philosophical Society had elected more than a very few members from Virginia there was organized at Williamsburg on November 20, 1773, "The Virginia Society for the Promotion of Useful Knowledge." The charter was signed by six prominent Virginians, including the Hon. John Page, then lieutenant governor, who was elected vice-president, the president being John Clayton. Of the six who signed the constitution, John Walker was already a member of the American Philosophical Society, which James McClurg joined in the following year, and Mann Page later.

The notices regarding the activities of this Society were published in the Virginia Gazette at Williamsburg. There is no reference to Jefferson in any of them, but he was presumably a member, for in a letter written in 1787 in answer to one from John Page, who had urged him to accept the presidency, he wrote that "he should feel himself out of his true place to stand before McClurg," who was probably president at the time.

In its early years the society seems to have been well received by the people of the colony; but after 1774 there are few published notices of it, although it appears to have kept up an organization for a considerable time.

Jefferson was in France from August 6, 1784, to October, 1789, succeeding Benjamin Franklin as Minister in 1785. Dumas Malone writes that, rightly regarded in France as a savant, he carried on the tradition of Franklin, but until the end of his stay he was overshadowed by Franklin's immense reputation. His attitude toward Franklin, whom he regarded as the greatest American, was one of becoming modesty, without a tinge of jealousy.

At that time France was regarded as the leader in the biological sciences; but Jefferson thought little of French science. He vigorously combated what he considered the disparagement of the American fauna by Georges Louis Leclerc, Comte de Buffon, who maintained that the animals common to both the Old and the New World are smaller in the latter; that those peculiar to the New World are on a smaller scale; that those which have been domesticated in both have degenerated in America; and that, on the whole, America exhibits fewer species. In order to correct these impressions, Jefferson procured from America at his own expense and presented to the Comte de Buffon the bones and skin of a moose, the horns of another individual of the same species, and horns of the caribou, the elk, the deer, the spiked horned buck, and the roebuck of America. Buffon also maintained, much to the annoyance of Jefferson, that the American mastodon, or "mammoth," was the same as the elephant of Africa and Asia.

He does not seem to have had a very high regard for Buffon. In a letter to President Madison of William and Mary he wrote: "Speaking one day with M. de Buffon on the present ardor of chemical inquiry, he affected to consider chemistry but as cookery, and to place the toils of the laboratory on a footing with those of the kitchen. *I* think it, on the contrary, among the most useful of sciences and *big* with future discoveries for the utility and safety of the human race."

Dumas Malone writes that Jefferson became associated with an extraordinary number of important societies in various countries of Europe, as he had long been with the chief learned, and almost all the agricultural, societies of America. Much, but by no means all, of this recognition was due to his political prominence. On December 26, 1801, he was elected an "associé étranger" of the Institute of France; if this was by virtue of his position at all, it was because of his presidency of the American Philosophical Society. Mr. Malone says that this signal honor, which during his lifetime was shared by no other man of American birth and residence, may be attributed to his reputation in France as the most conspicuous American intellectual. He himself modestly interpreted it as "an evidence of the brotherly spirit of science, which unites into one family all its votaries of whatever grade, and however widely dispersed throughout the different quarters of the globe."

Modern scholars, according to Mr. Malone, have recognized Jefferson as an American pioneer in numerous branches of science, notably paleontology, ethnology, geography, and botany. Living long before the age of specialization, he was a careful investigator, no more credulous than his learned contemporaries, and notable among them for his effort in all fields to attain scientific exactitude.

But Jefferson saw all these branches of science not as independent units but as integral parts of an all-embracing whole that should be developed for the sake of the future happiness and prosperity of mankind, for the ultimate good of his fellow men was always in his thoughts. It was this scientific foresight that led him to advocate so vigorously the idea that science would be the cornerstone of our Republic. In 1789 he wrote to President Willard of Harvard: "What a field we have at our doors to signalize ourselves in. The botany of America is far from being exhausted, its mineralogy is untouched, and its natural history or zoology totally mistaken and misrepresented ... It is for such institutions as that over which you preside so worthily, Sir, to do justice to our country, its productions, and its genius. It is the work to which the young men you are forming should lay their hands. We have spent the prime of our lives in procuring them the precious blessings of liberty. Let them spend theirs in showing that it is the great parent of science and virtue, and that a nation will be great in both always as it is free."

Such was the opinion of Thomas Jefferson, the most versatile and the most influential of our American scientific men.

Jefferson at 59.

PENCIL DRAWING BY BENJAMIN HENRY LATROBE, ABOUT 1802

Courtesy of the Maryland Historical Society, Baltimore

Jefferson at 61.

THOMAS JEFFERSON AND RELIGION

Marie Kimball

No discussion of Jefferson's literary tastes can be complete without mention of what many consider the greatest work of all time, the Bible. This, in turn, raises the question of his religion and of the many unjust charges that have been leveled against him. That the wise and liberal man who sponsored the "Statute of Virginia for Religious Freedom" should by some have been considered an infidel, is one of those amazing anomalies that occasionally occur. Perhaps the greatest harm Jefferson ever did himself was the observation in his "Notes on Virginia" that "it does me no injury for my neighbor to say there are twenty gods or no God." This was immediately taken up by his enemies, as well as by many right-thinking people with no critical faculty, as a confession of atheism, and to this day some of the stigma still clings to Jefferson's reputation. It is overlooked that he was elected a vestryman of Fredericksville parish in November 1767, and served there until St. Anne's parish was formed. Here he again served as vestryman from 1772-1785. Even in his old age, when religious services were held in the courthouse in Charlottesville, he would ride to town on horseback bringing his own seat, "some light machinery which folded up, was carried under his arm, and, when unfolded, served for a chair on the floor of the courthouse." That he was a faithful disciple of the principles of Jesus Christ, that he felt "there never was a more pure and sublime system of morality delivered to man than is to be found in the four evangelists," was as nothing in view of his independence in applying the principles of historical criticism to the divine word.

From *Jefferson: The Road to Glory, 1743 to 1776,* by Marie Kimball. Copyright 1943 by Coward-McCann, Inc. Reprinted by permission. With additions made by the author for this anthology.

Again quoting Edmund Randolph, we learn at first hand how Jefferson's contemporaries viewed this independence of spirit. "When Mr. Jefferson first attracted notice, Christianity was directly denied in Virginia only by a few. He was an adept however in the ensnaring subtleties of deism, and gave it, among the rising generation, a philosophical patronage; which repudiates as falsehoods things unsusceptible of strict demonstration. It is believed, that while such tenets as are in contempt of the gospel, inevitably terminate in espousing the fullest latitude in religious freedom, Mr. Jefferson's love of liberty, would itself have produced the same effects. But his opinions against restraints on conscience ingratiated him with the enemies of the establishment, who did not stop to enquire, how far those opinions might border on scepticism or infidelity. Parties in religion and politics rarely scan with nicety the peculiar private opinions of their adherents."

Some writers have felt that it was the reading of Bolingbroke's philosophical essays—"the blunderbuss charged against religion and morality," as Johnson said—that first caused Jefferson to question the Bible and probe into his own religious beliefs. It seems more likely that what he acquired from Bolingbroke was the critical attitude—the attitude that questions before it believes. This was undoubtedly augmented by his contact with William Small, to whom, as we have seen, Jefferson often paid tribute. He was one of the first truly liberal and broad-minded men with whom young Jefferson had come in contact, and his influence was proportionate. Furthermore, it was inevitable that Jefferson should share in the attempt of the eighteenth century to put religion on a rational basis. He was too intelligent and too broadly educated not to have been early puzzled and disturbed by problems concerning religious dogma. His open mind, his willingness to discuss the pros and cons of a question, was undoubtedly one of the bonds that linked the young Jefferson to the worldly Fauquier and the wise Wythe. The latter likewise suffered under the charge of being an heretic. Among the few papers of Wythe that are preserved is a statement he delivered on his attitude on this subject. "As to religion: I have ever considered it our best and greatest Friend, those glorious views which it gives of our relation to God, and of our destination in Heaven, on the easy terms of a good life, unquestionably furnish the best of all motives to virtue; the strongest disuasives from vice; and the richest cordial under trouble. . . . The Christian

religion (the sweetest and sublimest in the World) labours throughout to infix in our hearts this great truth, that God is love. . . . While
others, therefore, have been beating their heads, or embittering their
hearts with disputes about forms of baptism and modes of faith, it
has always, thank God, struck me as my great duty, constantly to
think of this—God is love; and he that walketh in love, walketh in
God and God in Him."

We have no actual statement from Jefferson's pen of his religious
opinions, his hopes and doubts and fears, at this early period, except
insofar as they are reflected in the excerpts he copied in his commonplace book. In a letter he was later to write to his young nephew,
Peter Carr, however, he discourses upon the religious crisis which
inevitably comes to young people of intelligence and independence
of spirit. In his gentle and wise words we see how forthrightly he
himself met the situation when a young man, for the letter can be
nothing but a reflection of his own experience.

"Your reason is now mature enough," he writes, "to examine this
object [religion]. In the first place, divest yourself of all bias in favor
of novelty and singularity of opinion. . . . On the other hand, shake
off all the fears and servile prejudices, under which weak minds are
servilely crouched. Fix reason firmly in her seat, and call to her tribunal every fact, every opinion. Question with boldness even the
existence of God; because if there be one, he must more approve of
the homage of reason, than that of blindfolded fear. You will naturally
examine first, the religion of your own country. Read the Bible, then,
as you would read Livy or Tacitus. The facts which are within the
ordinary course of nature, you will believe on the authority of the
writer, as you do those of the same kind in Livy and Tacitus. The testimony of the writer weighs in their favor, in one scale, and their not
being against the laws of nature, does not weigh against them. But
those facts in the Bible which contradict the laws of nature, must be
examined with more care, and under a variety of faces. Here you must
recur to the pretensions of the writer to inspiration from God. Examine upon what evidence his pretensions are founded and whether that
evidence is so strong, as that its falsehood would be more improbable than a change in the laws of Nature, in the case he relates. For
example, in the book of Joshua, we are told, the sun stood still for
several hours. Were we to read that fact in Livy or Tacitus, we
should class it with their showers of blood, speaking of statues, beasts,

etc. But it is said, that the writer of that book was inspired. Examine, therefore, candidly, what evidence there is of having been inspired. The pretension is entitled to your inquiry, because millions believe it. On the other hand, you are astronomer enough to know how contrary it is to the law of nature that a body revolving on its axis, as the earth does, should have stopped, should not, by that sudden stoppage, have prostrated animals, trees, buildings, and should after a certain time have resumed its revolution, and that without a second general prostration. Is this arrest of the earth's motion, or the evidence which affirms it, most within the law of probabilities?

"You will next read the New Testament. It is the history of a personage called Jesus. Keep in your eye the opposite pretensions: 1, of those who say he was begotten by God, born of a virgin, suspended and reversed the laws of nature at will, and ascended bodily into heaven; and 2, of those who say he was a man of illegitimate birth, of a benevolent heart, enthusiastic mind, who set out without pretensions of divinity, ended in believing them, and was punished capitally for sedition, by being gibbeted according to the Roman law, which punished the first commission of that offence by whipping, and the second by exile, or death in *furea*. . . . These questions are examined in the books I have mentioned, under the head of Religion, and several others. They will assist you in your inquiries; but keep your reason firmly on the watch in reading them all. Do not be frightened from this inquiry by any fear of its consequences. If it ends in a belief that there is no God, you will find incitements to virtue in the comfort and pleasantness you feel in its exercise, and the love of others which it will procure you. If you find reason to believe there is a God, a consciousness that you are acting under his eye, and that he approves you, will be a vast additional incitement; if that there be a future state, the hope of a happy existence in that increases the appetite to deserve it; if that Jesus was also a God, you will be comforted by a belief of his aid and love. In fine, I repeat, you must lay aside all prejudices on both sides, and neither believe nor reject anything, because any other persons, or descriptions of persons, have rejected or believed it. Your own reason is the only oracle given you by heaven, and you are answerable, not for the rightness, but uprightness of the decision. . . ."

These brave words express Jefferson's independence of spirit and indifference to cant as completely as anything he ever wrote. It may be charged, as it often was and has been, that he denied many of the articles of faith that distinguish the Christian religion as ordinarily taught and observed. Indeed, in the heat of the presidential elections of 1800, which were distinguished for their display of acrimony and vilification, his religious beliefs, or supposed lack of them, became a political issue. It was the major topic in the many pamphlets published at that time. The answer to these charges is best found in his own words. "I have a view of the subject," he wrote Dr. Benjamin Rush of Philadelphia at this period, "which ought to displease neither the rational Christian nor Deist, and would reconcile many to a character they have too hastily rejected. I do not know that it would reconcile the *genus irritabile vatum* who are all in arms against me. Their hostility is on too interesting ground to be softened." What this genus could not forgive Jefferson was his passion to shake off, as he said, "all the fears and servile prejudices," and "fix reason firmly in her seat." What was even more unforgivable was that, essentially, he was a religious revolutionist, that he was "a preacher of an American religion, of certain ideas which were not only destroying feudalism and monarchism, but were destined also to destroy the power of all mere priesthoods and of the creeds that had been inherited." Thus, in writing Horatio Spafford, he declared that "in every country and in every age, the priest has been hostile to liberty. . . . They have perverted the purest religion ever preached to man into mystery and jargon, unintelligible to all mankind."

Religion was thus a problem that occupied Jefferson's thoughts throughout his life. We see this reflected not only in early entries in his commonplace book, but in his correspondence over a long period of years, culminating in a constant interchange of letters on the subject with John Adams and others during the last decade. In a letter to Dr. Rush, while President, he speaks of "the delightful conversations" on the subject of the Christian religion they had in the evenings of 1798-99, when he was in Philadelphia. With this letter he enclosed a "Syllabus of the Estimate of the Doctrine of Jesus, compared with those of others," which is remarkable for the lucidity of its analysis of the figure that was Jesus Christ and of the historical development of the faith He inaugurated. Jefferson states that his views "are the result of a life of inquiry and reflection, and very different from that anti-Christian system imputed to me by those who know nothing of my opinions. To the corruption of Christianity I am, indeed, opposed;

but not to the genuine precepts of Jesus himself. I am a Christian, in the only sense He wished anyone to be; sincerely attached to His doctrines, in preference to all others; ascribing to Himself every human excellence; and believing that He never claimed any other." On another occasion he expressed similar sentiments in writing to William Short. "The greatest of all the reformers of the depraved religion of His own country, was Jesus of Nazareth. Abstracting what is really His from the rubbish in which it is buried, easily distinguished by its lustre from the dross of His biographers, and as separable from that as the diamond from the dunghill, we have the outlines of a system of the most sublime morality which has ever fallen from the lips of man."

In a letter written June 25, 1819 to Ezra Stiles, the eminent theologian and President of Yale College, with whom he had corresponded some thirty-five years, Jefferson gave a final expression to his faith—the fruit of a long life of benevolence and contemplation. "You say you are a Calvinist," he writes. "I am not. I am of a sect by myself, as far as I know. I am not a Jew, and therefore do not adopt their theology, which supposes the God of infinite justice to punish the sins of the fathers upon their children, unto the third and fourth generation; and the benevolent and sublime Reformer of that religion has told us only that God is good and perfect, but has not defined Him. I am, therefore, of His theology, believing that we have neither words nor ideas adequate to that definition. And if we could all, after this example, leave the subject as undefinable, we should all be of one sect, doers of good and eschewers of evil. No doctrines of His lead to schism."

Although Jefferson, as he said, rarely permitted himself to speak about religion and "never but in a reasonable society," any more than he would write on it—"should as soon as think of writing for the reformation of Bedlam," he observed—the result of his reflections on these topics was ultimately to be embodied in what has come to be known as the "Jefferson Bible." While he was President, "after getting through the evening task of reading the letters and papers of the day," he made certain extracts from the Bible which he called "the Philosophy of Jesus." It is a "paradigma of His doctrines, made by cutting the texts out of the book, and arranging them on the pages of a blank book, in a certain order of time or subject. A more beautiful or precious morsel of ethics I have never seen; it is a document in proof that I am a *real Christian*, that is to say, a disciple of the doctrines of Jesus, very different from the Platonists, who call *me* infidel and *themselves* Christians and preachers of the Gospel, while they draw all their characteristic dogmas from what its Author never said nor saw. They have compounded from the heathen mysteries a system beyond the comprehension of man, of which the great Reformer of the vicious ethics and deism of the Jews, were He to return to earth, would not recognize one feature."

The work of arranging this "precious morsel of ethics" occupied Jefferson "two or three nights only," as he tells us. It was his ambition to add to the English text "Greek, Latin and French texts in columns side by side." This he finally accomplished some time between January 1816, when he wrote the letter just quoted, and his last years. A handsome volume, bound in red leather with gold tooling, survives. Inscribed on the flyleaf, in the trembling hand of Jefferson's late years, are the words, "The Life and Morals of Jesus of Nazareth, Extracted textually, from the Gospels in Greek, Latin, French & English." Family tradition has it that this was the volume he read last each night, carrying out his own recommendation to others: "I never go to bed without an hour, or a half hour's previous reading of something moral, whereon to ruminate in the intervals of sleep."

THOMAS JEFFERSON AS A TRAVELER

Edward Dumbauld

Perhaps no genius America has produced—not even the venerable Benjamin Franklin—united such diversified gifts or displayed such versatility of talent as Thomas Jefferson. Accordingly, there has been no lack of literature treating various phases of Jefferson's activity. Many pages have been written of Jefferson as a statesman, as a political philosopher, as a party leader, as a diplomat, as a legislator, as a lawyer, as a man of letters, as student of languages and natural science, as an architect and designer of landscapes and gardens, as a family man, as a friend of the French, as a citizen of the world, and as a patron of education and religion. But no one has seen fit to present a comprehensive picture of Jefferson as a traveler. Yet this interesting aspect of Jefferson's life is well worthy of attention.

To be sure, many a modern globe-trotter would find nothing extraordinary in the voyages of Jefferson. It has been computed that the time he spent en route amounted to a year of his life. He visited no remote regions of the earth. Though one of the first to preach Pan-Americanism and the Monroe Doctrine, he was never in South America. Nor did he ever set foot in Spain, although by the purchase of Louisiana, formerly belonging to that country, he acquired for the United States a vast "empire for liberty." While in Italy he did not visit Rome, Florence, Venice, or Naples; Berlin, Vienna, and Budapest he never saw. Scarcely half a dozen European countries and twice as many states along the Atlantic seaboard comprised the territory Thomas Jefferson surveyed as a tourist.

George Washington traveled more extensively in America than Jefferson. Only the Eastern states were familiar ground to the master of Monticello, and late in life he advised a prospective pioneer: "You could not have applied for counsel to one less personally acquainted with the Western country than myself, having never been 50 miles westward of my own house." But for that matter few of Washington's contemporaries could equal his wide knowledge of America. Undoubtedly his travels played a significant part in the development of that comprehensive patriotism which so eminently qualified him for national leadership. Benefits of the same kind came to Jefferson. The long, slow journeys by coach and on horseback gave him an intimate knowledge of his country and the needs of its people.

Indeed, curiosity and pleasure were not the motives impelling Jefferson to travel. The illustrious Virginian boasted of having devoted three score years and one of his life, uninterruptedly, to the service of his country, and his journeys were usually undertaken for the purpose of transacting public business.

Born on April 13, 1743, at Shadwell, in what is now Albemarle County, Virginia, Jefferson attended college at Williamsburg. "When Jefferson started for William and Mary College in 1760, on horseback, a five days' ride, he had never been farther than twenty miles from home, and had never seen a town of more than twenty houses, and his acquaintance was limited to his school-fellows and the families of farmers around Shadwell. Yet within a few months we find this awkward youth of seventeen the favored and frequent companion of Francis Fauquier, the most elegant and accomplished gentleman Virginia had ever seen, Doctor William Small, the most learned man in the Colony, and George Wythe, the leader of its bar." (William E. Curtis, *The True Thomas Jefferson*, 68). Studying law under Wythe's mentorship, Jefferson came to the bar in 1767.

In May of the previous year he had obtained his first glimpse of the world beyond Virginia. In order to be inoculated for smallpox by the celebrated Dr. Shippen of Philadelphia, he had visited that city and then had gone on to New York.

In 1769 Jefferson was elected for his first term as a legislator, but had served only five days when the royal governor dissolved the House of Burgesses. However, he remained a member of that body until 1775, when it ceased to function. He attended the second Virginia Convention at Richmond in 1775; the preceding year he had set out for the first Virginia Convention at Williamsburg, but was taken ill of dysentery on the road and forced to be absent. However, he forwarded his *Summary View of the Rights of British America* for perusal by the members.

This clear and forceful statement, shortly afterwards published as a pamphlet, was a prelude to the Declaration of Independence. It enumerated in striking fashion the unlawful acts chargeable to the British monarch, and inquired: "But can his majesty thus put down all law under his feet? Can he erect a power superior to that which erected himself? . . . We know, and will therefore say, that kings are the servants, not the proprietors of the people. . . . The God who gave us life gave us liberty."

In 1775 Jefferson was elected as a Virginia delegate to the Continental Congress, and made two trips to Philadelphia to attend meetings of that body. The following year he was again in Philadelphia and won lasting renown as author of the Declaration of Independence. In the fall of 1776 he left Congress and returned to Virginia, where he entered the House of Delegates and initiated his program of law reform. His service in the legislature continued until his election as governor in 1779.

Succeeding Patrick Henry, Jefferson was the second governor of Virginia as an independent commonwealth, after its liberation from English rule. While he was in office, the Old Dominion was invaded by the British Army. The task of resisting and eluding the enemy obliged him to spend many hours on horseback. That by experience and study he had acquired a comprehensive knowledge of his native state was manifested in Jefferson's *Notes on Virginia,* written shortly after he retired as governor.

This work was originally prepared for the information of Barbé-Marbois, French consul in Philadelphia; its publication in Europe several years later won for its author considerable reputation as a man of learning. In accordance with the habits of industry and precision acquired in Wythe's office, it was Jefferson's practice, in conversation with persons of any station in life, to discuss the topic most familiar to those with whom he talked and to reduce to writing any information thus obtained which he thought might later on prove useful. Not only did he prepare the *Notes on Virginia* from such memoranda, but when traveling in Europe he similarly recorded his observations.

After the death of his wife, in 1782, when for the third time Congress chose him to undertake a diplomatic mission abroad, Jefferson accepted the appointment. He spent several months in Philadelphia and Baltimore attempting to find a vessel to take him across the Atlantic. But when news came that the peace negotiations terminating the Revolutionary War were already so far advanced that his attendance would not be required, Jefferson returned home.

Little over a month later he was re-elected to Congress. At Princeton, New Jersey, on November 4, 1783, he took his seat in that body, which adjourned the same day to reconvene at Annapolis. In 1784, Jefferson was appointed as an envoy to act with John Adams and Benjamin Franklin in negotiating treaties of commerce with foreign nations. Leaving Annapolis on May 11, he made a point of informing himself about the commerce of the states through which he passed on his way to embark for France. He sailed from Boston on July 5, 1784, and reached Paris a month and a day later.

With him went his daughter Martha, not yet twelve. He left his younger children, Mary, aged six, and Lucy, two, in the care of their maternal aunt, Mrs. Eppes. The youngest died shortly thereafter, and in the summer of 1787 Mary joined her father and elder sister in Paris.

In 1785, Jefferson succeeded Franklin as minister plenipotentiary to the French court. While stationed in Paris, he made three noteworthy trips. In 1786 he joined Adams in England in order to participate in diplomatic negotiations. In 1787 he made a tour of southern France and northern Italy. In 1788 he hastened to The Hague to find Adams and conclude arrangements for a loan from the Dutch bankers at Amsterdam who financed the struggling American government. From Holland he returned to Paris by way of Germany.

Jefferson remained abroad until 1789. In that year he became secretary of state in the cabinet of George Washington. From March to September, 1790, he was in New York, where the seat of the new government was first located. In August he accompanied President Washington on a brief visit to Rhode Island. In November he arrived in Philadelphia, then the temporary capital of the nation. With James Madison he made a trip through New England during the summer of 1791.

On December 31, 1793, Jefferson resigned as secretary of state, but on March 4, 1797, was sworn in as vice president of the United States. In 1800 the pastoral city of Washington became the capital of the United States. The following year Jefferson was inaugurated as president. At the end of his second term, in 1809, he retired to Monticello, where he passed the remainder of his days and died on the Fourth of July, 1826.

Jefferson constantly combined business with sightseeing. On his first trip to Philadelphia to be vaccinated, he went on to New York. Traveling through New England with Madison, he found time to report to President Washington about conditions along the Canadian border. When he had settled the affairs which brought him posthaste to Holland from Paris, he returned leisurely by the round-about route through Germany. Called to London, he proceeded to make a methodical tour of the countryside, with Whately's book on gardening in his hand. When, after an injury to his wrist, he was advised by his physician to try the effect of mineral waters as a remedy, he chose those of Aix-en-Provence in preference to others, because from that place he could commence a tour of the French seaports concerned in commerce with America. From Aix he wrote to his daughter Martha: "My journey hitherto has been a very pleasing one. It was undertaken with the hope that the mineral waters of this place might restore strength to my wrist. Other considerations also concurred—instruction, amusement, and abstraction from business, of which I had too much at Paris." Indeed, the characteristic many-sidedness of the man, by his enemies called duplicity, revealed itself in the adroit management of Jefferson the tourist no less than in the skillful maneuvers of Jefferson the political leader.

Doubtless the dangers and discomforts which beset the wayfarer in those days were sufficient to discourage Jefferson from undertaking any unnecessary travel. To be sure, highway robbery was all but unknown in America, if Jefferson's reply to a Frenchman submitting a scheme for suppressing that evil is to be believed. In France travelers went armed; Jefferson's passport authorized him to carry the usual weapons. Even in the United States a gun might be helpful in protecting a stranger from indignities.

But the roads, though not infested by brigands, were ill defined and often impassable. On the main thoroughfare between Philadelphia and Baltimore the ruts and gullies were so deep that, in order to keep the stage coach from upsetting, the passengers were obliged to lean to the right or left in unison at the driver's direction. Often they had to descend and walk in the mud, occasionally helping to push the coach when the horses' efforts were not sufficient. When progress became impossible, a new roadway was opened by felling trees. In some places there were a dozen such routes to the same spot, all full of stumps, rocks, and trees.

Near the close of the Revolution, the French traveler de Chastellux got lost in the woods while on the road to Monticello to visit Jefferson. In 1800, Mrs. John Adams met with the same predicament on her way from Baltimore to the new capital at Washington, wandering aimlessly through forest land for two hours until set aright by directions from a straggling black. Jefferson himself seems to have encountered similar difficulty while traveling to Philadelphia in 1775 to attend the Continental Congress. His account book shows that more than once he was obliged to employ guides.

In Europe the condition of the highways was hardly superior, though their location was not so uncertain. Indeed, entries in Jefferson's account book of sums paid for repairs to carriage or harness appear oftener during his journeys abroad than at home. In 1796 he informed Madison: "The roads of America are the best in the world except those of France and England."

About to return from Amsterdam to the French capital, Jefferson wrote to William Short, his *élève* and secretary at Paris: "What route I shall take will depend on information not yet received relative to the roads, and partly too on the weather's becoming milder than it now is." Jefferson finally determined to follow the Rhine as far as Strasbourg if the roads would permit, but to turn toward Paris whenever they became impassable. A letter to Short from Frankfort-on-the-Main narrates the vicissitudes of the trip: "I arrived here on the 6th. inst., having been overtaken at Cleves by the commencement of a storm of rain, hail & snow which lasted to this place, with intermissions now and then. The roads however continued good to Bonne, there beginning to be clayey & to be penetrated with the wet. They became worse than imagination can paint for about 100 miles which brought me to the neighborhood of this place where the chaussee began." The heavy road tax Jefferson "paid cheerfully, however, through the territory of Frankfort and thence up the Rhine, because fine gravelled roads are kept up; but through the Prussian, and other parts of the road below Frankfort, the roads are only as made by carriages, there not appearing to have been ever a day's work employed on them."

In his tour of France Jefferson had also been troubled by bad weather. A letter from Lyons informed Short: "So far all is well. No complaints; except against the weather-maker who has pelted me with rain, hail & snow, almost from the moment of my departure to my arrival here." Two weeks later, at Aix-en-Provence, Jefferson again complained of the constant storm of wind, hail, snow, and rain that pursued him. To cross the Alps it was necessary to travel ninety-three miles on mules, "as the snows are not yet enough melted to admit carriages to pass. I leave mine here, therefore, preparing to return by water from Genoa." Writing to his daughter Martha, he described the hardships of mountain and sea travel: "From Genoa to Aix was very fatiguing—the first two days having been at sea, and mortally sick—two more clambering the cliffs of the Appenines, sometimes on foot, sometimes on a mule, according as the path was more or less difficult—and two others travelling through the night as well as day without sleep. I am not yet rested, and shall therefore shortly give you rest by closing my letter."

Jefferson was extremely susceptible to cold. "I have often wondered," he declared, "that any human being should live in a cold country who can find room in a warm one. I have no doubt but that cold is the source of more sufferance to all animal nature than hunger, thirst, sickness, and all the other pains of life and of death itself put together. I live in a temperate climate, and under circumstances which do not expose me often to cold. Yet when I recollect on one hand all the sufferings I have had from cold, and on the other all other pains, the former preponderate greatly. What then must be the sum of that evil if we take in the vast proportion of men who are obliged to be out in all weather, by land and sea." Sojourning in southern France he exclaimed: "I am now in the land of corn, vines, oil, & sunshine. What more can man ask of heaven? If I should happen to die in Paris I will beg of you to send me here, and have me exposed to the sun. I am sure it will bring me to life again." He wondered why anyone possessing sufficient means to live in that pleasant region should remain in Paris, for though "money will carry to Paris most of the good things" of that section, "it can not carry thither its sunshine, nor procure any equivalent for it."

In October, 1791, Jefferson and Washington had to push on "through five days of North East storm" in order to reach Philadelphia before the opening of Congress, which took place a week earlier than anticipated. Fortunately, Mrs. Washington had taken possession of Jefferson's young daughter, Mary, at Mount Vernon and restored her to her father only after their arrival. Another peril enlivened the earlier portion of the trip. "The first part of our journey was pleasant, except some hair-breadth escapes by our new horse occasioned in going down hill the first day or so, after which he behaved better, and came through the journey preserving the fierceness of his spirit to the last."

On his trip to New York in 1766 Jefferson's horse ran away with him twice, and he was nearly drowned in fording one of the twelve rivers between Monticello and his destination. Between Monticello and Washington, Jefferson wrote to his attorney general in 1801, "of eight rivers ... five have neither bridges nor boats. When the one on which I live is fordable it will be a signal that the others are. This may be to-day, and in that case if it has ceased to rain, I shall set out and be with you on the fourth day." Five days later, Jefferson had arrived at Washington and was sending word to Madison about the condition of the roads. There was a stretch of two miles, he thought, which a carriage could not safely traverse. He had passed a wagon stuck in the mud and was of the opinion that no four-wheeled vehicle could have gotten through that spot without suffering the same fate. While in Philadelphia as head of the Department of State, he wrote on one occasion to a friend living at Stenton, on the outskirts of the city: "Th: Jefferson presents his compliments to Dr. Logan, and is sorry that a great mass of business just come on him will prevent him the pleasure of waiting on him tomorrow. The hope of dryer roads is some consolation for postponing the visit awhile."

In Virginia the highways were execrable. The best extended from Williamsburg to Richmond, a distance of sixty-three miles, which could be covered in two days. The last seventeen miles on the way from Philadelphia to Monticello were so hilly that when coming home in 1792, Jefferson feared that this bad stretch of road would injure his horses more than all the rest of the trip. Accordingly, he directed that plow or wagon horses should meet him to undertake the final stage of his journey. Coaches were rarely seen in Virginia; traveling was almost exclusively by horseback. At the time the Constitution was ratified, there were thousands of respectable men in the state who had never seen any other four-wheeled vehicle than a wagon, and there were thousands who had never even seen a wagon.

When going to Philadelphia in 1766, Jefferson rode in a one-horse chair. In 1775 he traveled in a phaeton, with two spare horses. Later on, when he had to make regular and frequent trips from his country estate to the seat of government, it was his practice to travel by the public stage in bad weather and in his own carriage when practicable.

Some of Jefferson's stopping places on his way between Monticello and the seat of government are identified by markers erected by the Roads Commission of Maryland. These include Spurrier's Tavern (spelled "Spuryear's" by Jefferson, who visited it frequently, as did George Washington), Van Horn's Tavern, Rhode's Tavern, and the Red Lion Tavern. Rodger's Tavern, east of the Susquehanna River, is still standing.

In March, 1790, when he had come to New York to take up his duties as secretary of state, Jefferson wrote to his son-in-law: "I arrived here on the 21st. instant, after as laborious a journey, of a fortnight from Richmond, as I ever went through; resting only one day at Alexandria and another at Baltimore. I found my carriage and horses at Alexandria; but a snow of eighteen inches deep falling the same night, I saw the impossibility of getting on in my own carriage; so left it there, to be sent to me by water, and had my horses led on to this place, taking my passage in the stage, though relieving myself a little sometimes by mounting my horse. The roads, through the whole way, were so bad that we could never go more than three miles an hour, sometimes not more than two, and in the night but one."

Jefferson could have gone faster on foot. In a curious memorandum made while in France, he records his rate of walking. "I walk a French mile in 17½ minutes. A French mile is 1.21 or 1¼ English miles. I walk then at the rate of 4 3/20 miles or 4 miles 264 yards an hour." Noting further that he paces off a French mile in 1254 steps, "walking moderately in the summer," he reckons that an English mile would require 2066½ steps, which "the brisk walk of winter" would reduce to 1735, a difference of 331 steps.

A week to ten days usually sufficed Jefferson for the trip from Monticello to Philadelphia. From the Quaker City to New York was a two days' journey. Annapolis was four days distant from Philadelphia. The same interval separated Monticello from Washington. Traveling in leisurely fashion, Jefferson spent almost a fortnight on the road between New York and Boston; although the highway between those cities was considered the best in the country and was usually covered in a week.

Travel was not only laborious but expensive as well. In the winter of 1793 Congress met in Germantown. The city of Philadelphia was then suffering the ravages of yellow fever. Leaving Monticello on October 25 Jefferson rode on horseback to Fredericksburg. From that place his servants, James and Bob, returned with the horses, while their master went on to Baltimore by public stage. There Jefferson joined President Washington, and the two were obliged to hire a private conveyance to bring them to their destination. On November 2, Jefferson wrote to his son-in-law: "After having experienced on my journey the extremes of heat, cold, dust & rain, I arrived here yesterday. I found at Baltimore that the stages run no further North, and being from that circumstance thrown into the hands of the harpies who prey upon travellers, was pretty well fleeced to get here. I think from Fredericksburg here with a single servant cost me upwards of seventy dollars." From his meticulously kept account book it appears that the precise sum was $77.65. The same day Jefferson wrote warning Madison and Monroe to be on their guard against a similar fate. The usual charge for passengers on the stage was six cents a mile, and the distance from Monticello to Philadelphia was two hundred and sixty miles.

Experiences of the same sort had befallen Jefferson in Europe. He affirmed that Rousseau had wronged the inhabitants of a certain French city in singling them out as a people accustomed to victimize strangers, for the practice was common everywhere among the menial class of "hackneyed rascals" with whom a traveler is most frequently in contact. "I have not yet been to Montpelier, but I can pronounce that Rousseau has done it injury in ascribing to it the character of pillaging strangers, as if it was peculiar to that place. It is the character of every place on the great roads along which many travellers pass. He should also have confined the character to postillions, voituriers, tavern keepers, waiters & workmen. The other descriptions of people are as good to strangers as any people I have ever met with."

This evil was not a purely French trait. When the advisability of locating the temporary seat of government at Princeton, New Jersey, was being considered, Jefferson commented on the the deficiency of accommodations there, "exposing ye attending members to the danger of indignities & extortions discouraging perhaps the fitest men from undertaking the service & amounting to a prohibition of such as had families from which they would not part." While attending the Continental Congress at Princeton, Madison complained to Jefferson: "I am obliged to write in a position that scarcely admits the use of any of my limbs, Mr. Jones & myself being lodged in a room not 10 feet square and without a single accommodation for writing."

Jefferson's experience with the Princeton townsmen may have colored his impressions of the college there. Although the degree of LL.D. had been conferred on him by that institution in 1791, Jefferson did not refrain from declaring to an inquiring parent that: "As far as I am acquainted with the colleges and academies of the U. S., and I will say more especially of Princeton, which you name, I have found their method of instruction very superficial & imperfect, carrying their pupils over the ground like race horses to please their parents and draw custom to their school."

An English traveler, who likewise considered "Princeton, a place more famous for its college than its learning," resolved to make the best of the notoriously deficient accommodations which American hostelries provided and not to grumble. But in Philadelphia he could not resist the superior attractions offered by the establishment of a French innkeeper. In a southern state, the same traveler consumed without complaint a dinner of cornmeal mush, without milk, or sugar, or even molasses. "Beshrew the Traveller," he exclaims, "who would let fall a reflection over the dinner I have made. Though plain, it was wholesome; and, instead of wishing it was better, I thanked God it was not worse."

Another Englishman was compelled to dance by a group of wagoners at a tavern, who wielded their whips when he hesitated to comply with their commands. Upon the arrival of his groom, the irate Briton, taking his guns from the saddlehorse, turned the tables on his tormentors. He was greatly complimented by the landlord in consequence of this feat. The Indian Queen, where Jefferson sometimes stopped in Philadelphia, was on one occasion the scene of a robbery in which several Congressmen lost their linen and thirty thousand dollars' worth of securities.

One journeying by water was not immune from molestation by "the harpies who prey upon travellers." Just before sailing from Cowes for America, Jefferson advised his bankers that his final draft on them would be for a larger sum than had been anticipated, since he must go by a particular ship or lose passage that season. The terms which the shipowner exacted provided that the cost of passage for ship and ship's provisions should be 100 guineas; that the passenger should at his own expense furnish any fresh provisions, wines, and delicacies desired; and that he should forfeit 50 guineas for detention of the ship in case of his failure to reach Cowes during the three days the ship was to wait there for him.

Navigation, moreover, had its own drawbacks and perils. Favorable winds were necessary. Jefferson's departure from Europe was delayed three weeks on this account. Certain times of the year were most propitious for passage. "By advice of those skilled in sea voiages" Jefferson chose the period between the autumnal equinox and winter for his departure. March and September, "the boisterous equinoctial months," he regarded as the most disagreeable seasons to be passed at sea.

Even coastwise sailing was apt to prove difficult. While on his way to the seat of government to assume his duties as vice president, Jefferson wrote from Chestertown, Maryland, to his daughter: "I have got so far, my dear Martha, on my way to Philadelphia which place I shall not reach till the day after to-morrow. I have lost one day at Georgetown by the failure of the stages, and three days by having suffered myself to be persuaded at Baltimore to cross the bay & come by this route as quicker & pleasanter. After being forced back on the bay by bad weather in a first attempt to cross it, the second brought me over after a very rough passage, too late for the stage.—So far I am well, tho' much fatigued." Likewise, adverse winds on Lake Champlain compelled Jefferson and Madison to turn back during the course of their tour through New England in 1791.

Hostile sea power constituted another hazard to ocean travel. Jefferson's inability to get to Europe as envoy in the winter of 1782-83 was due chiefly to the British blockade. Passage on a French ship, the *Guadeloupe*, was offered Jefferson; but after observing that "she sweats almost continually on the inside, in consequence of which her commander and several of the crew are now laid up with rheumatism," he concluded that it would not be right to jeopardize a ship belonging to a friendly nation by exposing it to the danger of falling into enemy hands.

A danger not dissimilar existed in time of peace. The Barbary

pirates were a menace to the ships of nations which had not purchased immunity by paying tribute. Those on board the captured
vessels were made prisoners and held for ransom. The principal
maritime powers of Europe—England, France, Spain and the States-
General of Holland—submitted to these degrading conditions and
bought off the pirates. Jefferson, while at the French court, sought to
form a combination of the lesser maritime powers to protect their
commerce by patrolling the Barbary coast with a fleet of a half-dozen
frigates. Congress failed to furnish its quota of one frigate, however,
and the plan fell through. It was not until Jefferson's administration
as president that the pirates were subdued by the American Navy.

When making arrangements for his younger daughter, Mary, to
be brought to France, Jefferson believed it would be prudent to
"confide my daughter only to a French or English vessel having a
Mediterranean *pass*. This attention, though of little consequence in
matters of merchandise, is of weight in the mind of a parent which
sees even possibilities of capture beyond the reach of any estimate.
If a peace be concluded with the Algerines in the mean time, you
shall be among the first to hear it from myself. I pray you to believe it
from nobody else, as far as respects the conveyance of my daughter
to me."

The anxious father likewise prescribed strict standards of sea-
worthiness for the ship which was to carry his child: "I must now
repeat my wish to have Polly sent to me next summer. This, however,
must depend on the circumstance of a good vessel sailing from Virginia in the months of April, May, June or July. I would not have her
set out sooner or later on account of the equinoxes. The vessel
should have performed one voyage at least, but not be more than four
or five years old. We do not attend to this circumstance till we have
been to sea, but there the consequence of it is felt. I think it would
be found that all the vessels which are lost are either on their first
voyage or after they are five years old; at least there are few excep-
tions to this. . . . I would rather live a year longer without her than
have her trusted to any but a good ship and a summer passage."

And then there was seasickness. Jefferson was nearly always a
sufferer from this malady when traveling by water. At the time of his
return to the United States from France, he was willing to pay
twenty to thirty guineas more if the ship would carry him directly

from a French port and spare him the ordeal of crossing the English Channel.

If the dangers and discomforts confronting the traveler by land or water were not sufficient to discourage Jefferson from voyages undertaken exclusively for pleasure or gratification of his curiosity, the tranquil felicities of domestic life at Monticello would have dissuaded him. He never tired of contrasting the burdens of public office with the charms which he found in his family, his friends, his farms, and his books.

The attractiveness of his own fireside increased with the passing years. As a young man he felt the wish to travel. In 1764, when he was a student at Williamsburg, he was unwilling to make a categorical proposal of marriage to his youthful flame, Rebecca Burwell, because he desired first to go abroad. "I shall visit particularly England, Holland, France, Spain, Italy (where I would buy me a good fiddle) and Egypt," returning home by way of Canada, he wrote to his confidant, John Page. The young lady was not inclined to postpone matrimony for two or three years until Jefferson's return from Europe (although in fact two decades were to elapse before he set foot on foreign soil), and she promptly married Jacquelin Ambler. The bridegroom, it is said, unwittingly or unfeelingly asked Jefferson to be best man at the wedding. A daughter of the couple later became the wife of Jefferson's lifelong enemy, Chief Justice John Marshall.

But although the thought of separation from Miss Burwell did not deter Jefferson from planning an extensive voyage, absence from home was far less endurable after the wedding ceremony of New Year's Day, 1772, when the comely widow, Martha Wayles Skelton, became mistress of Monticello. Twice Jefferson refused appointment as a diplomatic envoy on account of the precarious condition of his wife's health. To Lafayette, who communicated the news of his appointment the second time and offered to be useful to him in France, Jefferson avowed: "I lose an opportunity, the only one I ever had, and perhaps ever shall have, of combining public service with private gratification, of seeing countries whose improvements in science, in arts, and in civilization, it has been my fortune to admire at a distance, but never to see."

The attractions of Paris, when Jefferson at length was able to gratify his wish to go there, did not diminish his eagerness to hear the news of everything that happened "in the neighborhood of Monticello" or his affection for "my lazy & hospitable countrymen." He wistfully affirmed: "I often wish myself among them, as I am here burning the candle of life without present pleasure, or future object. A dozen or twenty years ago this scene would have amused me, but I am past the age for changing habits." To a European friend he declared: "I am now of an age which does not easily accomodate itself to new manners and new modes of living; and I am savage enough to prefer the woods, the wilds, and the independence of Monticello, to all the brilliant pleasures of this gay capital."

Even to sojourn in Philadelphia was painful. While attending the Continental Congress Jefferson exclaimed: "I have never received the script of a pen from any mortal in Virginia since I left it, nor been able by any inquiries I could make to hear of my family. . . . The suspense under which I am is too terrible to be endured. If anything has happened, for God's sake let me know it." In the midst of political quarrels which embittered personal relations and social intercourse in the Pennsylvania metropolis during the period preceding Jefferson's election to the presidency, he averred: "I envy those who stay at home enjoying the society of their friendly neighbors." Philadelphia he found "a dreary scene; where envy, hatred, malice, revenge, and all the worst passions of men, are marshalled to make one another as miserable as possible." He fumed with "impatience to leave this place, and everything which can be disgusting, for Monticello and my dear family, comprising every thing which is pleasurable to me in this world."

Toward the close of his administration as president, Jefferson awaited with eagerness "the day of retirement" to the pleasures of private life, although he was grateful to his constituents for their support and good will. "But I am tired of a life of contention, and of being the personal object for the hatred of every man, who hates the present state of things," he declared to his daughter Martha. "I long to be among you where I know nothing but love & delight, and where instead of being chained to a writing table I could be indulged as others are with the blessing of domestic society & pursuits of my own choice."

"Nature intended me for the tranquil pursuits of science by rendering them my supreme delight," the statesman confessed at the end of his political career. "The whole of my life has been a war with my natural taste, feelings & wishes. Domestic life & literary pursuits were my first & my latest inclination, circumstances and not my desires led me to the path I have trod. And like a bow tho long bent, which when unstrung flies back to its natural state, I resume with delight the character and pursuits for which nature designed me." To a friend abroad he declared: "I at length detach myself from public life which I never loved to retire to the bosom of my family, my friends, my farms and books, which I have always loved."

An occasional letter from an old acquaintance, however, revived fond memories of other scenes and other days, particularly "recollections of our charming coterie in Paris," and of the dauntless band of patriots at Philadelphia in that stirring era when American independence was declared. But in the midst of these delightful reveries was heard the mournful voice of Lafayette: "You remember our happy hours, and animated conversations at Chaville—how far from us those times, and those of the venerable Hotel de la Rochefoucauld! And we who still number among the living, do we not chiefly belong to what is no more?"

THOMAS JEFFERSON, SOIL CONSERVATIONIST

Hugh H. Bennett

Thomas Jefferson was in his own eyes first and always a farmer.

Between 1767 and his marriage in 1772, he successfully managed the farms [more than 2,000 acres in Albemarle County] left him by his pioneer father. Before his marriage, he more than doubled the acreage and maintained the farms as a successful business enterprise, yielding the rather substantial income for those days of about $2,000 a year.

Colonial Virginia at this time depended largely on English markets for the sale of its agricultural products. In the 150 years since the New World was opened by colonization, tobacco had become the chief cash crop, and this, combined with corn, the staple food crop, had already taken heavy toll from much of the originally productive soil. Erosion and soil exhaustion followed rapidly in the wake of the pioneers, as sloping land was cleared of trees and planted continuously to the same soil-depleting crops.

Jefferson's own words describe the current system of land usage:

> The highlands, where I live, have been cultivated about sixty years. The culture was tobacco and Indian corn as long as they would bring enough to pay the labor. Then they were turned out. After four or five years rest they would bring good corn again, and in double that time perhaps good tobacco. Then they would be exhausted by a second series of tobacco and corn. (Letter to President Washington, 1793.)

Under this endless crop sequence of tobacco and corn, planted in rows that usually ran uphill and downhill, much of the virgin topsoil was lost. By Jefferson's time the original surface layer of soil had been washed off many Virginia hillside fields by the rains and carried down into the rivers, leaving raw subsoil exposed.

Excerpts from *Thomas Jefferson: Soil Conservationist*, by Hugh H. Bennett. Soil Conservation Service, United States Department of Agriculture. Washington, 1944.

Jefferson's farm management [over long periods] necessarily was largely absentee. The actual operations were intrusted to the overseers who supervised the plantations. Jefferson's holdings in 1794 covered more than 10,000 acres since the property brought him by his wife about equalled his own. During the five years he was in Europe, however, Jefferson sent his overseers detailed instructions as to farm plans. He also forwarded seeds of European grasses, rice, olives, and other plants to be tested in different soils and climates in America. Moreover, he studied agricultural details of the European scene and, as time permitted, noted his findings and sent them home.

Jefferson's return to Monticello was marked by disappointment. In May 1794 he wrote President Washington:

> . . . I find on a more minute examination of my lands than the short visits heretofore made to them permitted, that a ten years' abandonment of them to the ravages of overseers, has brought on them a degree of degradation far beyond what I had expected. . . . I am not yet satisfied that . . . much will be done this year toward rescuing my plantations from their wretched condition. Time, patience and perseverance must be the remedy. . . .

Jefferson undertook to rebuild his depleted fields, and during the next few years he initiated an ambitious program of soil conservation.

This first phase of his conservation activities emphasized chiefly development of a system of crop rotations, including legumes, the use of fertilizers, and the practice of deep plowing. "Horizontal ploughing," the principal cultural practice by which Jefferson's conservation efforts are remembered today, is not mentioned in his agricultural records of this period. His approval of contouring as a measure of erosion control came somewhat later.

From 1794 to 1797, Jefferson maintained active contact with all operations on his several farms and strove earnestly to repair the damage inflicted by careless overseers. Almost daily his spare figure—the lean straight form of the skilled horseman—could be seen riding across the broad acres as he checked details of field arrangement, crop yields, food needs for the plantation population of almost 180 slaves, and the production of Monticello's miniature factories, where nails, cloth, grist, and other essentials were produced for the upkeep of the self-sufficient community.

During these years Jefferson exchanged agricultural information with and sought advice from the leading farmers of the day, including James Madison, George Washington, and John Taylor.

He strongly advocated the use of red clover—a good soil-conservation plant. He recommended it as an important part of a crop rotation to offset the exhausting effects of such crops as wheat. It had, he believed, multiple benefits: it furnished an excellent cover crop, highly preferable to bare fallow or even "spontaneous herbages," and it supplied good pasture at the same time. Moreover, he found that it would grow in fields "considerably harassed with corn."

Jefferson was interested in other soil-improving plants as well, particularly vetch. He experimented with various types of vetch to determine their effectiveness for winter cover and in rotation. He said: "I think it important to separate my exhausting crops by alternations of amelioraters."

Perhaps the most significant of all were Jefferson's recognition of the eroding effects of clean-tilled crops and his attempts to introduce substitute crops that would better protect his fields, which were mostly sloping and erodible. In June 1793, he wrote to President Washington: "Good husbandry with us consists in abandoning Indian corn and tobacco, tending small grain, some red clover following...."

Later, in December 1794, in a letter to John Taylor, he wrote: "The first step towards the recovery of our lands is to find substitutes for corn and bacon. I count on potatoes, clover, and sheep. The two former to feed every animal on the farm . . . and the latter to feed [the Negroes], diversified with rations of salted fish and molasses . . ." This quotation notes the principal points in Jefferson's farm conservation program; his recognition of the dangers of row crops; his belief in soil-building and soil-holding legumes in the rotation; a plan for diversified farming; and his interest in animal husbandry, principally sheep, partly for the sake of manure for fertilizer.

Jefferson understood that nature herself may gradually restore the fertility of the soil "in a long course of years," but because this natural process is so slow, he recommended manuring in addition to the use of rotations that included clover as a means of accomplishing "more in one than the atmosphere would require several years to do." He also publicized the experiments being carried on with plaster, or gypsum.

In Jefferson's time, comparatively few colonial farmers were concerned with returning to the earth any of the vital elements withdrawn by cropping, or with crop rotations, fertilizers, and cultural methods. But Jefferson was concerned not only with current returns from the land but also with the effects of abusive farming on posterity. He acknowledged the prevailing circumstances in a letter to President Washington in 1793: ". . . we can buy an acre of new land cheaper than we can manure an old acre." Nevertheless, he himself constantly looked for and tested ways of maintaining the soil's productiveness.

One of the most interesting items in his Farm Book—in which for nearly 50 years he jotted down bits of farm data such as plans, yields, and techniques—outlines an experiment on dung. He was not content merely to assume that animal manure would revitalize the soil and produce better crops; he planned tests to determine exactly how many cattle and how much time would be required to fertilize in this manner a given area of land and to measure its effectiveness by comparing the yield of wheat on the manured area with that from an equal area unmanured.

In his tests of legumes and grasses, Jefferson tried out numerous species, including the better known red clover, peas, and vetches, striving always to arrive at the best adjustment between environment and plant. He sought good grasses to bind the soil against washing by rain, to control gullies, and to improve hard-used land.

Jefferson's original 7-year rotation, outlined in his letter to Taylor, was as follows:

1. Wheat, followed the same year by turnips, to be fed on by the sheep.
2. Corn and potatoes mixed, and in autumn the vetch to be used as fodder in the spring if wanted, or to be turned in as a dressing.
3. Peas or potatoes, or both according to the quality of the fields.
4. Rye and clover sown on it in the spring. Wheat may be substituted here for rye. . . .
5. Clover.
6. Clover, and in autumn turn it in and sow the vetch.
7. Turn in the vetch in the spring, then sow buckwheat and turn that in, having hurdled off the poorest spots for cowpenning [so these bad spots could be improved by the manure.]

Jefferson's main objectives in this rotation seem evident. He must have been aiming at a sharp reduction of clean-tilled crops—corn only once in 7 years. Wheat, apparently, was to be depended on as "the only one which is to go to market to produce money"; clover and vetches were to be soil "amelioraters" and provide pasture. However, because of the drain on farm output by a large plantation population and constant numerous guests, Jefferson apparently was not able to put his plan fully into practice. A simplified and shorter rotation seems to have been the actual system of crop succession generally followed.

The plows of Jefferson's time were crude wooden implements. The design had never been standardized; each plow was the product of either a local artisan or the farmer himself. The average eighteenth-century plow penetrated the soil to only a slight depth, and for many years Jefferson sought some means whereby "deep ploughing" could be done. He had observed the bad effects of shallow plowing, which often merely loosened the topsoil so that it would wash away more easily.

Out of Jefferson's researches on this problem came his moldboard of "least resistance." This moldboard for the plow, developed according to the principles of physics, made it possible to plow to a depth of about 6 inches. It was one of the first attempts to standardize agricultural machinery and was so designed that the moldboard could be duplicated by any farmer.

Jefferson's moldboard for the plow has contributed, strangely enough, to both soil saving and soil wastage. On the positive side are its usefulness for contour ridging of erodible fields, for plowing out shallow open ditches, for broad ridging imperfectly drained flat lands, and for other uses. On the other side, this moldboard made it easier to tear up land indiscriminately. It contributed to "clean plowing," and we adopted this method far and wide, overlooking the fact that on some lands it is much better to maintain a vegetal covering.

Jefferson's agricultural and soil-conserving interests followed him into the White House. White House dinner-table conversation is said to have been as likely to touch on some problem of cultivation at Monticello as on the fate of democracy in Napoleonic France. During these years, Jefferson's property was managed by his son-in-law, Thomas Mann Randolph, a "man of science, sense, virtue and competence." Randolph had introduced into this hilly Virginia country a new method of cultivation that was destined more than a hundred years later to make over the face of America. This method was "horizontal ploughing," which we know today as contouring.

Jefferson for many years watched Randolph's efforts to prove the effectiveness of horizontal plowing in preventing erosion of sloping land. After he retired to Monticello permanently, he became an enthusiastic supporter of this method. In recounting to William Burwell (1810) a violent storm in which 3 inches of rain fell in a single hour, he wrote:

> Every hollow of every hill presented a torrent which swept everything before it. I have never seen the fields so much injured. Mr. Randolph's farm is the only one which has not suffered; his horizontal furrows arrested the water at every step till it was absorbed, or at least had deposited the soil it had taken up.

This conviction as to the value of contouring remained with Jefferson throughout the rest of his life, spent in agricultural pursuits at Monticello. In 1813 he wrote to Charles Peale:

> Our country is hilly and we have been in the habit of ploughing in straight rows whether up and down hill, in oblique lines, or however they lead; and our soil was all rapidly running into the rivers. We now plough horizontally, following the curvatures of the hills and hollows, on the dead level, however crooked the lines may be. Every furrow thus acts as a reservoir to receive and retain the waters, all of which go to the benefit of the growing plant, instead of running off into the streams. In a farm horizontally and deeply ploughed, scarcely an ounce of soil is now carried off from it.

Contour cultivation also is definitely labor-saving, as Jefferson pointed out: "The horses draw much easier on the dead level, and it is in fact a conversion of hilly grounds into a plain." Moreover, Jefferson found it easy to mark out the contours: "To direct the plough horizontally, we take a rafter level . . . A boy of thirteen or fourteen is able to work it round the hill, a still smaller one with a little hough marking the points traced by the feet of the level. The plough follows running through these marks."

The best description of this practice is given in a letter to Tristam Dalton, written in May 1817:

> Our practice is . . . to lay off guide lines conducted horizontally around the hill or valley from one end to the other of the field, and about 30 yards apart. The steps of the level on the ground are marked by a stroke of a hoe, and immediately followed by a plough. . . We generally level a field the year it is put into Indian corn laying it into beds 6 ft. wide, with a large water furrow between the beds, until all the fields have been once leveled. The intermediate furrows are run by the eye of the ploughman governed by these guide lines. . .

Jefferson also had constructed an excellent bench terrace for the vegetable garden almost at the top of Monticello's steep slopes. The nearby orchard and vineyard sites have the appearance of land that has long been contoured.

After 1809, when he retired from the Presidency, Jefferson was able to throw himself completely into agricultural and domestic affairs. His farming system is described in a letter to Jean Baptiste Say in 1815:

> Our culture is of wheat for market, and of maize, oats, peas, and clover, for the support of the farm. We reckon it a good distribution to divide a farm into three fields, putting one into wheat, half a one into maize, the other half into oats or peas, and the third into clover, and to tend the fields successively in this rotation. Some woodland in addition, is always necessary . . .

As compared with his proposed 7- year rotation of 1794, this system was simpler and shorter. For the rolling clay loam land of Monticello and vicinity, this plan of Jefferson's represents fairly good land use, especially under contour cultivation. That this plan was actually followed for several years seems substantiated by Jefferson's records. In his Farm Book, an entry for Monticello for 1809 reads as follows:

> . . . 3 fields of 60 acres each.
> 1 for half corn, half oats, peas or millet
> 1 for wheat 60 acres
> 1 for clover 60 acres
> and aim at a fourth for clover also as soon as we can.

The entry for 1811 on the crop system used on his Lego farm is almost identical.

Jefferson sought constantly for new crops adapted to his conditions of land and climate, and he instructed his overseer, Edmund Bacon, to conserve timber by "never cutting down a tree for firewood or any other purpose as long as one can be found ready cut down . . ."

Jefferson's promotion of improved methods of farming went beyond the confines of his own land. Through his amazingly voluminous correspondence, he publicized virtually every new and useful development in soil use and cultural practices. Jefferson's sponsorship of progressive conservation farming helped achieve an agricultural renaissance in the early part of the nineteenth century.

The flow of letters dealing with agricultural needs and practices, including conservation, in this age of restricted communication and transportation, functioned somewhat like a journal and did much to stimulate and spread agricultural advancement both at home and abroad.

Jefferson encouraged agricultural societies as a means of developing and spreading good farming techniques. Characteristic was his participation in the Albemarle Agricultural Society, founded in 1817. Composed of 30 leading landowners, with holdings in five counties, the society adopted a platform almost identical with that offered by Jefferson in 1811 in his "Scheme for a System of Agricultural Societies." The following three items from his "Scheme" reflect his preoccupation with soil conservation:

> 4th. Rotation of crops, and the circumstances which should govern or vary them, according to the varieties of soil, climate, and markets, of our different counties.
>
> 7th. Manures, plaster, green-dressings, fallows, and other means of ameliorating the soil.
>
> 9th. A succinct report of the different practices of husbandry in the county, including the bad as well as the good, that those who follow the former may read and see their own condemnation in the same page which offers better examples for their adoption . . . it would present every good practice which has occurred to the mind of any cultivator of the State for imitation, and every bad one for avoidance.

Each member of the society was to report on his own agricultural practices and to provide information on these points: Rotation of crops, average crop yield, acreage cultivated, amount of land cleared annually, the proportion of worn-out land, quantity of manure carried out, and quantity of plaster used and with what effect.

Recognizing that soil erosion could be conquered only through scientific treatment of the soil, Jefferson vigorously supported agricultural education and investigations at the university level. Agriculture "is a science of the very first order," he wrote to David Williams in 1803, urging the inclusion of agricultural techniques and experiments in college curricula; "It counts among its handmaids the most respectable sciences, such as Chemistry, Natural Philosophy, Mechanics, Mathematics generally, Natural History, Botany. In every College and University, a professorship of agriculture, and the class of its students, might be honored as the first."

Jefferson at 62.

PORTRAIT BY REMBRANDT PEALE, WASHINGTON, D. C., 1805

Courtesy of the New-York Historical Society, New York City

Jefferson at 62.

PORTRAIT BY GILBERT STUART, WASHINGTON, D. C., 1805

Courtesy of Mr. Ralph I. Straus, New York City

THOMAS JEFFERSON AND THE ARTS

Fiske Kimball

Among the founders of the Republic, who included other men of wide reading and high scientific attainments, Jefferson was unique in being also devoted to the arts—as an amateur, as a collector, as a patron, and in architecture, as a gifted creative artist of far-reaching influence.

This interest went much beyond any mere formal rounding of general cultivation. When among the French, as Minister from the United States, he wrote:

> Were I to proceed to tell you how much I enjoy their architecture, sculpture, painting, music, I should want words.... The last of them, particularly, is an enjoyment, the deprivation of which with us, cannot be calculated. I am almost ready to say, it is the only thing which from my heart I envy them, and which, in spite of all the authority of the Decalogue, I do covet.[1]

While it was in Europe that Jefferson first had opportunity to indulge to the full his enjoyment of the arts, an interest in them had begun very early in his life. This was the more remarkable since artistic stimuli and artistic opportunities were then so extremely meagre in America. This was especially true in the South, where the scattered plantations were not favorable to activities which flourish chiefly in towns. An effort to determine how Jefferson was able to form any adequate idea of the arts, as he very notably did, may be not without interest for the cultural history of America.

It is hard to realize how very few and inadequate were works of any of the arts in the Colonies generally, and in Virginia, at the time

A paper read April 23, 1943 before the American Philosophical Society in celebration of the Bicentennial of Thomas Jefferson. Published in the *Proceedings* of the Society, Volume 87, Number 3. Reprinted by permission, with corrections by the author.

[1] To Charles Bellini, September 30, 1785 (*Writings of Jefferson*, Lipscomb ed., 4: 154, 1903).

of Jefferson's youth. As late as 1781 he could write, in his *Notes on Virginia*, not unjustly of architecture there in its academic aspects: "The first principles of the art are unknown, and there exists scarcely a model among us sufficiently chaste to give an idea of them." Of sculpture, the first work to come to Virginia was the marble statue of Lord Botetourt voted by the Colony in 1771,[2] executed by Richard Hayward in 1773, and set up in the capitol at Williamsburg. Of paintings we know almost none in Virginia at that time except portraits, the best of them being scarcely more important than those at Westover attributed to Kneller but actually by lesser hands. Painters working in the colony were few and poor enough: John Wollaston, John Hesselius, John Durand. In 1768 was sent from London to Richard Henry Lee in Westmoreland the young Charles Willson Peale's heroic classical full-length of Pitt, but it is doubtful if Jefferson ever saw this ambitious and sophomoric work. It was only in 1774 that Peale first painted at Williamsburg.

Meanwhile Jefferson had one opportunity in youth to see something of what other colonies had to offer. In 1766 he came to Philadelphia to be inoculated against the smallpox by Dr. John Morgan, to whom he brought a letter of introduction from John Page; he passed through Annapolis and pressed on to New York. The figure of Pitt and the equestrian statue of the King, ordered in that year by the Assembly of New York, were not received and set up until 1770. Philadelphia, more than any other Colonial town, already had a small group of amateurs and collectors, including the men who had lately joined to send the young Benjamin West to Italy. Judge William Allen had copies of several Italian works, including a Venus of Titian, the Concert of Giorgione, and a Holy Family of Correggio.[3] John Penn's collection, according to Henry Pelham, Copley's half-brother, was "very great and elegant."[4] Former Governor James Hamilton had at

---

[2] One might expect Jefferson, then in the House of Burgesses, to have been on the committee regarding this, but he was not. *Cf. Journals,* 1770-1772: 138. We do not know that he was particularly a friend or admirer of Botetourt, as he had been of the preceding governor, Fauquier.

[3] Copley to Henry Pelham, September 29, 1771 (*Copley-Pelham Letters:* 163, 341, 1914).

[4] Henry Pelham to his mother, November 18, 1774 (ibid.: 272). For further evidences on Philadelphia collections, *cf.* C. and J. Bridenbaugh, *Rebels and Gentleman:* 213-215, 218, 1942.

Bush Hill what passed for an original by Murillo, a Saint Ignatius taken from a Spanish ship, and copies by West; in his garden were "seven statues of fine Italian marble curiously wrought." As early as 1761 John Morgan had paid tribute to both Allen and Hamilton, "from whom I have received so many favors,"[5] and we cannot doubt that he introduced the brilliant and fashionable young Virginian into their society.

It was doubtless to Morgan himself, however, that Jefferson owed his real initiation into the arts. Morgan was born in 1735 and was thus but eight years Jefferson's senior. Besides studying in London, Edinburgh, and Paris, he had made the Grand Tour of Italy,[6] had followed James Byers' "Course of Antiquities," in Rome, had a library including works on art, architecture, and archaeology, and had brought back from Italy a notable collection of copies of old masters as well as of drawings and engravings of both paintings and architecture. He owned, for instance, Vignola's work on the orders of architecture; he had been to Vicenza, and "visited several elegant palaces built by Palladio ... and the Theatrum Olympicorum," of which he had "procured a pretty exact plate." We shall not be mistaken in supposing that, during Jefferson's weeks in Philadelphia, Morgan found in him a receptive disciple, that in the field of art Morgan's example was as fruitful for Jefferson as that of Wythe, Small, and Fauquier in other fields, and that Jefferson promised himself not to fall behind him in the adornment of his own future dwelling.

Not until the year 1773 do we know definitely of any copies of old masters in Virginia. On March 4 of that year the painter Matthew Pratt, of Philadelphia, who, like Peale, had studied with West in London, advertised in the *Virginia Gazette* that he had brought with him to Williamsburg and was exhibiting and offering for sale "a small but very neat collection of paintings," six of these being after old masters. They included his own mediocre copy of West's copy of Correggio's "St. Jerome" (that is, the Holy Family with Saint Jerome), another "Holy Family," and his copy of Guido's "Jupiter and

---

[5] The Bridenbaughs (*ibid.:* 215) call Morgan the "foremost of the Philadelphia collectors," and chronicle the visits of John Adams and others to him.

[6] *Journal of Dr. John Morgan from Rome to London, 1764, with a fragment of a Journal at Rome 1764, and a Biographical Sketch, 1907.* This includes a list of articles collected by Dr. Morgan during his travels.

Europa." [7] By the 18th Pratt was evidently leaving Williamsburg to paint near Richmond and, later, at Hampton, but the pictures for a time remained visible near the Capitol. Jefferson's accounts show that he happened to be in Williamsburg for a week during this fortnight. We cannot doubt that he, who never failed to see any curiosity, improved the opportunity to visit the exhibition, but we shall see that the particular works shown cannot have made a favorable impression on him. He bought none, and did not add their subjects to his lists of desiderata.

It was in music that Jefferson first was able to indulge his tastes, through a serious mastery of the violin, which he had played since boyhood. In his earliest surviving pocket account books, which begin in 1767, we find frequent items for fiddlestrings. With Governor Fauquier, himself a musician, Jefferson formed one of a little group of amateurs who played often at the Palace, prior to Fauquier's death in 1768. Jefferson continued to study the violin with Alberti, a gifted virtuoso who had come to Williamsburg with some players, and to whom Jefferson's payments begin in 1769. Later Jefferson persuaded Alberti to come and live at Monticello, where he took lessons for several years. "I suppose," Jefferson wrote, "that during at least a dozen years of my life, I played no less than three hours a day." [8] He lost no opportunity of acquiring fine instruments, one in May 1768, which would seem to be the Cremona he still had when he died; another for which, "together with all his music composed for the violin," he pledged a large sum to John Randolph in 1771, and which he acquired when Randolph went to England in 1775. These two, he said, "would fetch in London any price." Nicholas Trist, who married Jefferson's granddaughter, quotes him as saying he had to lay aside his violin on the eve of the Revolution,[9] but we still find payments for fiddlestrings, as well as for a music stand, on his arrival in Paris, where in 1786 he bought a small violin, his third. Even after he had so seriously dislocated his right wrist in that year, indeed when he was Secretary of State, 1789-93; he had his fiddle bow mended, and

---

[7] W. Sawitzky, *Matthew Pratt:* 29 ff., 1942. These copies of Correggio and Guido survive and are there illustrated.

[8] Documents on Jefferson's early attainments in music are assembled by Marie Kimball, *The Road to Glory*, 1943, here supplemented by later entries in his manuscript account books. A fuller discussion will be published by Carleton Sprague Smith and Hellen Bullock.

[9] H. S. Randall, *Life of Jefferson* 1: 131, 1858.

on the eve of retirement laid in a good supply of strings.[10] In 1800 he was still buying music.

His musical interests were not limited by the violin. In 1771, during his courtship of Martha Wayles, herself musically gifted, he ordered a clavichord from Hamburg, then wrote: "I have since seen a Forte-piano and am charmed with it. Send me this instrument instead of the Clavichord."[11] Some keyed instrument he must always have. In Philadelphia in 1783 he bought a clavichord; in Paris he first hired a piano, then bought a harpsichord; in Philadelphia in 1792 he had a spinet; in 1800 he purchased a piano for $264.[12] Writing from Williamsburg to Paris in 1778, during a lull of the Revolution, he speaks of music as "the favorite passion of my soul" and makes his celebrated proposal to create a "domestic band of musicians" by importing workmen in various trades he ordinarily employed who could also "perform on the French horn, clarinet, or hautboy, and bassoon." Consolation for his unsuccess in realizing this plan he found, while abroad, in frequent attendance at the far from amateurish Concerts Spirituels at the Tuileries.

Very early he had sought, as Edward Randolph said, "to collect a library, not merely amassing a number of books, but distinguishing authors of merit and assembling them in subordination to every art and science." His library catalogue, preserved in manuscript, lists both his books on music and the musical compositions which he owned. By differences of ink and handwriting[13] it permits us to recognize which are the original entries for his earlier acquisitions and desiderata, down to his expected departure for Europe in 1782. Among the books then owned were Brenner's *Rudiments of Music*, Dr. Burney's *Present State of Music in Italy*, and *in Germany*, and manuals of instruction for the violin, the harpsichord, and the German flute. There are two pages of titles under Music—Vocal, with works ranging from Handel and Pergolesi, or Purcell's *Orpheus Britannicus*, to drinking songs, and two pages of Music—Instrumental, beginning with Corelli's concertos and Vivaldi's concertos. Later Jefferson made a table of all his instrumental music by over a score

[10] Accounts, October 12 and December 24, 1793.
[11] *Writings*, Lipscomb ed., 4: 231, 235, 1903.
[12] This would seem to be the one in a Hepplewhite case marked "Astor and Company," which descended in his family and was lately given back to Monticello by Laurence Gouverneur Hoes.
[13] *Cf.* Fiske Kimball, *Thomas Jefferson, Architect:* 90-91, 1916.

of authors, classified as sonatas, concertos, duets, and so forth, including also works later acquired, such as Haydn's 1st, 2nd, 3rd, 47th, and 48th sonatas, and his 51st and 52nd concertos. No later composers such as Mozart, not to speak of Beethoven, are listed. Considerable fragments of this great library of music are preserved (mostly deposited by the Thomas Jefferson Memorial Foundation at the Alderman Library of the University of Virginia). At Monticello are Jefferson's music stand for violin, and an ingenious four-sided music stand of his own design for playing quartettes.

Jefferson early dreamed of a house and garden of his own making. At twenty-one, we know, he bought "James on Gardening," translated from Leblond's manual of the French formal style of LeNôtre. In the next year, with the poet Shenstone's collected works, hymning nature and wide mountain prospects, he acquired the plan and description of the author's seat, The Leasowes, a famous example of the new English landscape garden. By 1767 he had determined to build on a site far more romantic than Shenstone's, on the summit of the little mountain rising above his birthplace, Shadwell, a site to which he then gave the name he was to make so famous, Monticello. Deep in books on architecture, of which he already owned a number, he gave his preference from the start to that of Palladio, with its appeal to the lawfulness of nature, to harmony of mathematical proportions. Making himself master of architectural drawing to a degree quite beyond the skill of any Colonial builders or amateurs down to this time, he designed a house with Palladian porticoes of an academic correctness new in the southern Colonies. By a genial adaptation to his mountain site of Palladio's schemes of colonnaded service wings, which he depressed below terraces, he gave his house an uninterrupted sweep of the superb panorama of plain, of valley, and of mountain range.

Pope asks:

"Who then shall grace, or who improve the soil?"

and answers:

"Who plants like Bathurst, or who builds like Boyle."

Jefferson, like Boyle—the architect Earl of Burlington—before him, was building in Palladian style; he early undertook ambitious planting also. "It has always been my passion," he wrote years later to the Comtesse de Tessé.[14] His ideas for it, in the landscape style, he must already have acquired with Shenstone's works in 1765. Shenstone's *ferme ornée* gave him an example of the method inaugurated by William Kent, when—as Walpole wrote—he "leaped the fence and saw that all nature was a garden." Jefferson was the first American to hold this belief, and to act on it.

Already his architectural skill was being laid under contribution by others: as in a design for his friend George Wythe, and one for an enlargement of the building of William and Mary College prepared in 1771-72 at Governor Dunmore's request, begun, and only suspended as Revolution neared. Here Jefferson made a plan with a great arcaded court reminiscent of the town-palaces of Italy as shown by Palladio. Perhaps thus early, rather than when he himself became Governor in 1779, he projected a transformation of the Palace at Williamsburg—by pedimented porticoes of eight columns, the "full width of roof"—into the form of a temple, prophetic of extremes of the classic revival not yet even proposed abroad.

For any broader idea of the other arts, he had also to look to books. The chapter on Sculpture in his library catalogue begins with Spence's *Polymetis*, first published in 1747. Then came François Perrier's folio *Signa et Statua Antiqua* (as Jefferson gives the title), a hundred statues drawn and engraved in Rome in 1638. Significant among the desiderata was the *Monumenti inediti* (1767-1768) of Winckelmann, whose epoch-making *History of Art* of 1764, first declaring the superiority of Greek art over the Roman, Jefferson later acquired while abroad.

The chapter on Painting begins with *Webb's Essay on Painting, An Inquiry into the Beauties of Paintings*, 1760, which Jefferson recommended to Robert Skipworth as early as 1771. Other books he surely had before he went abroad were Jonathan Richardson's *Theory of Painting and Essay on a Connoisseur*, which first appeared in 1715 and 1719, *Da Vinci on Painting*, William Gilpin's *Essay on Prints*, first published in 1768, and the *Aedes Walpoliana*, 1743. Webb, Richardson, and Gilpin were alike in expounding the academic style, with much emphasis on the handling of historical subject matter, classical

---

[14] Letter of January 30, 1803, in G. Chinard, *Trois amitiés françaises de Jefferson*: 125, 1927.

and Biblical. Among what seem also to be early entries in his catalogue are *The perfect painter*, 16°, and *Le vite de Pittore di Giorgio Vasari*, though we cannot be certain that these were actually acquired before he went abroad. One book, listed as a desideratum, he did not subsequently acquire: *Richardson's account of paintings, statues, etc. in Italy*, first published in 1722. It will be obvious, however, that he had seen and read this—perhaps indeed he had owned a copy before the fire of Shadwell in 1770—and that it was a chief source of his ideas regarding sculpture and painting.

Jefferson very early planned to adorn Monticello with casts and copies of famous works. About 1771 he listed these in his building notebook.[15] The list of statues desired is as follows:

> Venus of Medicis, Florence
> Hercules of Farnese, Rome
>
> Apollo of Belvedere, Rome
> Antinous, Florence
>
> Dancing Faunus
> Messenger pulling out a thorn
> Roman slave whetting his knife
> The Gladiator of Montalto
> Myrmillo expiring, Rome
> The Gladiator reposing himself after
>   the engagement (companion to the former)
> Hercules and Antaeus
> The two wrestlers
> The Rape of the Sabines (3 figures)

This selection is made with discrimination from among the works then most admired. It is interesting to canvass how the young enthusiast could arrive at such a list. Obviously his knowledge must have come from books; the field is narrowed to those he owned, or had seen and desired. Among these, we find that his chief source was indeed Richardson's critical work on the statues and paintings of Italy. Richardson speaks at one point (p. 156) of the Meleager, "one of the seven principal Antique statues; the others are the *Venus*, the *Apollo*, *Hercules*, *Gladiator*, *Laocoon* and *Antinoüs*." Most of these are de-

---

[15] *Thomas Jefferson, Architect*, fig. 79.

scribed singly elsewhere. Of them Jefferson included five, excluding the group of the Laocoon and the figure of Meleager, which Richardson merely mentions without describing it anywhere. Joseph Addison's *Remarks on Several Parts of Italy*, published in 1705, which Jefferson also owned before he went abroad, mentions at one point (p. 341) as among the most famous statues, "the *Venus de Medicis*, the *Silenus* with the Young *Bacchus* in his Arms, the *Hercules Farnese*, the *Antinous*." But that much of Jefferson's list was indeed from Richardson is shown by many evidences: the form of the names like "Venus of Medicis" or "Faunus dancing"; the inclusion of works not mentioned by Addison, like the "Myrmillo dying," at the Palazzo Pamfili, of which Richardson gives a long appreciation (p. 301). On the other hand, it is in Addison and not in Richardson that we find the forms "Roman slave whetting his knife" and "The two wrestlers," and mention and praise of the Hercules and Antaeus at the Pitti Palace.

Jefferson did not content himself merely with descriptions. We have seen already that he owned the folios of Spence and of Perrier. In the *Polymetis*, limited to representations of gods and demigods, were fine full-page plates of the "Venus of Medicis," the Apollo Belvedere, and the Hercules Farnese. In Perrier, published before the Medici collection was removed to Florence in 1677, were many more, not only the Hercules, the Apollo, the Venus, and the Antinous (Hermes) of the Vatican, but the Wrestlers, and the Myrmillo Expiring. Even these books were evidently not the end of his resources; a few scattered allusions not derived from them must have come from other works which he had somewhere seen. We observe that Jefferson did not merely follow any single list, but made his own independently, on the strength of his reading.

The building notebook also listed paintings: "St. Paul preaching at Athens; St. Ignatius at prayer; Jephtha meeting his daughter; Sacrifice of Iphigenia; History of Seleucus giving his beloved wife Stratonice to his only son Seleucus who languished for her, Florence; Diana Venetrix (see Spence's Polymetis)."[16] It is hard to know where he formed his idea of these works aside from the last. Among them only the St. Paul preaching at Athens, in Raphael's cartoon, receives special emphasis in the books we have mentioned.

---

[16] Shown there on plate XIII, figure 4, is an onyx of the subject "in Senator Buonaroti's collection at Florence."

In 1782 he added a note: "Bellini tells me that historical paintings on canvas 6 f. by 12 f. will cost £15 sterl. if copied by a good hand."

In that year, planning to go abroad, he obviously hoped to be able to secure such copies, as he transcribed his desiderata[17] with some additions, with the dimensions of certain of the paintings, and now significantly not merely with the subjects but some of the painters' names. The list of these then stood:

Belisarius from Salvator Rosa (Date obolum Belisario)
Jeptha meeting his daughter by Zocchi
St. Ignatius at prayer by
The Prodigal son from Salvator Rosa, 8f 3I high 65 5½I wide
Susanna & the two elders by Rubens, 6f high, 7f 8½I wide
The stoning of St. Stephen from Le Soeur, 9f 8½I high, 11f 3¾ wide
Curtius leaping into the gulph, from Mola, 6f 6¾I high, 11f 4½ wide
Cocles defending the bridge, companion to the other
Paul preaching at Athens, from a cartoon of Ra. Urbin
The sacrifice of Iphigenia
Seleucus giving his wife Stratonice to his son

Five of the additions to the earlier list, including the four for which dimensions are given, are selected from the collection of Sir Robert Walpole, at Houghton, catalogued by Horace Walpole in his *Aedes Walpoliana*. All the additions find mention in that work, and the dimensions are identical with those there stated. In the Introduction Walpole stresses particularly the genius of Salvator Rosa, mentioning both the Prodigal at Houghton and Lord Townshend's Belisarius, he praises Le Sueur's Saint Stephen as equal to Raphael, and he mentions with admiration Mola's Curtius which, like his Horatius Cocles, is very fully annotated. The Susanna of Rubens is not specially distinguished or described; this choice from among the many works listed by Walpole was Jefferson's own. Clearly all the paintings were chosen primarily for their subjects, with the moralizing character then so much valued. The artists were major figures of the admired academic canon, not excluding baroque masters.

The library catalogue also lists a few early desiderata in the way of prints, chiefly by Hogarth, with twelve "from dramatic and humorous paintings of Hayman (of Falstaff for the most part)." We have, alas, no list of the prints Jefferson ultimately owned, like that of

---

[17] In his library catalogue, after the desiderata in the way of books on art.

Washington's at Mount Vernon.[18] An inventory of taxable property at Monticello in 1815 lists, besides portraits in oil and crayon, "64 pictures, prints, engravings with frames more than 12 i, and 39 do, under 12 i. with gilt frames." As Jefferson's manuscript catalogue of his paintings, though incomplete, lists fifty-five with religious or mythological subjects, this would give him perhaps forty prints. As in the case of the major arts, his interests in prints became more and more specialized in historical and American subjects.[19] In his accounts for 1790 we find "Gave J. Trumbull order . . . for 2 sets of engravings from his Bunker Hill and Death of Montgomery"; in 1800, "Gave Birch an order . . . for 5. D. for plates"—doubtless William Birch's celebrated views of Philadelphia then appearing. One of Jefferson's sets of the Trumbull engravings now hangs again at Monticello. Although Jefferson bought engraving utensils in Paris in 1786, we do not know that he joined so many famous amateurs of that period, as diverse as Madame de Pompadour and Goethe, in attempting himself the practice of this art.

It was in Paris, the capital of the arts, that Jefferson had opportunity to indulge all his fondness for them, during his five years as Minister from 1784 to 1789.[20] He was not slow in forming close relations with leading figures. Baron Grimm, agent of the Empress Catherine and author of the *Correspondance littéraire*, which kept foreign courts abreast of the latest developments in letters and in the arts, was an intimate, who came often to Jefferson's elegant house in the Champs Elysées. In the salon of Madame d'Houdetot, friend of Rousseau and Saint-Lambert, in the intimacy of Madame de Tessé at her superb estate of Chaville, of the Duchesse d'Anville, of Madame de Staël, he knew all the leading figures of the world of taste.

The happiest picture of Jefferson's indulgence in these tastes is the record of the idyllic days of early September 1786, passed in company with the beautiful and passionate Maria Cosway, herself a painter: seeing the King's library, the châteaux of Madrid, of Marly, of Louveciennes, attending the Concert Spirituel, seeing the Garde Meuble, buying pictures, engravings and books, hiring a pianoforte—"after

[18] Manuscript inventories in the Library of Congress excerpted by R. T. H. Halsey, "Prints Washington Lived with at Mount Vernon," in *Bull. Metropolitan Mus. Art* 30: 63-65, 1935.

[19] *Cf.* Marie Kimball, "Jefferson, Patron of the Arts," in *Antiques*, April 1943.

[20] Marie Kimball, "Jefferson in Paris," in *North American Rev.* 248: 72-86, 1939.

dinner to Saint Cloud, from Saint Cloud to Ruggieri's, from Ruggieri's to Krumfolz"—no wonder that his heart for once nearly triumphed over his head!

Almost immediately on his arrival in Paris, in August 1784, Jefferson began buying casts and pictures,[21] at first rather casually and for small sums. These doubtless included such copies as that of a Holy Family of Raphael now at Monticello. Very soon, however, he was buying original works of some importance. From the De Billy collection, sold November 16-18, he acquired No. 21, a weeping Virgin catalogued as by Carlo Maratti. The next February he bought extensively at the sale of the cabinet of Dupille de Saint-Séverin, Nos. 36, 59, 248, and 306. They were a St. Peter of Guido Reni (72 francs), a Daughter of Herodias with the head of St. John the Baptist attributed to Simon Vouet (100 francs—the picture survives, at Monticello)[22], and a Prodigal Son by an unknown master (53 francs).[23] These and many more, which later adorned Monticello, were described by Jefferson in a manuscript catalogue with appropriate Biblical references and classical quotations.

Among fashionable living artists, it is very easy to patronize the ones who are soon forgotten. Jefferson showed in art the same prophetic insight as in politics. For assistance in drawing up his designs for the new Virginia capitol he turned to Clérisseau, author of the *Antiquités de Nismes* and a pioneer of classical enthusiasm in France. With Legrand and Molinos, Jefferson studied their method of building the great dome of the Halle au Blé, which he was later to recommend for the dome of the Capitol in Washington. To make for the Commonwealth of Virginia the statue of General Washington, commissioned for Virginia, he sent across the Atlantic in 1785 the sculptor Houdon, supreme in portraiture. Houdon also made the bust of Lafayette for the state as well as Jefferson's own bust. Jefferson had at Monticello plaster busts by Houdon of Franklin, John Paul Jones, Turgot, Voltaire, Lafayette, and Washington. His portrait of Franklin was by Greuze. He wrote in 1789, with a preference which time has

[21] *Cf.* Marie Kimball, *The Furnishings of Monticello:* 7, 1940.

[22] It does not correspond in composition with Vouet's treatment of the subject in a painting, now lost, engraved by Claude Mellan, but may well be another version, hitherto unknown, by the same artist.

[23] The sale-catalogue entries and prices were kindly transcribed for me by M. Michel Benisovitch.

ratified, "I do not feel an interest in any pencil but that of David."[24] Much later, after the death of Houdon, when the authorities of North Carolina sought Jefferson's advice as to a sculptor for a figure of Washington, it was to Canova that he sent them.

His patronage and encouragement of American painters were not less enlightened. He owned several works by West. He had Stuart twice paint his portrait. Trumbull, with his great project for historical paintings of the Revolution, he took into his house in Paris; the original composition for the Declaration of Independence was sketched there.

Sculpture, more difficult to acclimate in America, he made every effort to encourage. Besides sending Houdon, he patronized Joseph Wright and Giuseppi Ceracchi when they came to America. Later, as President, he brought over Andrei and Franzoni to work on the Capitol in Washington.

It was in architecture, however, that Jefferson was most to leave his mark. Even before he went to Paris he had made a design for the capitol of Virginia, first of all buildings projected to house the new republican governments of America. Not content with current fashions, he himself prepared drawings, taking as his model a Roman temple, the Maison Carrée at Nîmes, with its great portico—fitting within the body, pierced by windows, the houses of legislature. It was the earliest major affirmation of the ideals of the classic revival in an executed building, transcending the English garden temples which first followed such models, and preceding Napoleon's temple of victory, the Madeleine in Paris, by a score of years. Of a piece with the republican enthusiasm for the heroes of Plutarch, the Cincinnati, the building was a manifesto of classic monumentality, simplicity, and dignity, which established the character of the public buildings of the new states and of the nation.

When federal government was established by the Constitution, Jefferson, as the first Secretary of State, had further opportunity to implant his artistic ideas. He aided the French engineer, L'Enfant, in the planning of the new Federal City of Washington, and urged on him the adoption of classical models for the public buildings. When L'Enfant quarrelled with the authorities, Jefferson proposed holding a competition for designs for the Capitol and President's

[24] *Writings*, Lipscomb ed., 7: 308, 1903.

House, and himself submitted, anonymously, one for the latter based on Palladio's Villa Rotonda, while encouraging the gifted French architect Stephen Hallet to prepare one for the Capitol within the body of a peristylar temple.

Retired in 1793 from Washington's cabinet and, as he hoped, from public life, Jefferson planned a remodelling of Monticello on more Roman lines, adapted in part from the Hôtel de Salm, now the Palace of the Legion of Honor, which he had admired in Paris as one of the latest architectural novelties. Its effect of a single story, its Roman dome, had their influence on the house we know today, certainly one of the most beautiful, as it is one of the most original, of American buildings. Over many years Jefferson continued the development of the grounds, being the first to achieve, as he had been the first to propose, the adoption of the English style of informal, landscape gardening.

On his accession to the Presidency, Jefferson did not neglect the opportunity to foster the arts. He created the post of Surveyor of Public Buildings, appointing to it Benjamin Henry Latrobe, well trained in England, who had just built in the admirable Bank of Pennsylvania the first monument of the Greek revival in America. It was he who completed the wings of the old Capitol, and who began its rebuilding after it was burned by the British. To Jefferson himself, while he occupied the White House, are due its circular portico toward the Potomac and its long flanking colonnades.

For his friends in the Virginia Piedmont Jefferson gave the designs of such great houses as Edgehill, Farmington, Edgemont, Ampthill, and Barboursville, their tall Roman porticoes establishing the type to prevail in the ante-bellum South.

As a creative artist in architecture, Jefferson transcended the inherent philosophical weakness of the systems, academic and neoclassic, which he had espoused. A clear analysis of practical uses, an instinctive sense of form, tacitly directing his processes of mathematical determination, led him to a genial synthesis in which use and form were embodied with crystalline unity and perfection. This is evident above all in his greatest achievement in building, the University of Virginia. His brilliant conception of the "academical village," with its pavilions for the professors, their classrooms and living quarters, their balconies and gardens giving privacy in the midst of the communal life, its ranges of rooms for the students, their colonnades and arcades for communication under cover, its centralized and centralizing library as the heart of the institution, was given artistic form, within his classical allegiance, by the contrast of the "perfect models" of "cubical" and of "spherical architecture," by the dominance of the Rotunda, the unifying repetition of the porticoes, the melodious treble of the white columns against the warm thoroughbass of the brick walls.

Fortunate we are as a nation that among our great founders was a man of such artistic culture and creative power, who could endow us with his example and his works.

THOMAS JEFFERSON AND THE
DEMOCRATIC FAITH

John Dewey

Thomas Jefferson's republican convictions were formed early in his life, upon what was then the western frontier; when he was only twenty-two years old they seem to have been crystallized by a speech of Patrick Henry in opposition to the British Stamp Act. From that time on he was a leader in every movement for freedom and independence, usually somewhat in advance of other "rebels," finding what he said or wrote disapproved of at the time, only to win later assent. He developed with the experiences enlarged responsibilities gave him, but it was uninterruptedly in one direction. Political expediency may have caused him to deviate on special points, but there are few men in public life whose course has been so straight. Natural sympathies, actual experiences, and intellectual principles united in him to produce a character of singular consistency and charm. He was that rare person in politics, an idealist whose native faith was developed, checked, and confirmed by extremely extensive and varied practical experience. The pages of history may be searched to find another man whose native constitution destined him to espouse the liberal cause and whose career so happily furnished the conditions that gave him opportunity for articulate expression in deed and word.

I

Just as it was the "people" in whom Jefferson trusted as the foundation and ultimate security of self-governing institutions, so it was the enlightenment of the people as a whole that was his aim in promoting the advance of science. In a letter to a French friend, in which he says that his prayers are offered for the well-being of France, he adds that her future government depends not on "the state of science, no matter how exalted it may be in a select band of enlightened men, but on the condition of the general mind." What is hinted at in these remarks is openly stated in other letters. As the French Revolution went on from its beginnings, which aroused his deepest sympathies, to the despotism of Napoleon, he became increasingly skeptical of the social influence of a small band of enlightened men—like the French *philosophes*. His most extreme reaction is found in a letter to John Adams: "As for France and England, with all their preëminence in science, the one is a den of robbers, and the other of pirates. And if science produces no better fruits than tyranny, murder, rapine, and destitution of national morality, I should wish our country to be ignorant, honest, and estimable, as our neighboring savages are."

Jefferson's emphasis upon the relation of science and learning to practical serviceability had two sources. One of them was the newness of his own country, and his conviction that needs should be satisfied in the degree of their urgency. Political liberty—or as he calls it in one place, physical liberty—came first. A certain measure of material security was needed to buttress this liberty. As these were achieved, he was confident that the spread of education and general enlightenment would add what was lacking in the refinements of culture, things very precious to him personally.

The other cause of Jefferson's subordination of science and arts to social utility was his European experience. Science, no matter how "exalted," did not prevent wholesale misery and oppression if it was confined to a few. In spite of his very enjoyable personal relations with the leading intellectuals of Paris, his deepest sympathies went to the downtrodden masses whose huts he visited and whose food he ate. His affection for the "people," whose welfare was the real and final object of all social institutions, and his faith in the "will of the people" as the basis of all legitimate political arrangements made him distrust advances in knowledge and the arts that left the mass of the people in a state of misery and degradation.

The balanced relation in Jefferson's ideas between the well-being of the masses and the higher cultivation of the arts and sciences is best expressed in his educational project. Elementary popular schooling educated the many. But it also served a selective purpose. It allowed the abler students to be picked out and to continue instruction in the middle grade. Through the agency of the latter the "natural aristocracy" of intellect and character would be selected to go on to university education. State universities have carried forward Jefferson's idea of a continuous education ladder, that of Michigan being directly influenced by him.

II

Jefferson's stay in France gave rise to the notion that his political philosophy was framed under French intellectual influence. It is easy to understand why, after the reaction produced by the excesses of the French Revolution, Jefferson's political enemies put forward the idea as an accusation, extremists calling him a participant in Gallic atheism, licentiousness, and anarchy. Just why scholars have entertained the same idea, not as a charge against him, but as evidence of close intellectual relations between American social theory and the French Enlightenment is not so clear. Every one of Jefferson's characteristic political ideas—with one possible exception—was definitely formulated by him before he went to France. It is probable that his inclination toward the moral ideas of Epicurus, among the classic writers, dates from acquaintance made in Paris, but that did not affect his political ideas or even his working ethical views. Rousseau is not even mentioned by him. The moderate French Charter of Rights—a practical, not a theoretical, document—receives fairly extensive notice; the Rights of Man, the barest casual mention.

The fact is that in Jefferson's opinion the movement, intellectual and practical, was from the United States to France and Europe, not from the latter to America. The possible exception, alluded to above, is found in Jefferson's emphasis upon the moral inability of one generation to bind a succeeding generation by imposing either a debt or an unalterable Constitution upon it. His assertion that the "earth belongs in usufruct to the living; that the dead have neither powers nor rights over it" was general in scope. But his argument (in a letter written from Paris) closes with a statement of the importance of the matter "in every country and most especially in France." For, as he saw, if the new government could not abolish the laws regulating descent of land, recover lands previously given to the church, abolish feudal and ecclesiastical special privileges, and all perpetual monopolies, reformation of government would be hamstrung before it got started.

The genuine and undeniable influence of France upon Jefferson is shown in a letter he wrote expressing his amazement upon finding the prevalence of monarchical ideas upon his return to New York, when, as he says, "fresh from France, while in its first and pure stage," he was "somewhat *whetted up* in my own republican principles." The real significance of the question of French influence upon him is found in the larger matter of the sources of the ideas he expressed in the Declaration of Independence. I believe that it is true that he meant simply to write "an expression of the American mind in words so firm and plain as to command assent." There was nothing that was novel in the idea that "governments derive their just powers from the consent of the governed," nor did it find its origin in Locke's writings— "nearly perfect" as were the latter in Jefferson's opinion. Even the right of the people "to alter or abolish" a government when it became destructive of the inherent moral rights of the governed had behind it a tradition that long antedated the writings of even Locke.

There was, nevertheless, something distinctive, something original, in the Declaration. What was new and significant was that these ideas were now set forth as an expression of the "American mind" that the American will was prepared to *act* upon. Jefferson was as profoundly convinced of the novelty of the *action* as a practical "experiment"—a favorite word of his in connection with the institution of self-government—as he was of the orthodox character of the ideas as mere theory.

Jefferson used the language of the time in his assertion of "natural rights" upon which governments are based and which they must observe if they are to have legitimate authority. What is not now so plain is that the word *moral* can be substituted for the word *natural* whenever Jefferson used the latter in connection with law and rights, not only without changing his meaning but making it clearer to a modern reader. Not only does he say: "I am convinced man has no natural right in opposition to his social duties," and that "man was destined for society," but also that "questions of natural right are triable by their conformity with the moral sense and reason of man." In a letter to de Nemours, Jefferson developed his moral and political philosophy at some length by making a distinction "between the structure of the government and the moral principles" on which its administration is based. It was here that he said, "We of the United States are constitutionally and conscientiously democrats," and then went on to give the statement a moral interpretation. Man is created with a want for society and with the powers to satisfy that want in concurrence with others. When he has procured that satisfaction by instituting a society, the latter is a product which man has a right to regulate "jointly with all those who have concurred in its procurement." "There exists a right independent of force" and "Justice is the fundamental law of society."

So much for the moral foundation and aim of government. Its structure concerns the special way in which men jointly exercise their right of control. He knew too much history and had had a share in making too much history not to know that governments had to be accommodated to the manners and habits of the people who compose a given state. When a population is large and spread over considerable space, it is not possible for a society to govern itself directly. It does so indirectly by electing representatives to whom it delegates its powers. "Governments are *more or less* republican as they have more or less of the element of popular election and control in their composition." Writing in 1816, he said that the United States, measured by this criterion, were less republican than they should be, and he attributed this to the fact that lawmakers who came from large cities had learned to be afraid of the populace, and then unjustly extended their fears to the "independent, the happy and therefore orderly citizens of the United States." Anyone who starts from the moral principle of Jefferson as a premise and adds to it as another premise the principle that the only legitimate "object of the institution of government is to secure the greatest degree of happiness possible to the general mass of those associated under it" can, with little trouble, derive the further tenets of Jefferson's political creed.

The will of the people as the moral basis of government and the happiness of the people as its controlling aim were so firmly established with Jefferson that it was axiomatic that the only alternative to the republican position was fear, in lieu of trust, of the people. Given fear of them, it followed, as by mathematical necessity, not only that they must *not* be given a large share in the conduct of government, but that they must themselves be controlled by force, moral or physical or both, and by appeal to some special interest served by government — an appeal which, according to Jefferson, inevitably meant the use of means to corrupt the people. Jefferson's trust in the people was a faith in what he sometimes called their common sense and sometimes their reason. They might be fooled and misled for a time, but give them light and in the long run their oscillations this way and that will describe what in effect is a straight course.

I am not underestimating Jefferson's abilities as a practical politician when I say that this deep-seated faith in the people and their responsiveness to enlightenment properly presented was a most important factor in enabling him to effect, against great odds, "the revolution of 1800." It is the cardinal element bequeathed by Jefferson to the American tradition.

III

Jefferson's belief in the necessity for strict limitation of the powers of officials had both a general and a special or historic source. As for the latter, had not the Revolution itself been fought because of the usurpation of power by the officers of a government? And were not the political opponents of republicanism, in Jefferson's opinion, men so moved by admiration of the British Constitution that they wished to establish a "strong" government in this country, one not above the use of methods of corruption—not as an end in itself but as a means of procuring the allegiance of the populace more effectively and in a less costly way than by use of direct coercion? On general principles, Jefferson knew that possession of unusual and irresponsible power corrupts those who wield it; that officials are, after all, human beings affected by ordinary weaknesses of human nature, "wares from the same workshop, made of the same materials." Hence they were to be continually watched, tested and checked, as well as constitutionally limited in their original grant of powers.

There are, however, two important points in which popular representations of Jeffersonian democracy are often at fault. One of them concerns the basic importance of the will of the people in relation to the law-making power, constitutional and ordinary. There is no doubt that Jefferson was strongly in favor of specifying in the Constitution the powers that could be exercised by officials, executive, legislative, and judicial, and then holding them, by strict construction, to the powers specified. But he also believed that "every people have their own particular habits, ways of thinking, manners, et cetera, which have grown up with them from their infancy, are become a part of their nature, and to which the regulations which are to make them happy must be accommodated." Elsewhere he states the principle that "The excellence of every government is its adaptation to the state of those to be governed by it."

His idealism was a moral idealism, not a dreamy utopianism. He was aware that conclusions drawn from the past history of mankind were against the success of the experiment that was being tried on American soil. He was quite sure that Latin American countries would succeed in throwing off the yoke of Spain and Portugal, but he was decidedly skeptical about their capacity for self-government, and feared their future would be one of a succession of military despotisms for a long time to come. He was conscious that chances for greater success of the experiment in the United States were dependent upon events which might be regarded either as fortunate accidents or as providential dispensations: the wide ocean protecting the country from oppressive governments in Europe; the "Anglo-Saxon" tradition of liberties; even the jealousies of religious denominations that prevented the establishment of a state church, and hence worked for religious liberty; the immense amount of free land and available natural resources with consequent continual freedom of movement; the independence and vigor that were bred on the frontier; and so on. Even so, he had fears for the future when the country should be urbanized and industrialized.

In direct line with his conviction on this point was his belief in the necessity of periodic revisions of the Constitution, one to take place every twenty years, and his belief that the process of ordinary amendment had been made too difficult. His faith in the right of the people to govern themselves in their own way and in their ability to exercise the right wisely, provided they were enlightened by education and by free discussion, were stronger than his faith in any article of his own political creed—except this one. His own convictions as to the proper forms of government were strong, and he contended ably for their realization. But he was conciliatory by temperament and by practical policy. Students and historians have criticized him for not trying harder to put into effect after the "revolution of 1800" the reforms he had been urging before that time, especially as he based his opposition to Adams upon their absence. Doubtless he was moved by considerations of political expediency. But there is also no reason to doubt the sincerity of those expressions of his which set forth his willingness to subordinate his own political policies to the judgment of the people.

In any case, he was no friend of what he called "sanctimonious reverence" for the Constitution. He adhered to the view, expressed in the Declaration of Independence, that people are more disposed to suffer evils than to right them by abolishing forms to which they are accustomed. It was the more important, accordingly, to recognize that "laws and institution must go hand in hand with the progress of the human mind" and that institutions must change with change of circumstances brought about by "discoveries, new truths, change of opinions and manners." Were he alive, he would note and scourge that lack of democratic faith which, in the professed name of democracy, asserts that the "ark of the covenant is too sacred to be touched." Jefferson saw that periodical overhauling of the fundamental law was the alternative to change effected only by violence and repetition of the old historic round "of oppressions, rebellions, reformations, oppressions. . . ." There was but one thing that was unchangeable, and that was the "inherent and inalienable rights of man."

The other point on which Jefferson's ideas have not been adequately represented has to do with his belief that state governments "are the true barriers of our liberty," and his fear of centralized government at Washington—not that he did not have and hold with strong conviction the belief and the fear, but that the ideas with which he supplemented them have not received due attention. He attached much importance to self-governing communities of much smaller size than the state or even the county. He was impressed, practically as well as theoretically, with the effectiveness of the New England town meeting, and wished to see something of the sort made an organic part of the governing process of the whole country. Division of every county into wards was first suggested by him in connection with the organization of an elementary school system. But even from his early service in the legislature of Virginia to the latest years of his life he urged the adoption of his plan. In a letter written after he was seventy, he wrote, "As Cato concluded every speech with the words '*Carthago delenda est*' so do I with the injunction 'Divide the counties into wards'."

While the first purpose of the division into small local units was the establishment and care of popular elementary schools, the full aim was to make the wards "little republics, with a warden at the head of each, for all those concerns, which being under their eye, they would better manage than the larger republics of the county or State." They were to have the "care of the poor, roads, police, elections, nomination of jurors, administration of justice in small cases, elementary exercises of militia." In short, they were to exercise directly with respect to their own affairs all the functions of government, civil and military. In addition, when any important wider matter came up for decision, all wards would be called into meetings on the same day, so that the collective sense of the whole people would be produced. The plan was not adopted. But it was an essential part of Jefferson's political philosophy. The significance of the doctrine of "states' rights" as he held it is incomplete both theoretically and practically until this plan is taken into the reckoning. "The elementary republics of the wards, the county republics, the State republics and the Republic of the Union would form a gradation of authorities." Every man would then share in the government of affairs not merely on election day but every day. In a letter to John Adams, written in 1813, he wrote that he still had great hope that the plan would be adopted, and would then form "the keystone of the arch of our government." It is for this reason that I say this view of self-government is very inadequately represented in the usual form in which it is set forth—as a glorification of state against Federal governments, and still more as a theoretical opposition to all government save as a necessary evil. The heart of his philosophy of politics is found in his effort to institute the small administrative and legislative unit as the keystone of the arch.

I V

As was suggested earlier, the essentially moral nature of Jefferson's political philosophy is concealed from us at the present time because of the change that has taken place in the language in which moral ideas are expressed. The "self-evident truths'" about the equality of all men by creation and the existence of "inherent [changed to 'certain' by Congress] and inalienable rights," appear today to have a legal rather than a moral meaning; and in addition, the intellectual basis of the legal theory of natural law and natural rights has been undermined by historical and philosophical criticism. In Jefferson's own mind, the words had a definitely ethical import, intimately and vitally connected with his view of God and nature. The latter connection comes out more clearly in the preamble, in which he refers to the necessity of the American people taking the "separate and equal station to which the laws of nature and of nature's God entitle them."

These phrases were not rhetorical flourishes, nor were they accommodated for reasons of expediency to what Jefferson thought would be popular with the people of the country. Jefferson was a sincere deist. Although his rejection of supernaturalism and of the authority of churches and their creeds caused him to be denounced as an atheist, he was convinced, beyond any peradventure, on *natural* and rational grounds of the existence of a divine righteous Creator who manifested His purposes in the structure of the world, especially in that of society and the human conscience. The natural equality of all human beings was not psychological or legal. It was intrinsically moral, as a consequence of the equal *moral* relation all human beings sustain to their Creator—equality of moral claims and of moral responsibilities. Positive law—or municipal law, as Jefferson termed it— and political institutions thus have both a moral foundation and a moral criterion or measure.

The word "faith" is thus applied advisedly to the attitude of Jefferson toward the people's will, and its right to control political institutions and policies. The faith had a genuinely religious quality. The forms of government and law, even of the Constitution, might and should change. But the inherent and inalienable rights of man were unchangeable, because they express the will of the righteous Creator of man embodied in the very structure of society and conscience. Jefferson was not an "individualist" in the sense of the British laissez-faire liberal school. He believed that individual human beings receive the right of self-government "with their being from the hand of nature." As an eighteenth-century deist and believer in natural religion, Jefferson connected nature and nature's God inseparably in his thought. He wrote that he had "no fear but that the result of our experiment will be that men may be trusted to govern themselves without a master. Could the contrary of this be proved, I should conclude either that there is no God, or that he is a malevolent being."

These words are to be taken literally, not rhetorically, if one wishes to understand Jefferson's democratic faith. The connection of justice—or equity—with equality of rights and duties was a commonplace of the moral tradition of Christendom. Jefferson took the tradition seriously. His statements about the origin of the Declaration of Independence are confirmed in what he wrote shortly before his death: "We had no occasion to search into musty records, to hunt up royal parchments, or to investigate the laws and institutions of a semibarbarous ancestry. We appealed to those of nature, and found them engraved on our hearts."

Other days bring other words and other opinions behind words that are used. The terms in which Jefferson expressed his belief in the moral criterion for judging all political arrangements and his belief that republican institutions are the only ones that are morally legitimate are not now current. It is doubtful, however, whether defense of democracy against the attacks to which it is subjected does not depend upon taking once more the position Jefferson took about its moral basis and purpose, even though we have to find another set of words in which to formulate the moral ideal served by democracy. A renewal of faith in common human nature, in its potentialities in general and in its power in particular to respond to reason and truth, is a surer bulwark against totalitarianism than is demonstration of material success or devout worship of special legal and political forms.

A SHEAF OF POEMS

THE DEATH OF JEFFERSON

Hezekiah Butterworth

I

'Twas midsummer; cooling breezes all the languid forests fanned,
And the angel of the evening drew her curtain o'er the land.
Like an isle rose Monticello through the cooled and rippling trees,
Like an isle in rippling starlight in the silence of the seas.
Ceased the mocking-bird his singing; said the slaves with faltering
    breath,
"Tis the Third, and on the morrow Heaven will send the Angel
    Death."

II

In his room at Monticello, lost in dreams the statesman slept,
Seeing not the still forms round him, seeing not the eyes that wept,
Hearing not the old clock ticking in life's final silence loud,
Knowing not when night came o'er him like the shadow of a cloud.
In the past his soul is living as in fifty years ago,
Hastes again to Philadelphia, hears again the Schuylkill flow—

III

Meets again the elder Adams—knowing not that far away
He is waiting for Death's morrow, on old Massachusetts Bay;
Meets with Hancock, young and courtly, meets with Hopkins, bent
    and old,
Meets again calm Roger Sherman, fiery Lee, and Carroll bold,
Meets the sturdy form of Franklin, meets the half a hundred men
Who have made themselves immortal,—breathes the ancient morn
    again.

From *Songs of History*, by Hezekiah Butterworth. Boston, 1887.

IV

Once again the Declaration in his nerveless hands he holds,
And before the waiting statesmen its prophetic hope unfolds,
Reads again the words puissant, "All men are created free,"
Claims again for man his birthright, claims the world's equality,
Hears the coming and the going of an hundred firm-set feet,
Hears the summer breezes blowing 'mid the oak-trees cool and sweet,

V

Sees again tall Patrick Henry by the side of Henry Lee,
Hears him cry, "And will ye sign it?—it will make all nations free!
Fear ye not the axe or gibbet; it shall topple every throne.
Sign it for the world's redemption!—All mankind its truth shall own!
Stars may fall, but truth eternal shall not falter, shall not fail.
Sign it, and the Declaration shall the voice of ages hail.

VI

"Sign, and set yon dumb bell ringing, that the people all may know
Man has found emancipation; sign, the Almighty wills it so."
Sees one sign it, then another, till like magic moves the pen,
Till all have signed it, and it lies there, charter of the rights of men.
Hears the small bells, hears the great bell, hanging idly in the sun,
Break the silence, and the people whisper, awe-struck, "It is done."

VII

Then the dream began to vanish—burgesses, the war's red flames,
Charging Tarleton, proud Cornwallis, navies moving on the James,
Years of peace, and years of glory, all began to melt away,
And the statesman woke from slumber in the night, and tranquil lay,
And his lips moved; friends there gathered with love's silken footstep
    near,
And he whispered, softly whispered in love's low and tender ear,—

VIII

"It is the Fourth?" "No, not yet," they answered, "but 'twill soon be
  early morn;
We will wake you, if you slumber, when the day begins to dawn."
Then the statesman left the present, lived again amid the past,
Saw, perhaps, the peopled future ope its portals grand and vast,
Till the flashes of the morning lit the far horizon low,
And the sun's rays o'er the forests in the east began to glow.

IX

Rose the sun, and from the woodlands fell the midnight dews like
  rain,
In magnolias cool and shady sang the mocking-bird again,
And the statesman woke from slumber, saw the risen sun, and heard
Rippling breezes 'mid the oak-trees, and the lattice singing bird,
And, his eye serene uplifted, as rejoicing in the sun,
"It is the Fourth?" his only question,—to the world his final one.

X

Silence fell on Monticello—for the last dread hour was near,
And the old clock's measured ticking only broke upon the ear.
All the summer rooms were silent, where the great of earth had trod,
All the summer blooms seemed silent as the messengers of God;
Silent were the hall and chamber where old councils oft had met,
Save the far boom of the cannon that recalled the old day yet.

XI

Silent still is Monticello—he is breathing slowly now,
In the splendors of the noon-tide, with the death-dew on his brow;—
Silent save the clock still ticking where his soul had given birth
To the mighty thoughts of freedom that should free the fettered earth;
Silent save the boom of cannon on the sun-filled wave afar,
Bringing 'mid the peace eternal still the memory of war.

XII

Evening in majestic shadows fell upon the fortress' walls;
Sweetly were the last bells ringing on the James and on the Charles.
'Mid the choruses of freedom two departed victors lay,
One beside the blue Rivanna, one by Massachusetts Bay.
He was gone, and night her sable curtain drew across the sky;
Gone his soul into all nations, gone to live and not to die.

Jefferson at 62.

PROFILE MEDALLION BY GILBERT STUART, WASHINGTON, D. C., 1805

Photograph courtesy of the Library of Congress from C. W. Bowen's "History of the Centennial Celebration of the Inauguration of George Washington"

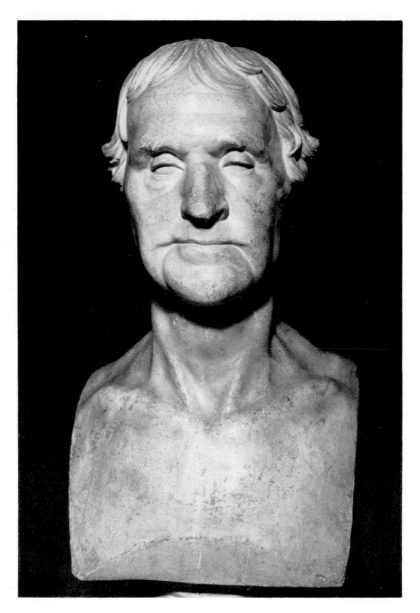

Jefferson at 75.

BUST BY WILLIAM JOHN COFFEE, MONTICELLO, 1818

(Replica from the lost original which belonged to Jefferson.)

Courtesy of Miss Olivia Taylor, Washington, D. C. Photograph by Woltz Studio

ON THE FATHER OF LIBERTY

Allen Tate

Jefferson had many charms;
Was democratic; still—and yet
What should one do? The family arms
On coach and spoon he wisely set
Against historical alarms:
For quality not being loath,
Nor quantity, nor the fame of both.

From *The Sewanee Review*, January 1930. Copyright 1930 by *The Sewanee Review*. Reprinted by permission of *The Sewanee Review* and Allen Tate.

MONTICELLO

LAWRENCE LEE

I

Once burned his late lamp as a little moon
Among the dark trees shining.
His house still stands, a symbol, on this hill,
The dome sun-white in summer noon,
Darkened with day declining.

The hill is vacant and the fields are still—
Only a slow bird flying.
Even the earth and air seem empty now
And only deepening shadows fill
The woods where crows went crying.

We shall not have from seasons peace, nor know
Comfort in red leaves shaking.
There is but coldness in this chiselled stone.
No autumn wind will ever blow
This dust to waking.

Let the firm hills remember greatness gone,
And limbs to shrill wind bending.
When thunder rolled and the great trees were split
He kept this upper way alone
Although a world seemed ending.

From *Monticello and Other Poems*, by Lawrence Lee. Copyright 1937 by
Charles Scribner's Sons. Reprinted by permission.

II

What shall man do for love except create?
Here once were only the stiff trees shaken
And not the ear to hear the singing wind
And not the eye to see how great
A yellow woods the gale had taken.

Now the stark winter, howling in blank boughs,
Screams past the stone, past the body broken.
Here was the ground where he had set his will
And in his love had built this house,
Here moved to act the strong word spoken.

Another year this hill was full of light,
This house was wakeful with the living.
By memory now we must make painful way,
Wishing less dark on such a night,
More hope than sounds of storm are giving.

There is a tempest raging at the world.
If in these hearths some spark would quicken,
Some antique candle scatter from the door
Old light where a new dark is curled
And all he loved is stricken. . . .

BRAVE NEW WORLD

Archibald MacLeish

But you, Thomas Jefferson,
You could not lie so still,
You could not bear the weight of stone
On the quiet hill,

You could not keep your green grown peace
Nor hold your folded hand
If you could see your new world now,
Your new sweet land.

There was a time, Tom Jefferson,
When freedom made free men.
The new found earth and the new freed mind
Were brothers then.

There was a time when tyrants feared
The new world of the free.
Now freedom is afraid and shrieks
At tyranny.

Words have not changed their sense so soon
Nor tyranny grown new.
The truths you held, Tom Jefferson,
Will still hold true.

What's changed is freedom in this age.
What great men dared to choose
Small men now dare neither win
Nor lose.

Freedom, when men fear freedom's use
But love its useful name,
Has cause and cause enough for fear
And cause for shame.

We fought a war in freedom's name
And won it in our own.
We fought to free a world and raised
A wall of stone.

Your countrymen who could have built
The hill fires of the free
To set the dry world all ablaze
With liberty—

To burn the brutal thorn in Spain
Of bigotry and hate
And the dead lie and the brittle weed
Beyond the Plate:

Who could have heaped the bloody straw,
The dung of time, to light
The Danube in a sudden flame
Of hope by night—

Your countrymen who could have hurled
Their freedom like a brand
Have cupped it to a candle spark
In a frightened hand.

Freedom that was a thing to use
They've made a thing to save
And staked it in and fenced it round
Like a dead man's grave.

You, Thomas Jefferson,
You could not lie so still,
You could not bear the weight of stone
On your green hill,

You could not hold your angry tongue
If you could see how bold
The old stale bitter world plays new—
And the new world old.

JEFFERSON

KARL SHAPIRO

If vision can dilate, my noble lord,
Farther than porticos, Italian cells,
Newtonian gardens, Haydn, and cuisine,
Tell us, most serious of all our poets,
Why is the clock so low?

I see the tender gradient of your will;
Virginia is the Florence of your soul,
Yes, ours. The architecture of your hands
Quiets ambition and revives our skill
And buys our faithlessness.

So temperate, so remote, so pure of phrase,
Your music sweeps a continent, a sphere,
Fashions a modern language for a war
And by its cadence makes responsible
Our million names to you.

When you were old the god of government
Seemed to recede a pace, and you were glad.
You watched the masons through your telescope
Finish your school of freedom. Death itself
Stood thoughtful at your bed.

And now the surfaces of mind are rubbed
Our essence starts like serum from our eyes.
How can you not assume the deities
That move behind the bloodshot look and lean
Like saints and Salem devils?

◇◇

THE OPINIONS OF FOUR PRESIDENTS

"THE PRINCIPLES OF JEFFERSON ARE THE DEFINITIONS AND AXIOMS OF FREE SOCIETY"

ABRAHAM LINCOLN

A LETTER TO H. L. PIERCE AND OTHERS

Springfield, Ill., April 6, 1859

Gentlemen: Your kind note inviting me to attend a festival in Boston, on the 28th instant, in honor of the birthday of Thomas Jefferson, was duly received. My engagements are such that I cannot attend.

Bearing in mind that about seventy years ago two great political parties were first formed in this country, that Thomas Jefferson was the head of one of them and Boston the headquarters of the other, it is both curious and interesting that those supposed to descend politically from the party opposed to Jefferson should now be celebrating his birthday in their own original seat of empire, while those claiming political descent from him have nearly ceased to breathe his name everywhere.

Remembering, too, that the Jefferson party was formed upon its

From *Abraham Lincoln: Complete Works, Comprising His Speeches, Letters, State Papers, and Miscellaneous Writings*, edited by John G. Nicolay and John Hay. New York, 1894.

supposed superior devotion to the personal rights of men, holding the rights of property to be secondary only, and greatly inferior, and assuming that the so-called Democracy of to-day are the Jefferson, and their opponents the anti-Jefferson, party, it will be equally interesting to note how completely the two have changed hands as to the principle upon which they were originally supposed to be divided. The Democracy of to-day hold the liberty of one man to be absolutely nothing when in conflict with another man's right of property; Republicans, on the contrary, are for both the man and the dollar, but in case of conflict the man before the dollar.

I remember being once much amused at seeing two partially intoxicated men engaged in a fight with their great-coats on, which fight, after a long and rather harmless contest, ended in each having fought himself out of his own coat and into that of the other. If the two leading parties of this day are really identical with the two in the days of Jefferson and Adams, they have performed the same feat as the two drunken men.

But, soberly, it is now no child's play to save the principles of Jefferson from total overthrow in this nation. One would state with great confidence that he could convince any sane child that the simpler propositions of Euclid are true; but nevertheless he would fail, utterly, with one who should deny the definitions and axioms. The principles of Jefferson are the definitions and axioms of free society. And yet they are denied and evaded, with no small show of success. One dashingly calls them "glittering generalities." Another bluntly calls them "self-evident lies." And others insidiously argue that they apply to "superior races." These expressions, differing in form, are identical in object and effect—the supplanting the principles of free government, and restoring those of classification, caste, and legitimacy. They would delight a convention of crowned heads plotting against the people. They are the vanguard, the miners and sappers of returning despotism. We must repulse them, or they will subjugate us. This is a world of compensation; and he who would be no slave must consent to have no slave. Those who deny freedom to others deserve it not for themselves, and, under a just God, cannot long retain it. All honor to Jefferson—to the man who, in the concrete pressure of a struggle for national independence by a single people, had the coolness, forecast, and capacity to introduce into a merely revolutionary document an abstract truth, applicable to all men and all times, and so to embalm it there that to-day and in all coming days it shall be a rebuke and a stumbling-block to the very har-bingers of reappearing tyranny and oppression. Your obedient servant,

A. LINCOLN

WHAT JEFFERSON WOULD DO

WOODROW WILSON

The circumstances of our day are so utterly different from those of
Jefferson's day that it may seem nothing less than an act of temerity
to attempt to say what Jefferson would do if he were now alive and
guiding us with his vision and command. The world we live in is no
longer divided into neighbourhoods and communities; the lines of
the telegraph thread it like nerves uniting a single organism. The
ends of the earth touch one another and exchange impulse and purpose. America has swung out of her one-time isolation and has joined
the family of nations. She is linked to mankind by every tie of blood
and circumstance. She is more cosmopolitan in her make-up than
any other nation of the world; is enriched by a greater variety of
energy drawn from strong peoples the world over. She is not the
simple, homogeneous, rural nation that she was in Jefferson's time,
making only a beginning at development and the conquest of fortune; she is great and strong; above all she is infinitely varied; her
affairs are shot through with emotion and the passion that comes
with strength and growth and self-confidence. We live in a new and
strange age and reckon with new affairs alike in economics and politics of which Jefferson knew nothing.

And yet we may remind ourselves that Jefferson's mind did not
move in a world of narrow circumstances; it did not confine itself to
the conditions of a single race or a single continent. It had commerce
with the thought of men old and new; it had moved in an age of
ample air, in which men thought not only of nations but of mankind,
in which they saw not only individual policies, but a great field of
human need and of human fortune. Neither did he think in abstract
terms, as did the men with whom he had had such stimulating commerce of thought in France. His thought was not speculation; it was

Part of an Address delivered at the Jefferson Day Banquet, Waldorf-Astoria
Hotel, New York, April 13, 1912. From *The Public Papers of Woodrow Wilson*,
edited by Ray Stannard Baker and William E. Dodd. Copyright 1925 by Edith
Bolling Wilson. Reprinted by permission of Edith Bolling Wilson.

the large generalization that comes from actual observation and experience. He had had contact with plain men of many kinds, as well as with philosophers and foreign statesmen. He thought in a way that his neighbours in Virginia could understand, in a way which illuminated their own lives and ambitions for them. And though he was deemed a philosopher, he was nevertheless the idol of the people, for he somehow heard and voiced what they themselves could have said and purposed and conceived. For all the largeness of his thought, it was bathed in an everyday atmosphere; it belongs to the actual, workaday world; it has its feet firmly on circumstances and fact and the footing all men are accustomed to who reflect at all on their lives and the lives of their neighbours and compatriots. He was holding up for the illumination of the things of which he spoke a light which he had received out of the hands of old philosophers. But the rays of that light as he held it fell upon actual American life; they did not lose themselves vaguely in space; they were for the guidance of men's feet every day.

We may be sure, therefore, that had Jefferson lived in our time he would have acted upon the facts as they are. In the first place, because he would have seen them as they actually are, and in the second place because he would have been interested in theory only as he could adjust it to the reality of the life about him. He would not have been content with a philosophy which he could fit together only within the walls of his study.

To determine what Jefferson would have done, therefore, requires only that we should ourselves clearly see the facts of our time as they are, whether in the field of government or in the field of our economic life, and that we should see how Jefferson's principle of the rule and authority of the people stands related to these facts. We are constantly quoting Jefferson's fundamental thought: it was that no policy could last whose foundation is narrow, based upon the privileges and authority of a few, but that its foundations must be as broad as the interests of all the men and families and neighbourhoods that live under it. Monopoly, private control, the authority of privilege, the concealed mastery of a few men cunning enough to rule without showing their power—he would have at once announced them rank weeds which were sure to choke out all wholesome life in the fair garden of affairs. If we can detect these things in our time; if we can see them and describe them and touch them as they are, then we know what Jefferson would have done. He would have moved against them, sometimes directly, sometimes indirectly, sometimes openly, sometimes subtly; but whether he merely mined about them or struck directly at them, he would have set systematic war against them at the front of all his purpose.

As regards the real influences that control our Government, he would have asked first of all: Are they determined by the direct and open contacts of opinion. He would have found that they were not; that, on the contrary, our Government as it has developed has supplied secret influences with a hundred coverts and ambushes; that the opinion of the Nation makes little noise in the committee rooms of legislatures; that it is certain large, special interests and not the people who maintain the lobby; that the argument of the lobby is oftentimes louder and more potent than the argument of the hustings and the floor of the representative body. He would have found, moreover, that until very recent years opinion had had very difficult access, if any at all, in most seasons, of the private conferences in which candidates for office were chosen, candidates for both administrative and legislative office, and that in the private conferences where it was determined who should be nominated and, therefore, of course, who should be elected, the same influences had established themselves which ruled in the legislative lobby. That money, the money that kept the whole organization together, flowed in, not from the general body of the people, but from those who wished to determine in their own private interest what governors and legislators should and should not do.

It is plain in such circumstances that he would have insisted, as we are insisting now, that if there could be found no means by which the authority and purpose of the people could break into these private places and establish their rule again, if the jungle proved too thick for the common thought to explore, if the coverts where the real power lurked were too difficult to find, the forces of genuine democracy must move around them instead of through them, must surround and beleaguer them, must establish a force outside of them by which they can be dominated or overawed. It is with the discussion of just such affairs that the public mind is now preoccupied and engrossed. Debate is busy with them from one end of the land to the other.

As regards the economic policy of the country it is perfectly plain that Mr. Jefferson would have insisted upon a tariff fitted to actual conditions, by which he would have meant not the interests of the few men who find access to the hearings of the Ways and Means Committee of the House and the Finance Committee of the Senate, but the interests of the business men and manufacturers and farmers and workers and professional men of every kind and class. He would have insisted that the schedules should be turned wrong side out and every item of their contents subjected to the general scrutiny of all concerned. It is plain, also, that he would have insisted upon a currency system elastic, indeed, and suited to the varying circumstances of the money market in a great industrial and trading Nation, but absolutely fortified and secured against a central control, the influence of coteries, and leagues of banks to which it is now in constant danger of being subjected. He would have known that the currency question is not only an economic question but a political question, and that, above all things else, control must be in the hands of those who represent the general interest and not in the hands of those who represent the things we are seeking to guard against.

In the general field of business his thought would, of course, have gone about to establish freedom, to throw business opportunity open at every point to new men, to destroy the processes of monopoly, to exclude the poison of special favours, to see that, whether big or little, business was not dominated by anything but the law itself, and that that law was made in the interest of plain, unprivileged men everywhere.

Jefferson's principles are sources of light because they are not made up of pure reason, but spring out of aspiration, impulse, vision, sympathy. They burn with the fervour of the heart; they wear the light of interpretation he sought to speak in, the authentic terms of honest, human ambition. And the law in his mind was the guardian of all legitimate ambition. It was the great umpire standing by to see that the game was honourably and fairly played in the spirit of generous rivalry and open the field free to every sportsmanlike contestant.

Constitutions are not inventions. They do not create our liberty. They are rooted in life, in fact, in circumstance, in environment. They are not the condition of our liberty but its expression. They result from our life; they do not create it. And so there beats in them always, if they live at all, this pulse of the large life of humanity. As they yield and answer to that they are perfected and exalted.

Indeed, the whole spirit of government is the spirit of men of every kind banded together in a generous combination seeking the common good. Nations are exalted, parties are made great as they partake of this aspiration and are permitted to see this vision of the Nation as a whole struggling toward a common ideal and a common hope.

We as Democrats are particularly bound at this season of expectation, and of confidence to remember that it is only in this spirit and with this vision that we can ever serve either the Nation or ourselves. As we approach the time when we are to pick out a President—for I believe that it is to be our privilege—we should fix our thought on this one great fact, that no man is big enough or great enough to be President alone. He will be no stronger than his party. His strength will lie in the counsel of his comrades. His success will spring out of the union and energy and unselfish cooperation of his party, and his party must be more than half the Nation. It must include, and genuinely include, men of every class and race and disposition. If he be indeed the representative of his people, there may be vouchsafed to him through them something of the vision to conceive what Jefferson conceived and understood—how the vision may be carried into reality.

JEFFERSON AND THE BILL OF RIGHTS

HERBERT HOOVER

Thomas Jefferson, of course, did not originate the Bill of Rights. He had much to do with its amplification and in securing that it be embedded in the Constitution. His flaming insistence in the Declaration that men "are endowed by their Creator with certain inalienable rights" had much to do with implanting them in the fibre of American life.

Jefferson knew well the centuries of struggle in which men had died fighting bitterly for these rights. Step by step they had been secured through the Magna Charta, the growth of common law, the "Petition of Rights," and the Declaration of Rights, until they reached full flower in the new republic.

During the first century and a half of our national life we saw no serious challenge to the Bill of Rights. We extended them and we accepted them as the air we breathed. But for the last quarter of a century they have been incessantly attacked both from without and within our country.

In the hurricane of revolutions which have swept the world since the Great War, men, struggling with the wreckage and poverty of that great catastrophe and the complications of the machine age, have in despair surrendered their freedom for false promises of security and glory. Whether it be Fascism, Nazism, Communism, or their lesser followers, the result is the same. Every day they repudiate every principle of the Bill of Rights. And where they have triumphed the first security of men has been lost.

Theirs is a form of servitude, of slavery—a slipping back toward the Middle Ages. Whatever these ideologies are, they have one common denominator—the citizen has no inalienable rights. He is submerged into the State. Here is the most fundamental clash known to

From *Thomas Jefferson Then and Now, 1743-1943, A National Symposium,* edited by James Waterman Wise. Copyright 1943 by Bill of Rights Sesqui-Centennial Committee. Reprinted by permission of Herbert Hoover.

mankind—that is, free men and women, cooperating under orderly liberty, as contrasted with human beings made pawns of government; men who are slaves of despotism, as against free men who are the masters of the State.

Even in America, where liberty blazed brightest and by its glow shed light on all the others, liberty is not only besieged from without but it is challenged from within. Many, in honest belief, hold that we cannot longer accommodate the growth of science, technology and mechanical power to the Bill of Rights. But men's inventions cannot be of more value than men themselves. It would be better that we sacrifice something of economic efficiency than to surrender these primary liberties. In them lies a spiritual growth of men. Behind them is the conception which is the highest development of the Christian faith—the conception of individual freedom with brotherhood. From them is the fullest flowering of individual human personality.

Those who proclaim that the Machine Age created an irreconcilable conflict in which Liberty must be sacrificed should not forget the battles for these rights over the centuries, for let it be remembered that in the end these are undying principles which spring from the souls of men. We imagine conflict not because the principles of liberty are unworkable in a machine age, but because we have not worked them conscientiously or have forgotten their true meaning.

Neither would sacrifice of these rights add to economic efficiency nor would it gain in economic security, or find a single job or give a single assurance in old age. The dynamic forces which sustain economic security and progress in human comfort lie deep below the surface. They reach to those human impulses which are watered alone by freedom. The initiative of men, their enterprise, the inspiration of thought, flower in full only in the security of these rights.

And by practical experience under the Bill of Rights we have tested this truth. Down through a century and a half this American concept of human freedom has enriched the whole world. From the release of the spirit, the initiative, the cooperation, and the courage of men, which alone comes from these freedoms, has been builded this very machine age with all its additions of comfort, its reductions of sweat. Wherever in the world the system of individual liberty has been sustained, mankind has been better clothed, better fed, better housed, has had more leisure. Above all, men and women have had more self-respect. They have been more generous and of finer spirit.

Those who scoff that liberty is of no consequence to the under-privileged and the unemployed, are grossly ignorant of the primary fact that it is through the creative and the productive impulses of free men that the redemption of those sufferers and their economic security must come. Any system which curtails these freedoms and stimulants to men destroys the possibility of the full production from which economic security alone can come.

Nor is respect for the Bill of Rights a fetter upon progress. It has been no dead hand that has carried the living principle of liberty over these centuries. Without violation of these principles and their safeguards we have amended the Constitution many times in the past century to meet the problems of growing civilization. We will no doubt do so many times again. New inventions and new ideas require the constant remolding of our civilization. The functions of government must be readjusted from time to time to restrain the strong and protect the weak. That is the preservation of liberty itself.

Jefferson was eternally right when he held that liberty comes only and lives only where the hard-won rights of men are held inalienable, where governments themselves may not infringe, where governments are indeed but the mechanisms to protect and sustain these principles. It was this concept for which America's sons have died on a hundred battlefields.

The purification of liberty from abuses, the restoration of confidence in the rights of men, from which come the release of the dynamic forces of advancing spirit and enterprise, are alone the methods through which the purpose of American life can be assured.

"A DEBT LONG OVERDUE . . ."

Franklin D. Roosevelt

ADDRESS AT DEDICATION OF THE
THOMAS JEFFERSON MEMORIAL, WASHINGTON, D. C.

April 13, 1943

Today, in the midst of a great war for freedom, we dedicate a shrine to freedom.

To Thomas Jefferson, Apostle of Freedom, we are paying a debt long overdue.

Yet, there are reasons for gratitude that this occasion falls within our time; for our generation of Americans can understand much in Jefferson's life which intervening generations could not see as well as we.

He faced the fact that men who will not fight for liberty can lose it. We, too, have faced that fact.

He lived in a world in which freedom of conscience and freedom of mind were battles still to be fought through—not principles already accepted of all men. We, too, have lived in such a world.

He loved peace and loved liberty—yet on more than one occasion he was forced to choose between them. We, too, have been compelled to make that choice.

Generations which understand each other across the distances of history are the generations united by a common experience and a common cause. Jefferson, across a hundred and fifty years of time, is closer by much to living men than many of our leaders of the years between. His cause was a cause to which we also are committed, not by our words alone but by our sacrifice.

From *The Public Papers and Addresses of Franklin D. Roosevelt,* compiled by Samuel I. Rosenman. 1943 Volume. New York: Harper and Brothers, 1950.

For faith and ideals imply renunciations. Spiritual advancement throughout all our history has called for temporal sacrifices.

The Declaration of Independence and the very purpose of the American Revolution itself, while seeking freedoms, called for the abandonment of privileges.

Jefferson was no dreamer—for half a century he led his State and his Nation in fact and in deed. I like to think that this was so because he thought in terms of the morrow as well as the day—and this was why he was hated or feared by those who thought in terms of the day and the yesterday.

We judge him by the application of his philosophy to the circumstances of his life. But in such applying we come to understand that his life was given for those deeper values that persist throughout all time.

Leader in the philosophy of government, in education, in the arts, in efforts to lighten the toil of mankind—exponent of planning for the future, he led the steps of America into the path of the permanent integrity of the Republic.

Thomas Jefferson believed, as we believe, in Man. He believed, as we believe, that men are capable of their own government, and that no king, no tyrant, no dictator can govern for them as well as they can govern for themselves.

He believed, as we believe, in certain inalienable rights. He, as we, saw those principles and freedoms challenged. He fought for them, as we fight for them.

He proved that the seeming eclipse of liberty can well become the dawn of more liberty. Those who fight the tyranny of our own time will come to learn that old lesson. Among all the peoples of the earth, the cruelties and the oppressions of its would-be masters have taught this generation what its liberties can mean. This lesson, so bitterly learned, will never be forgotten while this generation is still alive.

The words which we have chosen for this Memorial speak Jefferson's noblest and most urgent meaning; and we are proud indeed to understand it and share it:

"I have sworn upon the altar of God, eternal hostility against every form of tyranny over the mind of man."

◇◇

A FURTHER VIEW DOWN THE YEARS

"THE PROUD CONSOLATION THAT
SUCH A MAN HAS LIVED"

Nicholas Biddle

The peculiar character of the mind of Jefferson was its entire original-ity. There was nothing feeble nor ordinary in the structure of that intellect which, rejecting the common-places which pass, only be-cause they go unchallenged, through the world and seeking for truth rather in nature than in received opinions, examined for itself, thought for itself, and yielded its convictions only to reason. This temper was nourished by the severe studies which disciplined his youth, and confirmed by the indulgence in retirement of those deep and lonely moods of thought by which the noblest powers of the mind are nursed. In any country and at any time these powers would have rendered him distinguished; but while their direction was yet undetermined, the great conflict, which has occupied the last half century, between institutions and men, between the human race for freedom on one side and a few individuals for privileges on the other, found him on the verge of manhood, and awakened that impassioned devotion to freedom which shed its hues over all the studies and actions of his life. Among his contemporaries no one was more early or more deeply imbued with the spirit of his age, and few have contributed more to its diffusion. The youngest among the leaders of the revolution and at last almost the only survivor of them, he

From *Eulogium on Thomas Jefferson, delivered before The American Philo-sophical Society, on the eleventh day of April 1827*. By Nicholas Biddle. Pub-lished at the request of the Society. Philadelphia, 1827.

stood between two generations, and his free opinions which had startled the first race as hazardous innovations became during his life established truths among their posterity. This combination of an original mind impelled equally by the love of science and the love of freedom best reveals the true character of Jefferson and will best explain his whole history.

It is the first glory of his life, to have been one of the founders of a great and free empire, undoubtedly among the most distinguished events in the history of mankind. It was not, like the beginning of the Roman domination, a fellowship of outlaws, commenced in pillage and cemented by fratricide—nor yet the establishment of the obscure dynasties and the village empires of most of the ancient legislators; but it was the deliberate achievement of the proudest spirits of their age, who, in the eye of the world and at their own imminent hazard, built up the loftiest temple of free government ever reared among men. On its fairest column, among the companions of him who had no equal, is inscribed the name of Jefferson. From out that temple, this country, the young mother of nations, has poured forth her language, and her institutions, to cultivate and to bless the new world. The unnumbered people, the thronged empires which will hereafter fill these happy regions, will in the fulness of their prosperity turn with filial reverence to those ancestors who laid the deep foundations of their freedom, and eminently to him who drew its great charter. The fame of that instrument may yet survive the freedom it proclaimed. But even in the decay and overthrow of this country the pilgrim strangers from the remotest lands of this many-nationed continent, who may trace back to its source in these desolate places the stream of their own greatness, shall still find in the eternal freshness of the fountains of freedom the memory of Jefferson.

It is scarcely less glorious that even among his own great associates he was distinguished by being at once a scholar and a statesman. If, as is unquestionable, among all the intellectual pursuits, the master science is that of government, in the hierarchy of human nature the first place must be conceded to those gifted spirits who after devoting their youth to liberal studies are attracted to the public service and attain its highest honours, shedding over their course the light of that pure moral and intellectual cultivation which at once illustrates them and adorns their country. It is thus that philosophy best fulfils her destiny, when coming from her seclusion into the arena of life she shares and leads in defending the cause of truth and freedom. This is not easy: for many who were conspicuous in retirement have failed in action, over burthened by their preparation, as men sink under the weight of their own armour. But to succeed—to combine the knowledge of the schools and of the world—to be learned in books and things and yet able to govern men, to deserve that most illustrious of all names—a philosophical statesman; this is at once the highest benefit which study can bestow on the world and the noblest reward which the world can confer on learning. This was the singular merit of Jefferson. "The whole of my life," said he to a friend, "has been at war with my natural tastes, feelings, and wishes. Domestic life and literary pursuits were my first and latest desire. Circumstances have led me along the path I have trodden, and like a bow long bent I resume with delight the character and pursuits for which nature designed me." Yet the influence of these tastes over his whole career was equally obvious and beneficial. It is this exhaustless love of study which enables the finer intellects to sustain the burthen of public duties, to resist the encroachments of that selfishness, and to overcome that disgust, which intense devotion to the business of the world is too prone to inspire. From that outer scene of contention with the passions and interests of others their retreat is to the fountain within, calming by its repose and freshening with its coolness the overstrained energy of the mind. Such was the attachment of Jefferson to these pursuits, that in the course of his long and active life there were few departments of learning which his inquisitive mind had not explored. Of law, not merely its technical forms, but the spirit of jurisprudence, the author of the revised code of Virginia proved himself a master; and of his intimacy with that circle of knowledge which ministers to legislation and to international law, his successful execution of all the duties of a member of many legislative bodies, a minister, and a secretary of state, is the best testimony. The ample volume of ancient history and ancient languages,—of modern history and modern languages, was equally familiar to him. Mathematics, chemistry, astronomy, natural history, and natural philosophy, as well as the mechanic arts, were favourite pursuits, gracefully relieved by the studies of architecture and music: and all were connected and embellished by a wide range of miscellaneous literature. A greater mass of knowledge has often been accumulated by solitary students, and deeper researches have been doubtless made in all these sciences than consisted with the labours of an active statesman. But their prevailing charm lay in their perfect harmony with his social duties. They never obtruded, never out-grew their subordination to his public character, to which they imparted at once the strength of knowledge and the lustre of reputation. In a mind so vigorous they produced their natural fruits—perfect independence and simplicity. It is a truth of universal application, that they who are proud of their places confess their inferiority to them, and that the only true independence is the personal pride which is conscious that no position can exalt or humiliate it, and that in all times and under all circumstances the man predominates over the station. Jefferson accordingly felt that there are in the world much higher elevations than offices and far more alluring occupations than the struggles of political parties. He therefore neither sought nor shunned official stations, occupying them when they were voluntarily tendered but leaving them as willingly, and always communicating more distinction than he derived from them. But having assumed, he filled them, perfectly and devotedly. Such indeed was the disciplined industry of his versatile mind, that after discharging all the duties of his station with a precision which the most laborious dulness might envy, his elastic spirit resumed his studies with fresh ardour or escaped to the charms of that social intercourse which he knew so well how to enjoy and adorn. He enjoyed and adorned it the more, because he carried in to it that which in men, as in things, marks the last stage of refinement—entire simplicity. Too strong to need concealment—and too proud to descend to those artifices of dignity by which little minds dexterously veil their weaknesses, he was distinguished by the frankness and boldness with which all his thoughts were breathed to those around him—and for the unaffected simplicity of his manners. Even on that bleak eminence the presidency of his country, he was still only its first citizen, blending with admirable grace the simple dignity of a grave ruler with the varied acquirements of philosophy and the frank and cordial affability of a gentleman.

His writings are all imbued by the same spirit. The declaration of independence, the revised code, the Notes on Virginia, like the various reforms which he executed or meditated, are the joint efforts of that originality which led the way in every advance towards improvement, of the learning by which they were defended, and of the honest enthusiasm for freedom which nothing could dispirit nor subdue.

His very style partook of that character. Its felicity consisted in the freshness and originality of its expression and the terse form into which his strength of thought was compressed. There might be discovered, by a critical eye, some tendency towards new shades of expression as well as of thought, and something too of that tinge of gallicism imputed to Hume and Gibbon as the result of their residence abroad. But the general mould of his style was formed at an early age before he left America, and preserved its peculiarity through life. His correspondence was particularly attractive, combining the natural graces of manner with the rich materials of thought and presenting in an endless variety the vivacity and the captivating unreserve which form the charm of epistolary writing. That however which we may most usefully imitate is its conciseness. It would be a signal addition even to his services, if his example could wean us from that fatal love of words, that declamatory profusion, by which all the real business of life is oppressed and which threaten to confine the knowledge of our public affairs to those only who possess diligent leisure.

The same temper accompanied him to his highest station, and rendered him a bold and fearless chief magistrate,—qualities singularly valuable in this country. The tendency and the danger of other governments is subserviency to courts, that of ours is submission to popular excitement, which statesmen should often rather repress than obey. Undoubtedly the public councils should reflect the public sentiment; but that mirror may be dimmed by being too closely breathed on, nor can all the other qualities of a public man ever supply the want of personal independence. It is that fatal want which renders so many ostensible leaders in fact only followers, which makes so many who might have been statesmen degenerate into politicians, and tends to people the country with the slaves and the victims of that mysterious fascination, the love of popularity. Jefferson felt himself strong in his own originality. His administration was a conflict between those who had gained the power from which they had deemed themselves proscribed—and those who, outnumbered yet not vanquished, yielded with a stubborn resistance the heights from which they were descending. But the self possessed and balanced mind of the leader bore him proudly through the struggle. His commanding spirit restrained the ardour of his followers, and even in the flush of victory his triumph was stained by no excesses. But the mildest use of authority is obnoxious to reproach, and—as the want of power to persecute each other for religion has driven all our fanaticism into politics—the enmities against him were so embittered as to form almost a reproach on our nature, were it not redeemed by the reflection that he outlived all these calumnies till even the most violent of his enemies were subdued into admiration of him. It was indeed a rare example of magnanimity to see this magistrate, the perpetual object of scorn and obloquy, content with the consciousness of its injustice, and never tempted to employ his influence or the power of the law to suppress it, satisfied to use his own happy expression, that "error of opinion may be safely tolerated where reason is left free to combat it." He did wisely in this. The press in our country, like the monitor in the Roman triumph who stood beside the victor to guard him against the illusions of prosperity, is privileged to pour its warnings into the ear of successful ambition; and its rough licence may well be borne as the price of freedom, and the tax on distinction.

But, whatever might be deemed of the measures of his administration, the accomplishments requisite for his station could not be denied to him. The chief magistracy of this country,—the highest political elevation to which any private man can now aspire without crime or revolution—that reward of ambition whose temptations allure so many and should make us forgive so much,—may be not ingloriously administered by fortunate mediocrity, if it be content meekly to inscribe its name on our political olympiads. But when the man adorns the station—when its powers are nobly exercised and its honours gracefully worn, he may not yield in dignity of place to any whom the accidents of birth or fortune have raised to supreme authority. In the bearings of his personal character, Jefferson can be safely compared with the contemporary rulers of nations, not excepting him—the greatest of them all; nor need our patriotism shrink from the singular contrast between two men, chiefs for nearly an equal period of their respective countries, and models of their different species,— Napoleon, the emperor of a great nation—and Jefferson, the chief magistrate of a free people.

Of that extraordinary being it is fit to speak with the gentleness due to misfortune. Two centuries have scarce sufficed to retrieve the fame of Cromwell from that least expiable of crimes—his success over a feeble and profligate race, more fortunate in their historian than their history: and the memory of Napoleon must long atone equally for his

Jefferson at 78.

PORTRAIT BY THOMAS SULLY, MONTICELLO, 1821

("From Jefferson 1821. Finished 1830. T. S.")

Courtesy of the American Philosophical Society, Philadelphia

Jefferson at 82.

PLASTER LIFE MASK BY JOHN H. I. BROWERE, MONTICELLO, 1825

Courtesy of the New York State Historical Association, Cooperstown, New York

elevation and his reverses. There are already those who disparage his genius, as if this were not to humble the nations who stood dismayed before it. Great talents, varied acquirements, many high qualities, enlightened views of legislation and domestic policy, it were bigotry to deny to Napoleon. The very tide of his conquests over less civilized nations, deposited in receding some benefits even to the vanquished—and all that glory can contribute to public happiness, was profusely lavished on his country. But in the midst of this gaudy infatuation there was that which disenchanted the spell—that which struck its damp chill into the heart of any man who, undazzled by the vulgar decorations of power, looked only at the blessings it might confer, and who weighed, instead of counting, these victories. Such are the delusions which military ambition sheds in turn on its possessor and on the world, that its triumphs begin with the thoughtless applause of its future victims, and end in the maddening intoxication of its own prosperity. We may not wonder then if, when those who should have first resisted his powers were foremost in admiration and servility—when the whole continent of Europe was one submissive dependence on his will—when among the crowd of native and stranger suppliants who worshipped before this idol there was only one manly and independent voice to rebuke his excesses in a tone worthy of a free people—that of the representative of Jefferson, we may not wonder if all the brilliant qualities which distinguished the youth of Napoleon were at last concentered into a spirit of intense selfishness, and that the whole purpose to which his splendid genius was perverted was the poor love of swaying the destinies of other men—not to benefit, not to bless—but simply to command them, to engross every thing, to be every thing. It was for this that he disturbed the earth with his insane conquests,—for this that the whole freedom of the human mind—the elastic vigour of the intellect—all the natural play of the human feelings—all free agency, were crushed beneath this fierce and immitigable dominion, which, degrading the human race into the mere objects and instruments of slaughter, would soon have left nothing to science but to contrive the means of mutual destruction, and nothing to letters except to flatter the common destroyer. Contrast this feverish restlessness which is called ambition—this expanded love of violence which makes heroes—contrast these, as they shone in the turbulent existence of Napoleon, with the peaceful disinterested career of Jefferson: and in all the relations of their power—

its nature, its employment, and its result—we may assign the superiority to the civil magistrate.

Napoleon owed his elevation to military violence—Jefferson to the voluntary suffrage of his country. The one ruled sternly over reluctant subjects—the other was but the foremost among his equals who respected in his person the image of their own authority. Napoleon sought to enlarge his influence at home by enfeebling all the civil institutions, and abroad by invading the possessions of his neighbours—Jefferson preferred to abridge his power by strict constructions, and his counsels were uniformly dissuasive against foreign wars. Yet the personal influence of Jefferson was far more enviable, for he enjoyed the unlimited confidence of his country—while Napoleon had no authority not conceded by fear; and the extortions of force are evil substitutes for that most fascinating of all sway—the ascendancy over equals. During the undisputed possession of that power, Napoleon seemed unconscious of its noblest attribute, the capacity to make men freer or happier; and no one great or lofty purpose of benefiting mankind, no generous sympathy for his race, ever disturbed that sepulchral selfishness, or appeased that scorn of humanity, which his successes almost justified—But the life of Jefferson was a perpetual devotion, not to his own purposes, but to the pure and noble cause of public freedom. From the first dawning of his youth his undivided heart was given to the establishment of free principles—free institutions—freedom in all its varieties of untrammelled thought and independent action. His whole life was consecrated to the improvement and happiness of his fellow men; and his intense enthusiasm for knowledge and freedom was sustained to his dying hour. Their career was as strangely different in its close as in its character. The power of Napoleon was won by the sword—maintained by the sword—lost by the sword. The colossal empire which he had exhausted fortune in rearing broke before the first shock of adversity. The most magnificently gorgeous of all the pageants of our times—when the august ceremonies of religion blessed and crowned that soldier-emperor, when the allegiance of the great captains who stood by his side, the applauses of assembled France in the presence of assenting Europe, the splendid pomp of war softened by the smiles of beauty, and all the decorations of all the arts, blended their enchantments as that imperial train swept up the aisles of Notre Dame—faded into the silent cabin of that lone island in a distant sea.

The hundred thousands of soldiers who obeyed his voice—the will which made the destiny of men—the name whose humblest possessor might be a king—all shrunk into the feeble band who followed the captivity of their master. Of all his foreign triumphs not one remained, and in his first military conquest—his own country, which he had adorned with the monuments of his fame, there is now no place even for the tomb of this desolate exile. —But the glory of Jefferson became even purer as the progress of years mellowed into veneration the love of his countrymen. He died in the midst of the free people whom he had lived to serve; and his only ceremonial, worthy equally of him and of them, was the simple sublimity of his funeral triumph. His power he retained as long as he desired it, and then voluntarily restored the trust, with a permanent addition—derived from Napoleon himself—far exceeding the widest limits of the French empire—that victory of peace which outweighs all the conquests of Napoleon, as one line of the declaration of independence is worth all his glory.

But he also is now gone. The genius, the various learning, the private virtues, the public honours, which illustrated and endeared his name, are gathered into the tomb, leaving to him only the fame, and to us only the remembrance, of them. Be that memory cherished without regret or sorrow. Our affection could hope nothing better for him than this long career of glorious and happy usefulness, closed before the infirmities of age had impaired its lustre; and the grief that such a man is dead, may be well assuaged by the proud consolation that such a man has lived.

"I CANNOT RECKON JEFFERSON AMONG THE BENEFACTORS OF MANKIND"

Thomas Babington Macaulay

A LETTER TO JEFFERSON'S BIOGRAPHER, HENRY S. RANDALL

Holly Lodge, Kensington,
London, May 23, 1857.

Dear Sir,

The four volumes of the Colonial History of New York reached me safely. I assure you that I shall value them highly. They contain much to interest an English as well as an American reader. Pray accept my thanks, and convey them to the Regents of the University.

You are surprised to learn that I have not a high opinion of Mr. Jefferson, and I am a little surprised at your surprise. I am certain that I never wrote a line, and that I never, in Parliament, in conversation, or even on the hustings,—a place where it is the fashion to court the populace,—uttered a word indicating an opinion that the supreme authority in a state ought to be intrusted to the majority of citizens told by the head, in other words, to the poorest and most ignorant part of society. I have long been convinced that institutions purely democratic must, sooner or later, destroy liberty, or civilisation, or both. In Europe, where the population is dense, the effect of such institutions would be almost instantaneous. What happened lately in France is an example. In 1848 a pure democracy was estab-

From "What Did Macaulay Say About America?" by H. M. Lydenberg, in *Bulletin of the New York Public Library*, Volume 29, Number 7, July 1925.

lished there. During a short time there was reason to expect a general spoliation, a national bankruptcy, a new partition of the soil, a maximum of prices, a ruinous load of taxation laid on the rich for the purpose of supporting the poor in idleness. Such a system would, in twenty years, have made France as poor and barbarous as the France of the Carlovingians. Happily the danger was averted; and now there is a despotism, a silent tribune, an enslaved press. Liberty is gone, but civilisation has been saved. I have not the smallest doubt that, if we had a purely democratic government here, the effect would be the same. Either the poor would plunder the rich, and civilisation would perish, or order and property would be saved by a strong military government, and liberty would perish. You may think that your country enjoys an exemption from these evils. I will frankly own to you that I am of a very different opinion. Your fate I believe to be certain, though it is deferred by a physical cause. As long as you have a boundless extent of fertile and unoccupied land, your labouring population will be far more at ease than the labouring population of the old world; and, while that is the case, the Jeffersonian polity may continue to exist without causing any fatal calamity. But the time will come when New England will be as thickly peopled as old England. Wages will be as low, and will fluctuate as much with you as with us. You will have your Manchesters and Birminghams, and in those Manchesters and Birminghams, hundreds of thousands of artisans will assuredly be sometimes out of work. Then your institutions will be fairly brought to the test. Distress every where makes the labourer mutinous and discontented, and inclines him to listen with eagerness to agitators who tell him that it is a monstrous iniquity that one man should have a million while another cannot get a full meal. In bad years there is plenty of grumbling here, and sometimes a little rioting. But it matters little. For here the sufferers are not the rulers. The supreme power is in the hands of a class, numerous indeed, but select; of an educated class, of a class which is, and knows itself to be, deeply interested in the security of property and the maintenance of order. Accordingly, the malcontents are firmly, yet gently, restrained. The bad time is got over without robbing the wealthy to relieve the indigent. The springs of national prosperity soon begin to flow again: work is plentiful: wages rise; and all is tranquillity and cheerfulness. I have seen England pass three or four times through such critical seasons as I have described. Through such seasons the United States will have to pass, in the course of the next century, if not of this. How will you pass through them. I heartily wish you a good deliverance. But my reason and my wishes are at war; and I cannot help foreboding the worst. It is quite plain that your government will never be able to restrain a distressed and discontented majority. For with you the majority is the government, and has the rich, who are always a minority, absolutely at its mercy. The day will come when, in the State of New York, a multitude of people, none of whom has had more than half a breakfast, or expects to have more than half a dinner, will choose a Legislature. Is it possible to doubt what sort of a Legislature will be chosen? On one side is a statesman preaching patience, respect for vested rights, strict observance of public faith. On the other is a demagogue ranting about the tyranny of capitalists and usurers, and asking why anybody should be permitted to drink Champagne and to ride in a carriage, while thousands of honest folks are in want of necessaries. Which of the two candidates is likely to be preferred by a working man who hears his children cry for more bread? I seriously apprehend that you will, in some such season of adversity as I have described, do things which will prevent prosperity from returning; that you will act like people who should in a year of scarcity, devour all the seed corn, and thus make the next year a year, not of scarcity, but of absolute famine. There will be, I fear, spoliation. The spoliation will increase the distress. The distress will produce fresh spoliation. There is nothing to stop you. Your Constitution is all sail and no anchor. As I said before, when a society has entered on this downward progress, either civilisation or liberty must perish. Either some Caesar or Napoleon will seize the reins of government with a strong hand; or your republic will be as fearfully plundered and laid waste by barbarians in the twentieth Century as the Roman Empire was in the fifth;—with this difference, that the Huns and Vandals who ravaged the Roman Empire came from without, and that your Huns and Vandals will have been engendered within your own by your own institutions.

Thinking thus, of course, I cannot reckon Jefferson among the benefactors of mankind. I readily admit that his intentions were good and his abilities considerable. Odious stories have been circulated about his private life; but I do not know on what evidence those stories rest; and I think it probable that they are false, or monstrously exaggerated. I have no doubt that I shall derive both pleasure and information from your account of him.

I have the honor to be, dear Sir, your faithful servant,

T. B. MACAULAY.

H. S. Randall, Esq., etc., etc., etc.

"AFTER ALL DEDUCTIONS . . ."

Henry Adams

. . . According to the admitted standards of greatness, Jefferson was a great man. After all deductions on which his enemies might choose to insist, his character could not be denied elevation, versatility, breadth, insight, and delicacy; but neither as a politician nor as a political philosopher did he seem at ease in the atmosphere which surrounded him. As a leader of democracy he appeared singularly out of place. As reserved as President Washington in the face of popular familiarities, he never showed himself in crowds. During the last thirty years of his life he was not seen in a Northern city, even during his Presidency; nor indeed was he seen at all except on horseback, or by his friends and visitors in his own house. With manners apparently popular and informal, he led a life of his own, and allowed few persons to share it. His tastes were for that day excessively refined. His instincts were those of a liberal European nobleman, like the Duc de Liancourt, and he built for himself at Monticello a château above contact with man. The rawness of political life was an incessant torture to him, and personal attacks made him keenly unhappy. His true delight was in an intellectual life of science and art. To read, write, speculate in new lines of thought, to keep abreast of the intellect of Europe, and to feed upon Homer and Horace, were pleasures more to his mind than any to be found in a public assembly. He had some knowledge of mathematics, and a little acquaintance with classical art; but he fairly revelled in what he believed to be beautiful, and his writings often betrayed subtle feeling for artistic form,— a sure mark of intellectual sensuousness. He shrank from whatever was rough or coarse, and his yearning for sympathy was almost feminine. That such a man should have ventured upon the stormy ocean of politics was surprising, the more because he was no orator,

From *History of the United States of America During the First Administration of Thomas Jefferson,* by Henry Adams. New York: Charles Scribner's Sons, 1889. Volume I.

and owed nothing to any magnetic influence of voice or person. Never effective in debate, for seventeen years before his Presidency he had not appeared in a legislative body except in the chair of the Senate. He felt a nervous horror for the contentiousness of such assemblies, and even among his own friends he sometimes abandoned for the moment his strongest convictions rather than support them by an effort of authority.

If Jefferson appeared ill at ease in the position of a popular leader, he seemed equally awkward in the intellectual restraints of his own political principles. His mind shared little in common with the provincialism on which the Virginia and Kentucky Resolutions were founded. His instincts led him to widen rather than to narrow the bounds of every intellectual exercise; and if vested with political authority, he could no more resist the temptation to stretch his powers than he could abstain from using his mind on any subject merely because he might be drawn upon ground supposed to be dangerous. He was a deist, believing that men could manage their own salvation without the help of a state church. Prone to innovation, he sometimes generalized without careful analysis. He was a theorist, prepared to risk the fate of mankind on the chance of reasoning far from certain in its details. His temperament was sunny and sanguine, and the atrabilious philosophy of New England was intolerable to him. He was curiously vulnerable, for he seldom wrote a page without exposing himself to attack. He was superficial in his knowledge, and a martyr to the disease of omniscience. Ridicule of his opinions and of himself was an easy task, in which his Federalist opponents delighted, for his English was often confused, his assertions inaccurate, and at times of excitement he was apt to talk with indiscretion; while with all his extraordinary versatility of character and opinions, he seemed during his entire life to breathe with perfect satisfaction nowhere except in the liberal, literary, and scientific air of Paris in 1789.

Jefferson aspired beyond the ambition of a nationality, and embraced in his view the whole future of man. That the United States should become a nation like France, England, or Russia, should conquer the world like Rome, or develop a typical race like the Chinese, was no part of his scheme. He wished to begin a new era. Hoping for a time when the world's ruling interests should cease to be local and should become universal; when questions of boundary and nationality should become insignificant; when armies and navies should be reduced to the work of police, and politics should consist only in non-intervention;—he set himself to the task of governing, with this golden age in view. Few men have dared to legislate as though eternal peace were at hand, in a world torn by wars and convulsions and drowned in blood; but this was what Jefferson aspired to do. Even in such dangers, he believed that Americans might safely set an example which the Christian world should be led by interest to respect and at length imitate. As he conceived a true American policy, war was a blunder, an unnecessary risk; and even in case of robbery and aggression the United States, he believed, had only to stand on the defensive in order to obtain justice in the end. He would not consent to build up a new nationality merely to create more navies and armies, to perpetuate the crimes and follies of Europe; the central government at Washington should not be permitted to indulge in the miserable ambitions that had made the Old World a hell, and frustrated the hopes of humanity.

THE RETURN OF A VIRGINIAN

Dumas Malone

In late October, 1789, the year that revolution broke out in France and George Washington was inaugurated as president in the United States, a little American party embarked in the port of Cowes, England. The vessel was the *Clermont*, of 230 tons, and she was bound for Norfolk. The party consisted of the American Minister to France, Thomas Jefferson, now on furlough for a visit home; his daughters Martha and Maria (familiarly known as Patsy and Polly); two servants; and a shepherd bitch "big with pups." Jefferson had bought the dog at Havre, while waiting for a boat to cross the boisterous Channel, and she produced two puppies on the high seas. Otherwise, the voyage was almost without incident.

Some of the American captains detained at Cowes had predicted a nine weeks' passage, but the *Clermont* was only twenty-six days from land to land. After she weighed anchor at Yarmouth she soon got clear of fogs and had favorable winds until she neared the Virginia capes, while Jefferson and his little party, her only passengers, enjoyed the finest of autumn weather. Their seasickness was severe for a time but did not last long, and at the end he congratulated himself that he had crossed the Atlantic twice without running into anything that could be called a storm. He kept a simpler log than on his earlier voyage, he was not studying Spanish now, and he could have had little adult conversation with Captain Colley, a native of Norfolk and "a bold and judicious seaman." Patsy and Polly occupied much of his time no doubt, and after a while he could observe his new shepherd pups, but he probably spent many hours reminiscing.

From *Jefferson and the Rights of Man,* Volume Two of *Jefferson and His Time,* by Dumas Malone. Published by Little, Brown and Company. Copyright 1951 by Dumas Malone. Reprinted by permission of Dumas Malone; Little, Brown and Company; and the *Virginia Quarterly Review,* in which the present text, edited to stand alone, was published.

Surely he must have realized that he was leaving the Old World, after more than five years of honorable and devoted service, with an enormously enriched experience. If he had been a novice in diplomacy to begin with, this colleague of Franklin and John Adams who had talked with Vergennes and Montmorin and been snubbed by George III was one no longer. "I feel a degree of familiarity with the duties of my present office," he was soon to write to President Washington, and it was to those duties that he expected shortly to return, little dreaming of the lengthy part he was to play in the conduct of the foreign policy of the United States before he quitted the public stage. Since he anticipated no such career as he afterwards had as secretary of state and president, he could not have been expected to congratulate himself on his magnificent preparation for it, but the historian is in position to congratulate his country.

He himself thought of his international experience as no mere preparation for a particular sort of statecraft. Since it was a part of life he valued it for its own sake, and its significance extended far beyond technical diplomacy. He was more than a technician, more than a statesman as we ordinarily use the term. His was an omnivorous and highly sensitized mind and he had lived in a cockpit of ideas and world seat of culture. It is true that he did not need to go to Europe to get into the current of liberal thought which fertilized the reform movements of his age, for he had already done that before he wrote the Declaration of Independence. But he had found new and highly stimulating friends of light and liberty in the Old World and had become even more conscious of his membership in a noble international brotherhood. In certain respects it was an incongruous company—including as it did Condorcet, La Rochefoucauld, and Lafayette, along with Dr. Richard Price of England and Thomas Paine—and he was not in agreement with all its members at all points, but no one was quicker than he to perceive kinship of the spirit. With all his statesmanlike reservations, the revolution which had recently begun in France appeared to him the triumph of enlightened liberalism; and as he read his books afterwards and wrote to his friends he nourished in his own breast the sacred fire. His correspondence lagged in later years as terror increased at home and abroad, as friends of yesterday were engulfed in a revolution that lost its philosophical direction. But his ties with kindred European minds and spirits were never broken, and, both in Europe and America, he became a more conspicuous symbol of enlightened liberalism and the rights of man after the Revolution than he had ever been before. He could not have anticipated this as the *Clermont* sailed homeward, but he must have reflected that a bright chapter had been written in the story of his expanding thoughts and hopes, and have assured himself that the book would not be closed till death.

A bright chapter it was, despite the dark background of European despotism, and he must have thought it also an extraordinarily rich one. Perhaps not even he could completely catalogue his observations and acquisitions in the realms of art and architecture, agriculture and household furniture, science and invention. But he could think of the books and plants and drawings he had sent or was sending home, of the furnishings he had left in the Hôtel de Langeac, of the pictures he had bought or ordered, of the wines he was shipping, of the vineyards and rice fields he had observed in Burgundy and Bordeaux and Lombardy. Many of these things he could take with him. They could go in boxes or be preserved in letters and memoranda. They were his to give or keep for the rest of life. He could even put musical scores in boxes, as actually he did; but until he returned to Europe, such concerts as he had heard in Paris could be only a memory—less real than pictures of the Maison Carrée or the Hôtel de Salm. Only in Europe could the favorite passion of his soul be fully satisfied, and the music which had delighted him must have seemed like a lovely dream as he listened to the lapping of the waves.

II

The chief thrills of the voyage came at the very end of it. The coast of the American continent, like that of Europe, was obscured by mists when they neared it and a pilot could not have been seen had one appeared. The bold Captain, running in at a venture without being able to see the Virginia capes, managed to get inside and anchored at Lynhaven Bay, where Jefferson wrote a letter to his secretary William Short. Meanwhile, the wind rose, and when they beat up against it they lost their topsails and were almost run down by a brig going before the wind out of port.

The Jeffersons landed at Norfolk about midday on November 23, 1789, and went to Lindsay's Hotel. If the Minister did not take his official records ashore at once, he nearly lost them. Fire broke out on the vessel before the baggage was unloaded, though their belongings were all saved in the end. Jefferson had much liked the lines of a table on the *Clermont,* and had left with Captain Colley a memorandum to have one like it made for him in London, of the finest mahogany, and shipped to France. He got it in America after a year or so.

He now learned that something important with respect to him as a public man had happened on the very day that he left Paris, though he had been utterly oblivious of it when waiting at Havre and Cowes and while sailing in autumn sunshine on his voyage home. President Washington had nominated him as secretary of state, the Senate had confirmed him, and he was greeted in Norfolk as a high official of the new government and not merely as a diplomat at home on leave. It was three weeks before he got the letter which Washington had written him in October, and well into the new year before he accepted the appointment, but almost at the moment that he stepped on Virginia's soil he was confronted with what amounted to a *fait accompli.* The Mayor, Recorder, and Alderman of the Borough of Norfolk addressed him two days after his arrival—congratulating him on his safe arrival in his native land, thanking him for his eminent services to the trade of his State, and fervently wishing him happiness and continued success in the important station to which he had been called by a grateful country. His own reply was gracious, patriotic, and noncommittal. "That my country should be served is the first wish of my heart," he said; "I should be doubly happy indeed, were I to render it a service." In times past when he had said "my country" he nearly always meant Virginia, but now he must have been thinking of the Republic as a whole.

Toward the end of the month Jefferson took his little party by ferry across the Roads to Hampton, and then they drove through Williamsburg to Richmond. Nobody reported just how the dogs were transported, but the baggage went by stage to Richmond, where the travelers arrived after about a week, having lingered somewhat at the homes of friends along the way. In the capital city of the Commonwealth, Jefferson received addresses of welcome and congratulation from both houses of the General Assembly, then in session. Here he was described as "late Minister Plenipotentiary," but without direct reference to the secretaryship of state. This occasion was Virginian in flavor, the term "native country" had a more local connotation, and the two committees seem to have waited on him informally. He was back among old political associates and friends.

While he was in Richmond, Jefferson brought himself up to date on the political situation. North Carolina had accepted the new Constitution, but Rhode Island had again rejected it. The amendments Madison had designed to meet the major objections in the Virginia ratifying convention, and to provide the protection of individual rights which seemed so necessary to Jefferson and George Mason, had been ratified by the House of Delegates but not yet by the Senate. These seemed sure of adoption and presumably they cut the ground from under the feet of the antifederalists. Jefferson remarked that Patrick Henry, despite his continuing popularity, had been so often in the minority that he had quit the Assembly in disgust, "never more to return, unless an opportunity offers to overturn the new constitution."

He also observed the new state capitol for which he had sent a model; and he picked up numerous items of personal information, such as deaths and marriages among the Virginia gentry, which he passed on at the first opportunity to Short in Paris. This opportunity came at Eppington below the James, where his daughters—especially Polly—renewed ties with the Eppes family and he himself received a belated but important letter from the President of the United States. As he had ridden along the rough roads of his beloved Virginia he must have done some thinking about the position in the federal government to which he had been appointed, and about which he must say something. This he did about the middle of December when he was visiting other relatives of his dead wife, the Skipwiths in Chesterfield County.

He was probably as surprised by the title of the office as by the coupling of his own name with it, for John Jay had been "the Secretary for Foreign Affairs" in the old government. He soon learned, however, that Congress had put foreign affairs and the whole domestic administration, except for war and finance, into one department, to be headed by a secretary of state. He harbored no real doubts of his ability to handle the foreign business. Since Franklin was too old, John Adams was vice president, and John Jay was now chief justice—though continuing his old offices temporarily—the choice of Jefferson for the conduct of foreign affairs must have seemed little short of inevitable to him, as it did to many others. But the thought of the additional mass of domestic administration, carrying with it the probability of public criticism and censure, appalled him. As he wrote the President, his personal inclination was to remain in the position he was already familiar with. "But," he added, "it is not for an individual to choose his post . . . you are to marshal us as may be best for the public good." Having thus tried to avoid the responsibility of making a difficult decision, he wrote Short that he supposed he would remain as Minister. Perhaps this remark was designed to make his secretary feel better, but Short had already had letters from Jay and Hamilton assuring him that the President's desire could not be resisted. The matter was still unsettled when the Minister on leave received a welcome from his slaves at Monticello and his neighbors in Albemarle which must have reconciled this deeply sensitive man to his inability to return to France.

He got home two days before Christmas. The news of his coming, which he sent ahead in order that the house might be ready, had spread like wildfire through his farms, and the slaves had asked for and received a holiday. Their joyful reception of the Master and his daughters constituted a scene like no other that Martha ever witnessed. Accounts differ as to whether the slaves actually unhitched the horses and pulled the carriage up the last ridge of the mountain, but there can be little doubt about what they did when it reached the top. They carried the Master to the house in their arms, some blubbering and some laughing, kissing his hands and feet and the ground beneath him. To their simple minds it seemed that he had come home to stay, and he must have thought it good to be there—though he did not like to be the master of slaves or anyone else—though his wife was dead, and his red lands were wasted.

His neighbors addressed their congratulations to him soon after he got home, upwards of a dozen of them signing a paper: Dr. George Gilmer and Nicholas Lewis, James Monroe — a newcomer there though long a friend, Thomas Garth the steward, three by the name of Nicholas, and a half dozen others. They reminded him that twenty years earlier they had sent him to the House of Burgesses; they believed that his conduct in every stage of public life since then had been as satisfactory to those he served as it had always been to them; and they specially commended him for his strong attachment to the rights of all mankind.

His reply got into the newspapers of the time but since then it has attracted little or no attention. The draft which is preserved in his own papers shows by its many corrections and interlineations how carefully he prepared it; and it remains until this day one of the finest expressions of the thoughts and hopes of a philosophical statesman, of the sentiments of a good neighbor who extended the sunshine of his benevolence to all his countrymen and all the people of the earth. To these old friends, who had assigned him the first public part he ever played and whose affection was the source of his purest happiness, he said:

> ... We have been fellow-labourers & fellow-sufferers, & heaven has rewarded us with a happy issue from our struggles. It rests now with ourselves to enjoy in peace & concord the blessings of self-government so long denied to mankind: to shew by example the sufficiency of human reason for the care of human affairs and that the will of the majority, the natural law of every society, is the only sure guardian of the rights of man. Perhaps even this may sometimes err but it's errors are honest, solitary & shortlived. Let us then, my dear friends, for ever bow down to the general reason of society. We are safe with that, even in its deviations, for it soon returns again to the right way. These are lessons we have learned together. We have prospered in their practice, and the liberality with which you are pleased to approve my attachment to the general rights of mankind assures me we are still together in these it's kindred sentiments.

In the county of his birth this traveler, just returned from a continent in the throes of revolution against ancient despotisms, swore allegiance again to the holy cause of freedom, while announcing his undying faith in the sufficiency of human reason and his necessary reliance on the will of the majority. He wrote more famous papers, but never one which better summed up the philosophy by which his feet were guided.

III

Before he again left his Albemarle neighbors, in this first year of government under the new Constitution, he had to attend to certain important personal matters. He had to make a real decision about the secretaryship of state, for Washington was much too wise to make it for him; he soon found out that he had to give away his daughter Martha in marriage; and he must straighten out his financial affairs whether he returned to France or not.

He talked with James Madison about the secretaryship. While at home from Congress during the Christmas season, this great little architect of the new government, who was closer to George Washington at this stage than any other leader, rode over to Monticello from Orange County to greet and sound out his long-absent friend. Madison wrote Washington early in the new year that Jefferson had no enthusiasm whatever for the domestic business which had been attached to the Department of State and which he supposed would exceed the foreign. Madison himself thought that this would be trifling, that if any man could handle the whole business Jefferson surely could, and that there could be a new division of it if necessary.

These reflections commended themselves to the President and he forthwith repeated them in a characteristically kind letter. "I consider the successful administration of the general Government as an object of almost infinite consequence to the present and future happiness of the citizens of the United States," he said. "I consider the office of Secretary for the Department of State as *very* important on many accounts: and I know of no person, who, in my judgment could better execute the duties of it than yourself." He added the encouraging information that the appointment had given very extensive and very general satisfaction to the public.

It was obviously an admirable appointment, and although Washington said the appointee must make the decision, he left no possible doubt of his own desire. Jefferson was also impressed by the fact that others shared this—more of them, he said, than he expected. Hence he saw no real choice and, in the middle of February, he bowed to the inevitable. The complete sincerity of his frequently expressed preference for his old post in France may be questioned by some, just as he may be charged by some with false modesty, but if he cherished any considerable personal ambition he gave no sign of it even to those most intimate with him. What he did reveal clearly was the conflict of fears within his breast. His sensitiveness to the opinions of others was a major factor in his ultimate political success, but it was also his chief temperamental weakness and a main cause of personal unhappiness. In France, far from the public that he served, he would have been much safer from the public criticism and disapproval that he dreaded; but he would have wounded men whose good opinion he deeply valued if he had rejected this new task, and acceptance seemed the lesser evil. His fitness for high office was no accident, but there was much that was fortuitous in the precise form that his public service took. He had resolved forever to "bow down to the general reason of society," and he may well have thought that he was doing so by yielding to the polite urging of George Washington, the unanimously elected and deeply revered head of the American Republic.

Madison had written him from New York that "a universal anxiety" was expressed for his acceptance, sending him at the same time a newspaper account of Hamilton's first Report on the Public Credit, just submitted to Congress and not yet fully understood. Jefferson could hardly have realized that this report marked the beginning of a new phase of the administration of George Washington and that a fresh alignment of political forces was to emerge from the conflict over it. On February 11, 1790, in the House of Representatives, Madison opposed the form, though not the essential purpose, of one of Hamilton's major proposals. Jefferson had not had time to hear of it when he wrote his own letter of acceptance three days later; and there is no reason to believe that his friend's urging was due to the desire to gain political reinforcement for a pending domestic battle. It is uncertain whether Jefferson saw Hamilton's full report before he left Monticello on March 1, and even if he did he may have laid it aside for more careful and extended study at a more convenient season. He had his daughter's marriage to her cousin, Thomas Mann Randolph, Jr., on his mind. This took place on February 23. An important motion of Madison's was decisively beaten in the House of Representatives the day before, and Madison spoke on the question of the assumption of state debts the day after, but these facts were still unknown to Jefferson and purely coincidental.

IV

The marriage of Martha Jefferson was an extremely important domestic event, wholly unrelated to public questions. Since the death of her mother about seven and a half years before, she had been closer to her father's heart than any other person. Polly, nearly six years younger, had been with him much less and was never quite so harmonious with him in spirit. His relations with the Eppes family had remained close despite his long absence, but during his stay in France his ties with his own brothers and sisters, though maintained by occasional letters, had become attenuated. The year before he came home his youngest sister, Anna Scott, the twin of his brother Randolph, had made a late and unimpressive marriage with Hastings Marks, a former neighbor of his with whom he had no particular acquaintance. He had recognized the event and the new relationship by writing them both politely, but, whatever he might say, this circumstance did not touch him closely. Patsy's marriage was quite another matter.

His youngest sister was nearly thirty-three when she finally escaped the old maid's state. Martha was only a few months past seventeen, but early marriage was general in this society and he raised no objection on the score of age. Inbreeding was also common among the Virginia gentry and nobody looked askance at the union of cousins twice or thrice removed. The partner of his daughter's choice, then a little past twenty-one, was the son of Thomas Mann Randolph of Tuckahoe, whom Peter Jefferson had guarded during childhood and Thomas Jefferson had known all his life. Some three weeks before the wedding he wrote the Colonel: "The marriage of your son with my daughter cannot be more pleasing to you than to me. Besides the worth which I discover in him, I am happy that the bond of friendship between us, as old as ourselves, should be drawn closer and closer to the day of our death."

He found "worth" in young Randolph and accepted him without the slightest reservation as a son, but it is a question just how much he had seen of him in recent years. He had corresponded with the student at Edinburgh and given a full measure of advice, but, despite the enduring tradition, it is uncertain whether the young traveler made a visit to him in Paris. Hence one wonders just when and how the courtship was conducted. Perhaps the girls stayed for a time at Tuckahoe while their father was greeting old friends in Richmond, and young Randolph must have soon come visiting to Monticello. At all events, he paid his "addresses" to Martha after she returned to Virginia, and her father let her indulge her sentiments freely, scru-

pulously suppressing his own wishes until hers turned out to be identical. That is what he said, but his daughter could hardly have failed
to see that this young man would be highly acceptable to him.
Intellectually young Randolph was, or became, a man of parts and
his father-in-law found him companionable. Tall and lean and a bold
horseman, he was no doubt a dashing figure at this stage, though it
soon appeared that he needed much help in the management of his
affairs.

As for Martha, later descriptions emphasized the beauty of her
character, not her person, and a miniature made in Paris when the
bloom of youth was on her is less attractive than her portrait by
Sully as a matron. Her rather homely face, as seen by contemporaries
in daily life, was brightened by good will and animated by intelligence. She was tall, loosely made, and awkward in movement, but
her voice was sweet and her manners were gracious. She had blue
eyes and reddish hair, and was best summed up afterwards by the
remark that she was a delicate likeness of her father. The similarity
was more than physical but while close it was not complete, for she
had already revealed a more active sense of humor. Her father had
done his best to make her accomplished, but there were other things
which concerned him more. He once made some notes on the duties
of a wife, and presumably these were for his daughter on the eve of
marriage. As read now, his words have an old-fashioned and strongly
masculine flavor, and only by contrast do they suggest the salons and
boudoirs of Paris. "Sweetness of temper, affection to a husband and
attention to his interests, constitute the duties of a wife and form the
basis of domestic felicity," he wrote. "The charms of beauty, and the
brilliancy of wit, though they may captivate in the mistress will not
long delight in the wife: they will shorten their own transitory reign
if as I have often seen they shine more for the attraction of everybody else than their husbands." Martha had heard him say this sort
of thing many times before and did not need to be admonished now.
She was quite unspoiled, and time was to show that she fully lived
up to his standards for her as a wife and mother.

Colonel Randolph, who had been a widower for a year, offered to
convey to his son a tract of 950 acres in Henrico County called Varina,
with forty slaves on and belonging to it, and executed the deed
promptly on the insistence of the more businesslike Jefferson, who
promptly matched it, though he wisely made his gift to Martha and

her heirs, not to her husband. It consisted of 1000 acres of his Poplar Forest tract in Bedford County and twelve families of slaves, along with some stock. The young couple seemed well provided for.

He saw them wedded on February 23, bore the expense of the license, and paid the clergyman the marriage fee. On March 1 he left them and Polly at Monticello, and during the spring wrote the three of them in turn. His letters were affectionate, solicitous, and monitory; and theirs, when finally they came, were appealingly dependent. Before summer both girls were at Eppington, where Polly remained with her "dear Aunt Eppes," a serious rival of her father in her affections. Meanwhile, young Randolph looked over his farm at Varina, where he and Martha were determined to live despite the inconvenience of the place. He was not well, could not stand the heat, and seemed rather helpless and confused when he unburdened himself to his father-in-law. What the young pair most wanted was to find a place near Monticello, and in the course of time they did. Their financial prospects took a turn for the worse that summer, when Colonel Randolph, who was older than Jefferson, found a much younger lady for a wife and made another marriage settlement. Jefferson, who fully recognized the Colonel's susceptibility, urged his daughter to adjust herself to this confused situation, and he himself entered into negotiations with the elder Randolph in the autumn for the purchase of Edgehill, an admirable place for Martha and her husband in Albemarle. These dragged on for several years and need not concern us here.

Jefferson had gained a son but had not lost a daughter. Some years later, when Martha was several times a mother and he was about to return home from the seat of government, she said in the course of a sentimental letter: "The first sensations of my life were affection and respect for you and none others in the course of it have weakened or surpassed that." No *new* ties, she observed, "can weaken the first and best of nature." But she showed toward her husband the loyalty her father had instilled in her, and within the first year of marriage Thomas Mann Randolph, Jr., had accumulated an eternal debt of gratitude to Jefferson. From the beginning the young couple depended on him as on nobody else, and when complications arose he generally managed to straighten things out. But as he set out for Richmond on March 1, 1790, leaving his two daughters and his new son on the mountain, his immediate concern was to tidy up his own tangled finances before proceeding northward to new official duties in New York.

V

While at home he had not failed to observe that his farms had deteriorated during his long absence from them. He could not give them much personal attention now, and he left Nicholas Lewis in general charge of his local affairs, making a provisional arrangement with Thomas Garth in the event of the death of this friend and neighbor, whose health at the time was bad. Perhaps anticipating the sale of more distant holdings which he made later in the year, he rather conservatively estimated his lands as amounting to upwards of 10,000 acres and he now had about 200 slaves. His assets seemed to him sufficient to warrant an advance of money which he sorely needed, and accordingly he wrote to the bankers in Amsterdam with whom he had conducted official business, inquiring about a personal loan of one or two thousand dollars. Then, in Richmond, he formalized his arrangements with his English creditors. The bulk of his debt was attributable directly or indirectly to the burden with which his wife's estate was weighted when she got it from her father, John Wayles, and was owed to two chief houses. The total now was more than £7500, and the accumulated interest charges now amounted to more than fifty per cent of the principal. He provided for regular annual payments during the next seven years, thus completing an important part of the personal business which had brought him home, but as he signed his bonds he must have wondered if a thoroughly realistic balance sheet would have shown him to be solvent.

After a week in Richmond, he proceeded to Alexandria, where he received from the Mayor another address of congratulation and made another reply. A heavy snow fell on the night of his arrival, whether or not it amounted to the eighteen inches which were reported by this teller of large stories who so hated cold weather. It convinced him that he would have difficulties on the road, so he left his phaeton to be sent by water and went himself by stage, his horses being led by two of his own servants. He had been unable to visit George Mason at Gunston Hall, but in Philadelphia he was visited by Benjamin Rush, and he himself called for the last time on the bedridden and now emaciated Franklin.

Dr. Rush, who had known him in the Continental Congress, found him plain in dress and unchanged in manners, still attached to republican forms of government, still comparing American and European animals to the disadvantage of the latter. Jefferson found Dr. Franklin characteristically cheerful but feared that their animated conversation about the Revolution in France was really beyond the old man's strength. The dean of American diplomacy and chief luminary of philosophy died a month later, and surely the new Secretary of State was his spiritual heir if he left one. But when Jefferson arrived in New York on March 21, two weeks after leaving Richmond, it was his fellow Virginian, George Washington, that he reported to. He did this immediately, even though the day was Sunday, and at that moment a new era in his public life began.

It was to be national in setting, international in scope, and universal in spirit. The new Secretary of State had never been a mere localist, and he certainly was not one now. But he always loved the red hills of Albemarle more than the streets of any city, and he could be a great American and true citizen of the world without surrendering his birthright as a Virginian. He kept returning to his native region until finally he came home for good, and in his heart of hearts he was always there.

THE EARTH BELONGS TO THE LIVING

Adrienne Koch

Just before leaving Paris, Jefferson wrote down his deepest philosophical critique of constitutions and the ultimate ends of good government in a letter to Madison. It raised a question that Jefferson believed had never been raised before, but which, in his view, was one of the most fundamental in political philosophy: has one generation a right to bind another? This is the famous letter of September 6, 1789, usually identified by its powerful theme "The earth belongs always to the living generation."[1] When Madison received the communication, he instantly wrote a searching reply.[2]

The two letters together (Jefferson scholars have failed to consider Madison's reply) constitute a brilliant finis for Jefferson's long and profitable tour of duty in Europe and Madison's supreme fight in America to establish a strong constitution and a stable new government. Nowhere in the friendship of fifty years can we find a better expression of intellectual reciprocity, enabling Madison to sparkle with borrowed warmth, and Jefferson to discipline the humane overambitiousness of his proposals. The perfect courtesy that pervaded this and other intellectual encounters made it possible for stringent

Revised by Miss Koch for this anthology from *Jefferson and Madison: The Great Collaboration,* by Adrienne Koch. Copyright 1950 by Alfred A. Knopf, Inc. Printed by permission of Alfred A. Knopf, Inc. and Adrienne Koch.

[1] Jefferson to Madison, Paris, September 6, 1789. *Writings* (Ford), V, 115-124. Printed versions of this letter are not entirely correct. The Memorial Edition of Jefferson's Writings prints Jefferson's first version of this letter; but he corrected the important error of computing 34 years as the span of a "generation" to 19 years in the second version of the letter. There are other differences in this second version. The Ford Edition prints the corrected second version, but misreads several important sentences and phrases. For drafts, first version, and second version the Jefferson Papers at the Library of Congress must be consulted. For the original of the second version see Madison Papers, L. C.

[2] Madison to Jefferson, New York, February 4, 1790. *Writings* (Hunt), V, 437-41, n.

criticism to be received without hurt, and philosophical prodding to be tolerated without injury to pride. The impression one gathers here—an impression reinforced in other exchanges—is that Jefferson is more speculative and more daring in putting forward dynamic generalizations, and that Madison is the more astute politician. Jefferson's liberated spirit made it possible for Madison to achieve the flair that required more than political intuition, while Madison supplied the means for Jefferson to remain a philosopher in politics—a philosopher, that is, charged with real power.

II

Jefferson set up his argument in the letter on the "self evident" principle that the earth belongs to the living, and not to the dead. The dead have no powers and no rights, for they are nothing. Whatever powers or rights they had when alive cease naturally with their death. Therefore, since the dead have no rights, they have no right to bind the living.

The first application of this principle established that specific property rights are civil and not natural rights. The earth is made for the use of the living by natural law, but specific lands are owned by the living only by virtue of the laws of society. The portion of the earth occupied by any man ceases to be his with his death, and reverts to society. "Then no man can by natural right oblige the lands he occupied. . . . For if he could, he might during his own life, eat up the usufruct of the lands for several generations to come, and then the lands would belong to the dead, and not to the living, which would be the reverse of our principle. What is true of every member of the society individually, is true of them all collectively, since the rights of the whole can be no more than the sum of the rights of individuals."[3]

The second application Jefferson made of the principle that the earth belongs to the living concerned the public debt. Since the dead have no right to bind the living, the living are under no obligation to pay the debts of the dead. The living have no right to burden posterity with their own debts and are morally bound to pay them within their own time. "I suppose that the received opinion, that the public

[3] Jefferson to Madison, Paris, September 6, 1789. *Writings* (Ford), V, 116.

debts of one generation devolve on the next, has been suggested by our seeing habitually in private life that he who succeeds to lands is required to pay the debts of his ancestor or testator, without considering that this requisition is municipal only, not moral, flowing from the will of the society . . . but that between society and society, or generation and generation there is no municipal obligation, no umpire but the law of nature."[4]

In presenting this argument for a natural limit on the public debt, Jefferson had in mind the perpetuation of debts by France and Great Britain. Because no limit was accepted, these countries witnessed the dissipations of their rulers and the corruptions of war. These in turn put the people under ever accumulating burdens of taxation, with resulting poverty and oppression. "By reducing . . . the faculty of borrowing within its natural limits, it would bridle the spirit of war, to which too free a course has been procured by the inattention of money lenders to this law of nature, that succeeding generations are not responsible for the preceding[5] . . . and it will exclude . . . the contagious and ruinous errors of this quarter of the globe, which have armed despots with means not sanctioned by nature for binding in chains their fellow-men."[6]

To preserve the independence of the people and guard the rights of posterity, Jefferson proposed that governments should fix the ultimate terms for the redemption of public debts within the limits of their rightful powers. The law of nature prescribes the limits of their powers within the period of the life of the majority. This rule would prevent the creation of a perpetual or unjust public debt. The point is so important for Jefferson that he urged the consideration of a fundamental provision in the new French constitution: ". . . would it not be wise and just for that nation to declare in the constitution they are forming that neither the legislature, nor the nation itself can validly contract more debt, than they may pay within their own age . . . ?"[7]

In writing to Madison, however, Jefferson had more immediate concerns than a declaration of rights in the French constitution. He

---

[4] Ibid., V, 120.
[5] Ibid., V, 121.
[6] Ibid., V, 123.
[7] Ibid., V, 120.

proposed that Madison should consider the application of this principle to the United States. "It would furnish matter for a fine preamble to our first law for appropriating the public revenue. . . . We have already given, in example, one effectual check to the Dog of war, by transferring the power of letting him loose from the executive to the Legislative body, from those who are to spend to those who are to pay. I should be pleased to see this second obstacle held out by us also in the first instance. No nation can make a declaration against the validity of long-contracted debts so disinterestedly as we, since we do not owe a shilling which may not be paid with ease principal and interest, within the time of our own lives."[8]

The third and most important application of the principle that the earth belongs to the living concerned the constitution and laws of any society. Since each generation is independent of the one preceding, it has a right to choose its own constitution and laws. No constitution, no law, is too sacred to be changed. This is the heart of Jefferson's philosophy of constitutions:

> . . . no society can make a perpetual constitution, or even a perpetual law. The earth belongs always to the living generation. They may manage it then, and what proceeds from it, as they please, during their usufruct. They are masters too of their own persons, and consequently may govern them as they please. But persons and property make the sum of the objects of government. The constitution and the laws of their predecessors extinguished them, in their natural course, with those whose will gave them being. This could preserve that being till it ceased to be itself, and no longer . . . If it be enforced longer, it is an act of force and not of right.[9]

In closing his letter, Jefferson had called on Madison to take up the thesis and promote it with "that cogent logic so peculiarly yours." Only Madison, Jefferson thought, could create the opportunity to "force" the subject into discussion—so high did Madison stand "in the councils of our country." Aware of the theoretical cast of his suggestions, Jefferson apologized for what would "at first blush . . . be laughed at, as the dream of a theorist"—an apology which he softened,

8 Ibid., V, 123.
9 Ibid., V, 121.

in his second version of the letter, to "at first blush it may be rallied as a theoretical speculation."[10] These were very likely only conventional disclaimers, since Jefferson protested that examination would prove his theory "solid and salutary."

III

Despite Jefferson's friendly appeals, Madison was loath to employ his "cogent logic" in promoting a policy on the limits of constitutions, laws, and public debts that he considered unrealistic. The form taken by Madison in his reply was to agree in theory with his friend's fundamental principles, but to attack on the grounds of practicability virtually every specific proposal the letter contained. He detailed the reasons for his skepticism.

His first big gun was directed against Jefferson's recommendation that all constitutions require periodic revision every nineteen years in order to allow each generation to legislate for itself. Were such a limitation imposed on the fundamental laws of a society, what would be its effect? Madison objected that he could see three distinct disadvantages flowing from this mechanical limitation on constitutions. First, government would be subject to an interregnum, with all its attendant consequences. Secondly a government "too mutable & novel" loses its tradition and the cumulative respect of a patriotic citizenry. Probably every government requires "that share of prejudice in its favor which is a salutary aid to the most rational government." Third, Madison suspected that periodic total revisions of a constitution might encourage "pernicious factions . . . and agitate the public mind more frequently and more violently than might be expedient." [11]

The second big gun was trained on laws carrying some stipulation rendering them irrevocable at the will of the legislature. "If the earth be the gift of nature to the living, their title can extend to the earth in its natural state only." In a civil state, Madison pointed out, the "improvements made by the dead form a debt against the living, who take the benefit of them." [12] Therefore, those who initiated the

---

10 Ibid., V, 123; and Jefferson Papers and Madison Papers, L. C.
11 Madison to Jefferson, New York, February 4, 1790. *Writings* (Hunt), V, 438-9, n.
12 Ibid., V, 439, n.

improvements can properly impose obligations upon the future generations who will gain by them. Especially is this true of debts incurred in wars of national defense. There are also debts incurred principally for the benefit of posterity, and not necessarily dischargeable within the term of nineteen years. In general, Madison concluded this series of objections by stating that upon investigation there seemed to be some "foundation in the nature of things" to support the "descent of obligations from one generation to another.[13]

The third big gun of Madison's critique aimed at ordinary laws. Here Madison announced his objections were "merely practical," but so strong that they constituted very material objections indeed. Considering mainly positive laws concerning property, Madison foresaw "the most violent struggles . . . between the parties interested in reviving & those interested in reforming the antecedent state of property." [14] Anarchy, or at least a general confusion about the state of things would then "discourage every useful effort of steady industry pursued under the sanction of existing laws." [15]

The burden of the final section of Madison's letter of reply was philosophical. He properly interpreted Jefferson's position to imply a doctrine of "overt or express" declaration of the public will on the part of each generation, for constitutions and for laws affecting public debt and property. This assumption conditioned Jefferson's argument throughout, and in Madison's opinion led to the "embarrassments" he had just reviewed in his threefold critique of "the earth belongs to the living." The only escape from this unworkable doctrine, Madison thought, was to endorse the prevalent doctrine that there can be tacit assent to established governments and laws "and that this assent is to be inferred from the omission of an express revocation." [16] Without implied or tacit consent, civil society could not exist. This principle, in fact, is at the heart of the republican belief that the voice of the majority binds the minority. If one asks why majority rule, the answer can hardly be that it is decreed by a law of nature! For, Madison pointed out, a law of nature would strictly imply unanimity rather than mere majority. The answer,

---

[13] Ibid.
[14] Ibid.
[15] Ibid., V, 440, n.
[16] Ibid.

Madison thought, must be derived from "compact founded on utility," not from natural law at all. Finally, if one were to suppose that tacit or implied assent could not be allowed, "no person born in Society, could on attaining ripe age, be bound by any acts of the majority, and either a unanimous renewal of every law would be necessary, as often as a new member should be added to the Society, or the express consent of every new member be obtained to the rule by which the majority decides for the whole."

The grander vision of Jefferson's startling proposal, however, did not escape Madison's consideration. He readily granted that Jefferson's principle was of general importance for philosophical legislators. In the main, he himself accepted Jefferson's objective: to make constitutions sensitive to the majority will of each successive generation—for without this, as Jefferson had pointed out, a constitution would be "an act of force and not of right." Madison further welcomed the principle, and said it would give him pleasure "to see it first announced to the world in a law of the United States" to restrain living generations from placing "unjust and unnecessary" burdens on their successors.[17] For the present generation is morally bound to respect the natural rights—the basic needs—of coming generations, however much positive laws in any given society may depart from the moral ideal. In short, those who set the financial policy of democratic countries would be doing well to bear this principle in mind and apply it to the changing circumstances of their own day. But the limitation on debt policy, or legal or constitutional policy, could not be mechanical or automatic, restricted to nineteen or any other number of years. Nor could debts be restricted in intention to the present generation if the object of the debts could justly be claimed as a necessary burden on posterity, the debt having been incurred principally for the benefit of posterity. The debt incurred on account of the Revolutionary War, which the United States was still struggling with at the time of Madison's writing, was such a debt.

In general, the fundamental features of the theory that proved acceptable to both Jefferson and Madison were forward-looking and generous in their regard for the liberty and welfare of generations to come in America. Madison's agreement with Jefferson in regarding constitutions as subject to principled alteration was one of many

17 Ibid., V., 441, n.

convincing proofs that although he was a constitution-maker, he was not a constitution-idolater. Both men were liberal and experimental in their effort to provide a society that would meet the demands of each living being for conditions that would encourage growth and self-respect. That was why Jefferson really cared more for bills of rights than he did for constitutions. Bills of rights, declarations of fundamental political principles such as he had provided in the Declaration of Independence and had promoted while in France, were salutary reminders of the ends of good government and the restraints upon power that every free society would honor.

While Madison underwrote what he considered to be the sound part of Jefferson's theoretical letter, he made it clear that he was in no position to assure his friend of the readiness of the new American government to accept the principles they both valued. It would be a long time, he warned, before "truths . . . seen through the medium of Philosophy, become visible to the naked eye of the ordinary politician." [18]

IV

One cannot properly appreciate Jefferson's perspective on the theme that the earth belongs to the living without reference to his recent experiences abroad. France, on the eve and in the dawn of revolution, was the climax of his exciting opportunity to gain "the knowledge of another world." In the midst of the American Minister's momentous last year in Paris, he was permitted to play a unique role as American adviser to a group of influential and enlightened French leaders. For the liberal reform group headed by Lafayette, the group Jefferson referred to as "the Patriot Party," he became a subtle brain-truster, counseling deftly, urbanely, and without a suspicion of egotism. He kept a steady head, placed an effective historical perspective on unprecedented and chaotic events, never wavered in his faith in free government.

With all his liberal enthusiasm, however, Jefferson was cautious in assessing the realistic limits of the reform that France could bear. Had he had his way, the French Revolution would have ended with a humane charter of rights, such as the one he prepared and sent to

18 Ibid.

Lafayette and Monsieur de St. Etienne, for submission to the King.[19] The charter would have taken its place in a constitutional monarchy, Jefferson thought, designed to be no worse domestically than the British, and more restrained in its foreign ambitions. Possessed of a strong constitution of the sort Jefferson advocated, the French people, he decided, would have secured their basic liberties, and would be well placed for the gradual conquest of further popular rights and freedoms.

As the reform movement had gathered cumulative force in Paris, Jefferson's influence had even been felt in the French National Assembly. The opening of the fateful year 1789 found Jefferson busy with his intimate French friends, devising declarations of rights— the basic principles to guide a society that was ready to affirm the great truth that "the mass of mankind has not been born with saddles on their backs, nor a favored few booted and spurred, ready to ride them legitimately, by the grace of God." [20] Having advised Lafayette on the chief principles to include in his declaration of rights, Jefferson was asked in turn to revise it. Penciled corrections of Lafayette's declaration on the copy Jefferson retained have been interpreted to be Jefferson's own. Jefferson must also have requested another good friend of his, Dr. Gem, to submit another version. Both declarations of rights Jefferson carefully copied in the original French and enclosed in a letter to Madison, so that America might study what the French intellectuals in the cause of liberty were turning their thoughts to.[21] In the summer of 1789 the French National Assembly in its pre-Revolutionary work became strikingly busy with similar declarations of rights. Jefferson's friends and disciples had not done their preparatory work in vain.

v

A close investigation of manuscript sources in an attempt to evaluate Jefferson's claim of originality revealed an absorbing interchange of ideas, which appears to confirm his claim.

[19] Jefferson to M. de St. Etienne, Paris, June 3, 1789. *Writings* (Ford), V, 99-100.
[20] Jefferson to R. C. Weightman, Monticello, June 24, 1826. *Writings* (Memorial), xvii, 81-2.
[21] Jefferson to Madison, August ——, 1789. W. C. Rives Papers, L. C.

The intellectual interchange began in February 1788, in Paris, in Jefferson's handsome house which he rented from the Count de Langéac. A visitor, one of the many whom the hospitable Virginian entertained, arrived to spend the late winter and spring in Paris. He was Thomas Paine, inspired revolutionary propagandist, the journalistic hero of the American Revolution. Apart from his pleasure at reunion with his good friends Jefferson and Lafayette, Paine had a project that had brought him to Paris: to get support from the French Academy of Sciences for his engineering venture to build the first iron bridge. He knew that Lafayette would be particularly helpful in this matter, and that Jefferson's enthusiasm almost matched his own. But after the business of the day was over, there was time for conversation. And conversation must often have centered on the unprecedented political developments taking place in two countries peculiarly interesting to the company, America and France.

During the course of Paine's visit, there is proof that Jefferson turned the discussion in his home one night to the subject of natural rights. The receipt of news regarding James Wilson's arguments, some months earlier, in the Pennsylvania Convention for the ratification of the Constitution appears to have occasioned the discussion. Wilson had urged that a bill of rights was not desirable in the Constitution. Paine, upon returning to his own lodgings after the evening's discussion, reflected further and composed a four-page memorandum on "natural and civil rights and the distinction between them." He sent this brief sketch of ideas to Jefferson "to see how nearly we agree." The main drift of Paine's memorandum was a sharp distinction between natural rights, which he called rights of "personal competency" (such as thinking, speaking, forming and giving opinions), and civil rights or rights derived from compact, which secured individuals personal protection for acquiring and possessing property.[22]

The discussion that interested these two doughty champions of republican theory did not die with that interesting evening. Jefferson's letter on the principle that the earth belongs to the living, and Paine's brilliant summation of republican political theory in his *Rights of*

---

[22] Jefferson Papers, L. C. Not dated on original. Formerly attributed to 1789. Probable date February or May 1788. (Most of March and April Jefferson was away from Paris, and the meeting referred to in the memo could not have taken place then.)

Man, took up the theme and developed it in accordance with the interests of the two authors. Paine wrote:

> There never did, there never will, and there never can exist a parliament, or any description of men, or any generation of men, in any country, possessed of the right or the power of binding and controlling posterity to the "end of time" . . . therefore, all such clauses, acts or declarations, by which the makers of them attempt to do what they have neither the right nor the power to do . . . are in themselves null and void.
>
> Every age and generation must be as free to act for itself, *in all cases,* as the ages and generation which preceded it. The vanity and presumption of governing beyond the grave, is the most ridiculous and insolent of all tyrannies.
>
> Man has no property in man; neither has any generation a property in the generations which are to follow. . . .
>
> It is the living, and not the dead, that are to be accommodated.[23]

There is such a close parallelism between Jefferson's and Paine's formulation of the theme that the earth belongs to the living as to suggest that they continued their interchange on the elementary principles of good society and that one influenced the other. This suspicion is encouraged by the fact that when Paine returned to London in May 1788, he remained in close correspondence with Jefferson until the latter departed for America in the fall of 1789. But this correspondence gives no clue for the present inquiry.

Further quest in the elusive matter whether Jefferson or Paine originated the striking idea that the earth belongs to the living led to the dim figure of Dr. Gem as a likely link in the transmission to Paine of Jefferson's elaboration of this idea. The first telling piece of evidence is a declaration of rights, in French, in Dr. Gem's hand (and endorsed by Jefferson as Gem's). This is one of the two sets of principles Jefferson sent to Madison to show what leading French thinkers were devising on the subject of fundamental rights. Although Gem's list is undated, it must have been written in the winter of 1788 or early in January 1789, because the date of Jefferson's copy of these same "Principes généraux relatifs à un état politique" was on or before January 12, 1789, when he sent it as an enclosure in his letter to

---

[23] *The Complete Writings of Thomas Paine* (New York: The Citadel Press; 1945), I, 251.

Madison. Commenting to Madison on the two unusual enclosures, Jefferson identified Lafayette as the first author and Dr. Gem as the second:

> The one is by our friend . . . [Lafayette]. You will see that it contains the essential principles of ours accomodated as much as could be to the actual state of things here. [No wonder, since Jefferson apparently helped Lafayette to compose it.] The other is from a very sensible man, a pure theorist, of the sect called the Oeconomists, of which Turgot was considered as the head. The former is adapted to the existing abuses; the latter goes to those possible as well as to those existing.[24]

The definitive connection between the physiocrat theoretician Dr. Gem and the theme "the earth belongs to the living" is established by a second remarkable document. This is a brief memorandum, in English, in Dr. Gem's hand (and again endorsed so by Jefferson). Although this document is still in the vast repository of Jefferson's papers at the Library of Congress, there is no entry to cover its receipt in Jefferson's scrupulous epistolary ledger. It is probable, therefore, that Dr. Gem gave it to Jefferson personally. The time must have been before September 6, 1789, when Jefferson worked out his letter to Madison. Gem had written:

> That one generation of men in civil society have no right to make acts to bind another, is a truth that cannot be contested.
> The earth & all things whatever can only be conceived to belong to the living, the dead & those who are unborn can have no rights of property.
> Individuals have the power to alienate their property or to engage it for the payment of debts. Why may not a body [of] men, a nation, contract debts & engage their united property for the payment of them?
> In this no rights of posterity seem to be violated; because the property of the present generation does not belong to them.
> To repress the interested, ambitious & corrupt conduct of the administrators of nations, it may be expedient to declare by a law, that after a certain term of years the payment of a loan shall be

---

[24] Jefferson to Madison, Paris, January 12, 1789. *Writings* (Ford), V, 64.

void; creditors lending their money on these conditions suffer no wrong by the failure of payment.

As things are constituted in Europe, the indebted nations cannot without injustice refuse the payment of public debts.[25]

A close analysis of these critical notes indicates that Jefferson had already discussed these matters with Dr. Gem. The order in which the ideas are presented, and the language employed, partially substantiate this. The full substantiation is provided by the letter Jefferson sent to Dr. Gem on September 9, three days after Jefferson composed the final draft of the Madison letter. "The hurry in which I wrote my letter to Mr. Madison which is in your hands, occasioned an inattention to the difference between generations succeeding each other at fixed epochs, and generations renewed daily and hourly." [26] Since the final letter to Madison introduced the revised model of generations to which Jefferson referred, it is evident that Dr. Gem saw an earlier draft than the one dated September 6. Moreover, Jefferson's final draft of the letter to Madison apparently tried to answer Dr. Gem's principal criticism, to the effect that a nation may contract debts and engage its "united property" as payment. Although Jefferson recognized that individuals in private life have the power to engage their property to pay their debts, he asserted that this power is municipal only, not moral. "But a material difference must be noted between the succession of an individual and that of a whole generation. Individuals are parts only of a society, subject to the laws of a whole. . . . But when a whole generation, that is, the whole society dies . . . and another generation or society succeeds, this forms a whole, and there is no superior who can give their territory to a third society." [27] Therefore, there is no municipal obligation between society and society or generation and generation, "no umpire but the law of nature." [28]

One final item in this story of the interchange of ideas is a letter from Jefferson to Dr. Gem, some months after Jefferson had arrived in America and when he knew he would not be returning to Paris.

---

[25] Jefferson Papers, L. C. Undated, but probably August 1789.
[26] Jefferson to Dr. Gem, [Paris] September 9, 1789. Jefferson Papers, L. C.
[27] Jefferson to Madison, Paris, September 6, 1789. *Writings* (Ford), V, 117-18.
[28] Ibid., V, 120.

The letter shows the affection and unusual regard Jefferson had for the doctor.

> In bidding adieu, my dear Doctor, to the country which united our residence, I find the loss of your society and instructive conversation among the leading circumstances of regret. Be assured that I feel it most sensibly, and accept my warm acknowledgments for all your kindnesses and services to me and my family while at Paris. I hope that your philanthropy is by this time fully gratified by the final establishment of order, and equal government in a country which you love, and that you will still be pleased in seeing them extended to others—so as to found a rational hope that man is at length destined to be happy and free. . . . [29]

The case for Jefferson's influence on Paine through the intermediary of Dr. Gem can now be completed. All three were interested in natural rights and in the French cause of liberty. Jefferson had discussed these matters with each of them. It is probable that Dr. Gem met Paine when the latter visited Jefferson in Paris and that lively discussions ensued on the elementary principles of a good society. Dr. Gem, so far as we know, was the only one who had a copy of Jefferson's letter to Madison on "the earth belongs to the living." Soon after Jefferson drafted the letter and left France, Paine turned up in Paris, very much the favorite of the French liberal leaders. He would naturally have gravitated to another ardent British champion of the French Revolution, like Dr. Gem.

The hypothesis advanced here is that Paine saw a copy of Jefferson's letter to Madison. The vivid phrases would surely have appealed to Paine; and their reappearance in the Rights of Man would then be an altogether natural occurrence, an everyday borrowing from a cultural milieu to which Paine had contributed and in which he felt altogether at home.

VI

The defense of the rights of living, begun in Jefferson's letter, was brought into sharper focus in the controversy that gave rise to the writing of the *Rights of Man* and that followed upon its publication in the United States. Paine's main purpose was to refute the reaction-

[29] Jefferson to Dr. Gem, New York, April 4, 1790. Jefferson Papers, L. C.

ary political doctrine then being advocated in England by Edmund
Burke. Paine had been taken up by Burke in the summer of 1788. But
this odd alliance could not last long. Paine's vehement defense of
everything American, which in itself had alienated some of his distinguished new British friends, became insufferable to Burke when
it was coupled with an even more provoking defense of the accel-
erating French Revolution. Of the early stages of the Revolution,
Paine had written to Jefferson that the year 1789 would be immor-
talized as an "Anno Mundi or an Anno Domini."[30] As for Burke, the
former defender of the rights of the American colonies, the French
Revolution was anathema primarily because it was a break with the
past. His tolerant skepticism about philosophical abstractions in politics had given way under the pressure of the Revolution to an embittered metaphysical theory of society that outlawed all radical change.
This theory was published, one year after Jefferson's forceful letter,
in Burke's "Reflections on the Revolution in France."

Burke's position was the perfect ideological opposite of the one
defended by Jefferson and Paine. Contemptuous of the worship of
"reason" and the large social and political innovations promoted by
French Revolutionary republicans, he invoked the notion of a "Perpetual Charter" as a limit not only on revolutions, but on British
reform movements as well. Rejecting all utilitarian approaches to
society and politics, Burke made a mystical appeal to the spiritual
partnership that was presumably the state's peculiar kind of contract.
This contract was to be looked on with reverence since it extended
beyond government to all science, all art, every virtue, and all perfection.

> As the ends of such a partnership cannot be obtained in many
> generations, it becomes a partnership not only between those who
> are living, but between those who are living, those who are dead,
> and those who are about to be born. Each contract of each
> particular state is but a clause in the great primeval contract of
> eternal society, linking the lower with the higher natures; con-
> necting the visible and invisible world, according to a fixed com-
> pact sanctioned by the inviolable oath which holds all physical
> and all moral nature, each in their appointed place.[31]

[30] Paine to Jefferson, London, February 16, 1789. Jefferson Papers, L. C.
[31] Edmund Burke: *Reflections on the Revolution in France* (1790). *Works*
(Bohn Edition, London, 1861), II, 368.

Nothing could be less palatable to Jefferson and Paine than Burke's trans-empirical political philosophy. According to the two defenders of the view that the earth belongs to the living, there was something better than a spiritualistic interpretation of civilization—the belief in the rights of men and their legitimate demand for favorable conditions to promote happiness in society. Freedom was hard enough to purchase, especially when its purchase price was blood. They were not inclined to defeat that freedom by obscurantist metapolitics that irrevocably bound the living to the dead and the future to the past. By some complex historical irony, in our own day the philosophy of natural rights is said to be "abstract" and "metaphysical." But as Jefferson and Paine held this philosophy, it was an operational approach to establish sound conditions for human security and growth. "Rights," in short, could listen to "Reason," and "Reason" had no quarrel with "Utility." But a "Perpetual Partnership" like Burke's looked down on "low" concerns, was above mere reason, and was astrally removed from trading in "pepper and coffee, calico and tobacco." Burke's philosophy was what Jefferson elsewhere called the "Gothic" habit of mind, looking backward for its ideals, profoundly distrustful of keeping constitutions flexible to fit the changing needs of life. Truly, if Jefferson was not apprised of Burke's position when he wrote his forceful letter, he would have had to invent one like it for the sake of perfect opposition.

Jefferson soon had the opportunity, in an American setting, to endorse Paine's sharp attack on Burke in order to combat the developing opposition to true republicanism. After having read Paine's tract, Jefferson gave his blessings to the publication in a note that he intended to be private. As he wrote to Madison, he "was pleased to find that it was to be reprinted here, that something was at length to be publicly said against the political heresies which had of late sprung up among us, not doubting but that our citizens would rally again round the standard of Common Sense."[32] To Jefferson's great astonishment, however, the pamphlet appeared with his note employed for flamboyant advertisement. This indiscretion on the part of the printer was the origin of the open break between Jefferson and John Adams, since the "political heresies" referred to in Jefferson's note plainly characterized Adams's "Discourses on Davila." In the ensuing criticisms Jefferson and Paine were coupled; to which Jefferson re-

[32] Jefferson to Madison, Philadelphia, May 9, 1791. *Writings* (Ford), V, 331.

plied: "I certainly merit the same, for I profess the same principles."[33]

V I I

The gist of Jefferson's letter is his philosophy that laws and constitutions must be revised in the light of our reason and experience for the peace and good of mankind. He returned to the thesis that the earth belongs to the living on numerous occasions throughout his life, the latest when he was in his eightieth year.[34] His last letter on this subject is notable for the clarity of its statement, the first significant omission of the time limits which he had used to define a generation, and the momentous revision of his original letter by the incorporation of Madison's principle of tacit assent.

> That our Creator made the earth for the use of the living and not of the dead; that those who exist not can have no use nor right in it, no authority or power over it; that one generation of men cannot foreclose or burden its use to another, which comes to it in its own right and by the same divine beneficence; that a preceding generation cannot bind a succeeding one by its laws or contracts; these deriving their obligation from the will of the existing majority, and that majority being removed by death, another comes in its place with a will equally free to make its own laws and contracts; these are axioms so self-evident that no explanation can make them plainer; for he is not to be reasoned with who says that non-existence can control existence, or that nothing can move something. They are axioms also pregnant with salutary consequences. The laws of civil society indeed for the encouragement of industry, give the property of the parent to his family on his death, and in most civilized countries permit him even to give it, by testament, to whom he pleases. And it is also found more convenient to suffer the laws of our predecessors to stand on our implied assent, as if positively reenacted, until the existing majority positively repeals them. But this does not lessen the right of that majority to repeal whenever a change of circumstances or of

[33] Jefferson to James Monroe, Philadelphia, July 10, 1791. Ibid., V, 352.

[34] There are a number of letters in which Jefferson renewed the theme that the earth belongs to the living. The most important are: to John Eppes in 1813, to Samuel Kercheval in 1816, and to Thomas Earle in 1823.

will calls for it. Habit alone confounds what is civil practice with natural right. . . .[35]

In summing up, thirty-four years after the original letter to Madison, Jefferson reaffirmed his great theme and, by tacit assent, joined with Madison in a realistic appraisal of its operational meaning.

[35] Jefferson to Thomas Earle, Monticello, September 24, 1823. *Writings* (Memorial), xv, 470-1.

A PEPPERCORN FOR MR. JEFFERSON

Bernard Mayo

Early in the morning of New Year's Day, 1802, Parson John Leland proudly drove his heavily laden sleigh up to the front door of the President's House. For three weeks this Baptist preacher and his companion, Darius Brown, had been on the road to Washington from their home town of Cheshire, in the Berkshire hills of western Massachusetts. Over crisp and sparkling snow they had slowly traveled through one village after another, and in each had been loudly huzzaed by the farmers and mechanics whose votes in 1800 had helped elect Thomas Jefferson the "People's President." The Parson had spun yarns to Darius about Revolutionary days in Virginia, where he had fought not only for Mr. Jefferson's Declaration of Independence but for his world-famous Virginia Statute of Religious Freedom. He had talked about his own present struggle for religious liberty against the tax-supported Congregational clergy of Massachusetts. And all the way to the Federal City he had zealously guarded his precious cargo, a "Mammoth Cheese" which the people of Cheshire had lovingly made for Mr. Jefferson—"the greatest cheese in America, for the greatest man in America."

John Leland was a plain man, a pious, self-educated preacher-farmer. The chances are that he had never heard of the medieval tale of Our Lady's Tumbler. Yet there was something of the medieval acrobat's devotional spirit in the Parson and his fellow farmers of Cheshire. They had long been restive under the rule of the Hamiltonian Federalists, purse-proud and class-proud aristocrats who openly derided their Jeffersonian faith in the decency and dignity of the common man. When the glorious news came that Jefferson and his Democratic-Republicans had triumphed, the citizens of Cheshire had rejoiced with rank-and file Americans from Maine to Georgia, fired

From *The Virginia Quarterly Review*, Spring 1943. Reprinted by permission.

their muskets, and sung such spirited songs as "The People's Friend" and the very popular "Jefferson and Liberty"—

> Hail! long expected glorious day
> Illustrious. memorable morn;
> That freedom's fabric from decay
> Secures—for millions yet unborn.

But they had not been content with singing thanks and praises. They wished to express their joy in some tangible way. Now there was one thing the little town of Cheshire did supremely well, and that was the making of cheese. Why not, said Parson Leland, present Mr. Jefferson with the biggest and best cheese the world has ever seen? They agreed that every man and woman who owned a cow would give for this cheese all the milk yielded on a certain day. Not one drop of milk was to come from a Federalist cow!

A huge cider press was fitted up to make it in, and on the appointed day the whole community turned out with pails and tubs of curd, the girls and women in their best gowns and ribbons, the men in their Sunday-go-to-meeting coats and clean shirt-collars. The cheese was put to press with prayers by Parson Leland and the singing of hymns by the men and women of Cheshire. When it was well dried and put on the parson's sleigh, it was as large as a burr millstone and weighed—mark you—1,235 pounds!

Now it had arrived at its destination and there on the steps of the President's House was Thomas Jefferson himself, smiling and with hand outstretched.

When Mr. Jefferson shook hands with a man, so people related, he did so in a manner that said as plainly as words could, "I am your friend." His reddish hair had grayed, yet his slow smile and soft manner were as gracious as when Leland had last seen him in Virginia. This man of quiet dignity had filled the most important posts at home and abroad, yet he was "without any tincture of pomp, ostentation, or pride," and one could speak as freely with him as with any farmer in the hills of Berkshire or of Albemarle. Tall, thin, dressed in his customary suit of black, the Philosopher-President (according to a Federalist observer) on that day struck a new note in Jeffersonian innovation. He had "shoes on that closed tight round his ancles, laced up with neat leathern strings, and absolutely without buckles, considering them as superfluous and anti-republican, especially when a man has strings."

Delighted with the simplicity and warmth of his welcome, Leland and Darius presented him with the Mammoth Cheese "in behalf of all Cheshire." The Parson then read a prepared Address, a precious bit of homespun Americana. In it the citizens of Cheshire avowed their loyalty to a Constitution which the Federalists had tried to subvert, and thanked "that Supreme Father of the Universe, who . . . has raised up a Jefferson for this critical day, to defend Republicanism and baffle all the arts of Aristocracy.

"Sir, we have attempted to prove our love to our President not in words alone, but in deed and truth. With this Address we send you a Cheese, by the hands of Messrs. John Leland and Darius Brown, as a peppercorn of the esteem which we bear to our chief magistrate, and as a sacrifice to Republicanism. It is not the last stone in the Bastille, nor is it of any consequence as an article of worth; but as a free will offering, we hope it will be received. The Cheese was not made by his lordship, for his sacred majesty; nor with a view to gain dignified titles or lucrative offices; but by the personal labour of free born farmers (without a single slave to assist), for an elective President of a free people; with the only view of casting a mite into the scale of democracy. . . .

"May God long preserve your life and health for a blessing to the United States, and the world at large."

This peppercorn of esteem (small in itself compared to the love common people everywhere had for him), this gigantic democratic "mite," was accepted by Mr. Jefferson with heartfelt thanks. He had the great cheese placed in the East Room of the White House, a large and unfinished audience-hall which he that day christened "the Mammoth Room." The designation appealed to his sense of humor, since Federalist editors for years had jeered at his scientific interest in fossil bones and often called him "Mr. Mammoth" and "the Mammoth of Democracy."

At noon that day the President held his usual New Year's reception or levee. The scarlet-coated Marine Band played "Jefferson and Liberty" as citizens of Washington, government officials, army and navy officers, turbaned ladies, gold-braided diplomats, and blanketed Miami and Pottawatomie chieftains—a various and brilliant company—gathered to pay the compliments of the season to Mr. Jefferson.

It was a proud day for the Parson and his friend Darius. The good-humored President greeted each guest with dignified simplicity and invited them, one and all, to go to the Mammoth Room and partake of the Mammoth Cheese. First he cut out a huge wedge to be sent back to the donors, and then everybody sampled the cheese.

Republicans pronounced it the biggest and best ever. Federalists said the flavor was only so-so. Privately they grumbled about "this monument to human weakness and folly," and thought it strange that a *preacher* should have presented it to a man who ranked first on the Tory list of public enemies: Tom Jefferson, Tom Paine, and Tom the Devil. Manasseh Cutler, congressman and Congregationalist minister from eastern Massachusetts, was chagrined at the spirit of democratic unrest in his own state symbolized by this "poor, ignorant, illiterate, clownish preacher." Federalist editors only further increased the President's popularity by ridiculing this cheese-monger adulation of Thomas Jefferson, that wicked man who had inspired delusive hopes of a poor man's Millenium among "our American peasantry."

The Parson and Darius stayed on a few days to see the sights of the new Federal City. Before they left for Cheshire, Mr. Jefferson with characteristic delicacy and tact persuaded them to accept a sum of money far above the market value of the cheese. It was his rule never to accept presents while in office, and this money the Parson might expend in Cheshire as he saw fit.

And before they drove off in their sleigh for home (a journey on which Leland was to preach in almost every village), Mr. Jefferson, members of Congress, and the people of Washington went to the Capitol on Sunday to hear the Parson preach one of his rough-hewn and effective sermons. In the spirit of his Cheshire Address and not without an oblique allusion to President Jefferson and what he symbolized to the average American, the democratic Parson took for his text, "And behold a greater than Solomon is here."

II

John Leland and his fellow Americans could be pardoned for thinking that the Millennium had arrived. For their young Republic under Jefferson enjoyed peace in a world at war, and an unprecedented, widely diffused prosperity. The People's President had put the Argosy of state on a true republican tack, had done away with ceremonies of a dangerous monarchical tendency, and once again opened the doors of hospitality to refugees from Old World tyranny. He had abolished all internal taxes. At the same time he had drastic-ally reduced the public debt and piled up a surplus in the Treasury. No President before or since could ask his fellow countrymen, as he did in his second Inaugural Address: "What farmer, what mechanic, what laborer, ever sees a tax-gatherer of the United States?"

To crown all, his magnificent Louisiana Purchase of 1803 doubled the area of the Republic, removed foreign control of its vital Missis-sippi outlet, and made possible its greatness as a continental power. A vast empire as large as and more fertile than the Republic itself had been acquired, peaceably, and without taxation, for the tariff revenues at New Orleans alone would soon pay for the Purchase. It was, as Jefferson modestly said, a transaction replete with the bless-ings of freedom and equal laws for unborn millions.

In 1804 he was re-elected by Parson Leland's Massachusetts and every state in the Union except Connecticut and Delaware. A few die-hard Federalists continued to attack him, and often most scur-rilously. "This monied corps" of the great cities, "this mass of anti-civism," as he termed them, comprised only one twenty-fifth of the people, yet controlled three-fourths of the newspapers. With char-acteristic good humor he declared that the Federalist press was very useful: "It is like the chimneys to our dwellings; it carries off the smoke of party which might otherwise stifle the nation." The Fed-eralists made little headway against the People's President, who in 1808 disappointed thousands of Americans by refusing a third term in the presidency.

"Rarely ever did prince rule more absolutely than T. J.," growled a Federalist near the end of his presidency, still complaining of the people's adulation and the subserviency of a "rubber-stamp" Con-gress. "He can manage everything in the national legislature by his rod."

The man who wielded the rod of power, great as a statesman, adept as a politician, was a very practical idealist who translated democratic faith into democratic practice. He devoted his whole life to the wel-fare of his fellow man, as legislator, governor, congressman, diplomat, secretary of state, vice president, and president; as social reformer, inventor, scientist, architect, and educator. His many talents and great services have been generally acknowledged. But most historians, perhaps awed by the breadth and depth of his accomplishments, have failed to get beyond the impressive outer works to the warm, affectionate, and charming inner personality. They do a great injustice to Mr. Jefferson to treat him as a mere intellectual machine, or a political symbol. Some have even denied him a sense of humor!

A delightful play of humor and wit enlivens his thousands of letters. He loved to tell anecdotes of his much-admired friend, Dr. Benjamin Franklin, and of Paris of the *Ancien Régime*. On occasion he could tell a typically American tall story that a Davy Crockett or a Seba Smith would have appreciated. His intimate friend and lieutenant, James Madison, was in private life "a social, jovial, and good-humored companion, full of anecdote, sometimes rather of a loose description." During these Washington years Secretary Madison further endeared himself to his chief by relating the latest story or *bon mot*, many of them concocted by Federalists at Jefferson's expense, and making the President laugh until the tears came.

It was a very human President that John Leland and Darius Brown, and his Washington neighbors and friends, had the good fortune to meet, whether at his New Year's levee, his dinner table, or during his walks and rides about the new Federal City.

III

"There is a degree of ease in Mr. Jefferson's company that everyone seems to feel and to enjoy," said Benjamin H. Latrobe, the architect of the Capitol. This was especially true at the President's dinners. He had done away with pompous state dinners, but he gave nearly every day small dinner parties for ten or twelve. Mr. Latrobe's description of a dinner at the President's on a November afternoon in 1802 is typical of many contemporary accounts. Jefferson's two daughters, Mrs. Randolph and Mrs. Eppes, were there, having come up from their homes in Virginia. Present also were James and Dolly Madison, Mr. and Mrs. Carter from Virginia, Levi Lincoln, the Attorney General, Dr. William Thornton, the head of the Patent Office, and Mr. Jefferson's secretary, Meriwether Lewis.

They had a magnificent venison dinner, prepared by Monsieur Julien, the French chef. The excellent wines varied from rare old

sherry to champagne. Mr. Jefferson said little at dinner beside attending to the filling of plates, "which he did with great ease and grace
for a philosopher." But when the cloth was removed he became very
talkative, and the conversation was most agreeable and spirited:
"Literature, wit, and a little business, with a great deal of miscellaneous remarks on agriculture and building, filled every minute."
When Martha Randolph, at the request of Mr. Carter, drank a glass
of wine with him, Mr. Jefferson smilingly told his daughter that she
was breaking his law against drinking healths at table. "She said she
was not acquainted with it, that it must have been passed during her
absence. He replied that three laws governed his table—no healths,
no politics, and no restraint."

The ladies of Washington were especially charmed by his handsome way of entertaining. His compliments reminded them that he
had spent five years at the court of Louis XVI. One lady was once
congratulating herself that she never felt the cold in winter.

"Go where I will," she said, "I can always fancy it's summer."

Bowing as if he were back at Versailles, Mr. Jefferson replied:
"And whenever you come under my roof, Madam, I partake your
impression!"

On one occasion a rather obtuse lady caused his dinner guests to
gasp in astonishment. The Federalists for years had been satirizing
Jefferson for leaving Monticello during the Revolution when a British
force seized it. Instead of remaining there to be captured, like some
foolish Don Quixote, he had taken refuge on Carter's Mountain. The
name of this place had somehow been connected in the woman's
mind with that of the President. Wishing to make conversation, she
asked him if he did not live near Carter's Mountain.

"Very close," he said, "it is the adjoining mountain to Monticello."

"I suppose it is a very convenient pleasant place?" persisted the
lady, not noticing her husband's frowning red face or the efforts of
the other guests to conceal their amusement.

"Why, yes," answered Mr. Jefferson smiling. "I certainly found it so
in wartime.'

At his small dinner parties for gentlemen only, Jefferson's humor
sometimes took a broader turn. Like his friend Madison or any other
eighteenth-century gentleman he could appreciate a story reminiscent of "Tom Jones" or "Tristram Shandy."

Present at one of these dinners were Latrobe and three other gentlemen, "all men of science." The conversation, in deference to Latrobe, was turned to architecture. Then Jefferson skillfully led the talk to the experiments being made on the nature of light; to his friend, Dr. Joseph Priestly, the discoverer of oxygen; European emigration to America; the culture of the vine and American wines; and then to a favorite topic, the domestic manners of the Parisians.

"By this time the President became very entertaining," wrote Latrobe to his wife, and he told one of his amusing Franklin anecdotes. At a party given by Dr. Franklin in Paris a certain "Mrs. M." was making herself ridiculous by correcting the Doctor's wretched French, when her own was not much better. At that point the Doctor's grandson, Temple Franklin, entered the room, said Mr. Jefferson, "and, in one of his freaks of assurance, kissed the lady who stood nearest the door, and then went round the room saluting each of them, and last of all he kissed Mrs. Jay. Mrs. Jay, not being used to such gallantry, blushed so deeply that Dr. Franklin, observing it, asked why she blushed. Mrs. M. immediately answered, 'Parcequ'il a *lui* baisé *le derrière*'—instead of *la dernière*."

The President can "both hear and relate humorous stories as well as any man of social feelings," remarked Dr. Samuel L. Mitchill, a gay and sociable New York congressman, editor of the Medical Repository, and an eminent scientist whose universal knowledge had prompted Mr. Jefferson to nickname him "the Congressional Dictionary." It is doubtful whether Dr. Mitchill fully appreciated his stories at the expense of medical men, even though they were told in a characteristic tone of playful raillery. One of these was directed at a mutual friend, Dr. Benjamin Rush, who, for all his many virtues, had unfortunately popularized the practice of blood-letting. Once on a journey Jefferson had stopped at a tavern where the landlady returned from the funeral of a promising young man. The good woman wept and lamented his loss at great length, then, finally wiping her eyes, she said: "At least we have the consolation that the doctors did everything possible for him—he was bled six and twenty times."

For Federalist congressmen no less than Republican the President's House was an oasis of good food, good wines, and good humor. In the crude and sprawling city of Washington they were confined to stuffy boarding houses, "like bears, brutalized and stupefied . . . from hearing nothing but politics from morning to night." Men who lived on "hog, homminy, and hoe-cake" did not complain with sour

old Patrick Henry that "Tom Jefferson has abjured his native vittles."
A French dinner at Mr. Jefferson's, prepared by the incomparable
Julien, was well worth the hazard of being overturned or mired on
Pennsylvania Avenue, "when one can neither go backwards or for-
wards, and either loses one's shoes or one's patience."

The Reverend Manasseh Cutler, although displeased at not being
called upon to say a blessing, was fascinated by "His Democratic
Majesty" and his many foreign "jimcracks"—a strange soup called
bouilli, ice cream enclosed in *warm* pastry, and "a pie called macaroni, which appears to be a rich crust filled with the strillions of
onions." Senator Plumer of New Hampshire noted eight different
kinds of wine, including a superb Tokay costing a guinea a bottle!
Their host, as usual, was "very social and communicative." Plumer
wondered whether Mr. Jefferson was really in earnest when, noting
that many New Englanders thought horse-racing was immoral, he
made an elaborate defense of the sport: horse-racing improved the
breed, and the attendant betting was less injurious to the Southern
people than the heavy gambling at cards and dice in Calvinistic
Boston.

"But Mr. Jefferson tells large stories," remarked John Quincy
Adams of Massachusetts, a man so sober and precise that the President could never resist the impulse to startle him. Surely the President was mistaken when he said that once in Paris the thermometer
stood, not for a single day but for six weeks, at twenty degrees below
zero; or that when he went to Paris he left in Virginia some ripe
pears, sewed up in tow bags, and upon his return almost six years
later found them perfectly preserved—self-candied! "You never can
be an hour in this man's company without something of the marvel-
lous, like these stories."

IV

During Mr. Jefferson's eight years in the Federal City the people
of Washington and Georgetown developed a warm affection for him
as a neighbor and a friend. They appreciated his interest in every
civic enterprise and his generous contributions—whether toward a
market-house, a circulating library, a new church or academy, or to
the poor. His private charities (amounting in one year alone to nearly

a thousand dollars) were unpublicized, but Washingtonians knew that every time he returned from Monticello poor people again began their calls upon him, and were never disappointed.

The President was always accessible to every citizen or visitor. When guests dropped in he would come out of his study in his comfortable slippers and everyday dress, quite unlike the black suit he wore on formal occasions. On one day, for example, when he greeted an unexpected guest he was wearing "a blue coat, a thick gray-coloured hairy waistcoat, with a red under-waistcoat lapped over it, green velveteen breeches with pearl buttons, yarn stockings, and slippers down at the heels; his appearance being very much like that of a tall, raw-boned farmer."

That study was his refuge and his joy. There he had his books, his carpenter's tools, his palette and paints, his drafting board, his scientific instruments, maps, globes, and gardening tools. In the window recesses were stands for his roses and geraniums, among which was suspended the cage of his favorite mocking bird. Often he would open the cage and the bird would fly about, perch on his shoulder and take food from his lips, and sometimes hop upstairs after him to his bedroom. "How he loved this bird! How he loved his flowers! He could not live without something to love," said a Washington friend, Mrs. Samuel Harrison Smith; "and in the absence of his darling grandchildren, his bird and his flowers became the objects of tender care."

Mrs. Smith, a great friend of the family and beloved by the grandchildren, who were all too seldom at the President's House, exceedingly admired his flowers, and especially his geraniums. But the mocking bird was as much a favorite with Etienne Lemaire, the President's steward, as with Mr. Jefferson himself. Whenever the President was at Monticello, Lemaire took affectionate care of it, and he was proud that it could not only imitate all the birds of the woods but could sing popular American, Scottish, and French tunes.

Lemaire was the head of a household establishment of a dozen servants, all of them devoted to the President: Julien and Madame Julien, Joseph Dougherty, the coachman and general handyman, and Mrs. Dougherty, Edward Maher, Maria Murphy, and the others. The feeling that members of the household entertained toward Mr. Jefferson was perhaps best expressed by Isaac A. Coles, his private secretary during the latter years of his presidency. "His conduct is marked by so much delicacy, and his conversation is so frank, so open, so unreserved, that the great Executive Officer is constantly lost in the Man, and I declare to you that some of the most delightful moments of my life have been passed in his company. . . . From the President I receive nothing but kindness, and in truth I love him."

For eight years the people of Washington had seen Mr. Jefferson going about the city, mounted on his magnificent horse Wildair—riding on a Sunday to divine services, where he loved to sing old psalm tunes; to Theophilus Holt's nursery gardens on the Eastern Branch or Mr. Main's gardens in Georgetown; to the stores on the Avenue and F Street; to the Navy Yard, the Marine Barracks, the Great Falls of the Potomac, or on a botanizing expedition along the banks of Rock Creek. He had never missed a fall meeting of the Washington Jockey Club Races. And he had enjoyed at the little theatre on Pennsylvania Avenue such plays as the comedy, "I'll Tell You What, or, An Undescribable Something," the farce, "All the World's a Stage, or the Spouting Butler," and the favorite burlesque afterpiece, that "most Tragical, Comical, Operatical Tragedy that ever was Tragedized by any Comical Company of Tragedians, called 'The Life and Death of Tom Thumb the Great' "—his laughter and his delight smoothing out the lines in his face placed there by his presidental worries and labors.

When the time came for him to leave the President's House, there were addresses from all over the nation expressing gratitude for his forty years of services to his country and to mankind. The people of the Federal City made farewell calls upon him, and in their public addresses, their "peppercorns of esteem," struck a personal note. The citizens of Georgetown praised the domestic and social virtues of a neighbor whom posterity would honor "among the immortal benefactors of man." The Tammany Society of Washington, in their parting address to the author of the Declaration of Independence and the "Grand Sachem" of the seventeen American tribes, expressed the "spontaneous effusions" of men who had each passing day for eight years examined and approved his conduct. "The world knows you as a philosopher and a philanthropist," declared the citizens of Washington; "the American people know you as a patriot and statesman;—we know you, in addition to all this, as a *man*. And . . . there is not one among us whose predominant feeling at this moment is not that of affection."

In his felicitous manner Mr. Jefferson bade farewell to his fellow citizens, and prepared to retire to his family, his farms, and those tranquil pursuits of science which had ever been his supreme delight. Characteristic, and most felicitous, was the parting blessing he sent to Mrs. Samuel Harrison Smith, just before he rode back to Monticello:

"Th: Jefferson presents his respectful salutations to Mrs. Smith, and sends her the Geranium she expressed a willingness to receive. It is in very bad condition, having been neglected latterly, as not intended to be removed. He cannot give it his parting blessing more effectually than by consigning it to the nourishing hands of Mrs. Smith. If plants have sensibility, as the analogy of their organization with ours seems to indicate, it cannot but be proudly sensible of her fostering attentions. Of his regrets at parting with the society of Washington, a very sensible portion attaches to Mrs. Smith, whose friendship he has particularly valued. Her promise to visit Monticello is some consolation; and he can assure her she will be received with open arms and hearts by the whole family. He prays her to accept the homage of his affectionate attachment and respect."

THOMAS JEFFERSON, THE GENTLE RADICAL

Dixon Wecter

This is an ignorant year
Within a cruel time.
If he were here
We might rebuild
The firm wall raised by him,
The column felled.

> — Lawrence Lee
> *The Tomb of Thomas Jefferson* (1940)

I

Nature did not intend Thomas Jefferson for a hero. Temperament, physique, and background were all against it. If destiny had not plucked him from the ivory tower he built at Monticello, and hurled him into the thick of public turmoil, Jefferson would have lived and died a bookish, fastidious Virginia squire. He might have become, more easily than a hero, a writer of belles-lettres, a college don, or an amateur philosopher sunning himself on the leeward side of John Locke. He is like no other American leader, although there are faint resemblances in Woodrow Wilson and Franklin D. Roosevelt of which their friends have made the most.

Certainly Jefferson the idol was not hewn from the same stone as Washington, Israel Putnam, Francis Marion. He had a sedentary man's shrinking from military discipline. The drums and trumpets passed him by. His only sight of advancing redcoats was through a telescope, from a knoll near Monticello called Carter's Mountain, in June, 1781, and in later years his enemies were quick to assert that his headlong flight after that vision spoke for itself. He was a man of exquisite perceptions, an artist with nerves attuned to the age of sensibility. At the death of his wife he fell into a swoon so deep that his life was feared for; those who disliked Jefferson did not hesitate to call him "womanish" and "feline."

Loose-jointed in appearance and in talk—lacking Franklin's homely vigor without achieving the majesty of Washington—"Long Tom" Jefferson wore his elegance of mind and raiment with an insouciance that some misjudged for sloppiness. As President he received a British Minister in slippers and dressing gown (a democratic style that Huey Long once tried to copy, in receiving a German dignitary). Even at his inauguration Jefferson had quietly walked from Conrad's boarding-house to take the oath in the Senate chamber of the un-finished Capitol; though legend persistently repeats that he arrived on horseback, dismounted casually, and hitched his horse to the "palisades" of the Capitol fence. He owned ten thousand acres and two hundred slaves, and recoiled from courting the masses or play-ing the political bully-boy. Yet he became "the People's friend," a high-handed imperialist, and a saber-rattler before the Barbary pirates. For all his agrarian background, he was far less the full-blooded country gentleman than were Washington and Jackson. He raised tobacco but never used it, never kept a playing-card in his house, bred fine horses but never loved the race-track. Duelling did not tempt him. He drank no spirits, but was fond of French wines and cookery—one of those gentlemen, as Patrick Henry said, who "abjured their native victuals." He was virtually a vegetarian, as he told Doctor Ulley—and, like most vegetarians, proved to be a ter-rifying idealist, tinged with fanaticism. His mores were not those of the carnivorous mammal. And his mind was a brilliant, delicate, complex mechanism. In fact, as Henry Adams remarked, all our early Presidents save Jefferson can be drawn with "a few broad strokes of the brush—" but the master of Monticello, with his shifting lights and shades, nuances and translucencies, defies even the finest pencil. Did the People ever have a more extraordinary friend?

Let us see how Jefferson came to be a hero. Born in 1743 among the red clay hills of Albemarle County, Virginia, he sprang from good stock. His mother, Jane Randolph Jefferson, made him cousin to numerous purse-proud Tuckahoes. Jefferson affected to pass lightly over the old pedigree of the Randolphs, "to which let every one ascribe the faith and merit he chooses," and to stress the homespun simplicity of his father, Peter, whose "education had been quite neglected." With this help, legend has made Peter Jefferson into a clodhopper, stressing the democratic rather than the patrician heritage of his son. Late research, however, has shown that Peter Jefferson owned a great acreage of rich land, and five overseers, served as vestryman and justice of the peace and sheriff, and displayed a skill in map-making that bears witness to his cultivation of hand and brain. He was no Thomas Lincoln.

At William and Mary College young Thomas Jefferson was something of a bookworm, who as his classmate John Page recalled "could tear himself away from his dearest friends and fly to his studies." A century later, drawing heavily upon imagination, John Esten Cooke wrote a novel called *The Youth of Jefferson, or a Chronicle of College Scrapes*. Tom or "Sir Asinus," here figures as a tall, freckled, sandy-haired lad with a prankish temper. Thinking he is pursued by the proctor, he flies down the corridor in a faded dressing-gown, and barricades himself gun in hand, crying out: "Beware! I am armed to the teeth, and rather than be captured I will die in defence of my rights—namely, liberty, property, and the pursuit of happiness under difficulties!" (The mature Jefferson did not include "property" among the inalienables; that belonged to Hamilton's point of view.)

"Under temptations and difficulties," young Jefferson wrote, "I would ask myself what would Doctor Small, Mr. Wythe, Peyton Randolph, do in this situation?" His three youthful heroes were a Scotch mathematician, a jurist and college tutor, and a tidewater gentleman of Jefferson's own blue blood. To the end of his life, indeed, Jefferson's ideal was blended of two types, the scholar and the intellectual aristocrat, which have rarely been popular with the masses of Americans. It was the dash of liberalism which Jefferson himself added to the *beau ideal* that made him an unforgettable favorite. Meanwhile, Jefferson gained notice at the Virginia bar and in 1769 was chosen by his native county for the House of Burgesses. He fell under the spell of Patrick Henry, who "appeared to me to speak as Homer wrote." Sympathetic with Henry's hostility to the Crown, Jefferson was still cool enough to perceive the orator's defects in logic and learning. Jefferson came early to distrust the spell of rhetoric. In part it may have been a rationalization: a weak throat and unconquerable diffidence in large groups kept Jefferson from ever becoming himself a spell-binder. His pen was mightier than his voice. Three silent men—Franklin, Washington, Jefferson—were the first great idols of the Republic: the age of silver tongue and spread eagle, of Webster and Hayne, Grady and Bryan, was yet unborn.

Quickly gaining note as a pamphleteer for Independence, Jefferson was sent as a Virginia delegate to the Continental Congress. New Englanders liked him as a penman, even as they admired Washington as a soldier. "Though a silent member of Congress, he was so prompt, frank, explicit and decisive upon committees and in conversation," wrote John Adams, ". . . that he soon seized upon my heart." This popularity was very important to Jefferson's budding career. In June, 1776, as a tribute to his fine literary gift, legal training, and eagerness to work, he was named first of a committee of five to draft the Declaration of Independence.

Jefferson was not then aware of the world-shaking import of his document. Later he took it retrospectively in his stride, as it were. In the face of contrary facts he stated so vehemently that the Declaration had been signed by Congress on the Fourth of July—even to the extent of imagining a "paper" draft signed on that date, when confronted with the parchment undoubtedly engrossed on August 2— that indulgent posterity, in the main, has let Jefferson have his way. With due respect to his fellow-committeemen, Jefferson was truly the author of the Declaration—the proud boast of his tombstone, and his supreme claim among the Founding Fathers. If he is something less than the Divinely inspired creator of this noble document—whose theories, spirit, and even phrases are the products of a long evolution—he is surely the amanuensis of Americanism. To Lee in 1825 he wrote that the Declaration "was intended to be an expression of the American mind." Its clarity, vigor, beauty, and fighting affirmation of the democratic faith endear Jefferson forever to his countrymen. No one else could have seen so well or expressed so finely the ultimate, as well as the immediate, aims of the new American spirit. It was addressed to the people. Hence it omitted a few underlying subtleties. Chief of these was the vital distinction Jefferson saw between *natural rights* (those which man can exercise "without the aid of exterior assistance," such as freedom of thought and speech) and *civil* rights (like gaining and holding property, in which men agree to abdicate a measure of individualism, and to act only "under the guarantee of society"). This was the reason why property was not one of the "inherent and inalienable rights," since it lay under the hand of social control. Jefferson's individualism was one of rights plus duties; Hamilton's tended to stress property rights above other matters, and paved the way for that ideal later called "rugged individualism"—a term, said Herbert Hoover in 1934, which "I should be proud to have invented," but which to others meant an industrial philosophy active in the creation of slums and economic misery, while it destroyed the green countryside and the domestic handicrafts that Jefferson loved. But Jefferson did not put his distinction into writing until after he had quit Philadelphia and gone back home, "being alone and wanting amusement," and it remained unpublished for more than a century after his death. This was typical of the casualness of Jefferson.

After firing the salvo of the Declaration, Jefferson returned to Virginia, convinced that his next duty was to sow the liberal seed at home—by abolishing entails, revising the criminal code, setting up free schools, and cleaving Church from State. Jefferson had no stomach for soldiering; his aptitude lay in "mental fight." Certain keen partisans of Washington, Hamilton, and the Federalists have never forgiven Jefferson for failing to expose himself to hunger, frostbite, and bloodshed in the cause to which he had rallied his countrymen. The late Senator Beveridge, biographer of John Marshall, by playing up a phrase in one of Washington's letters, imagines the shivering soldiers in their smoky huts at Valley Forge thinking of the penman of their faith, asking each other with chattering teeth, "Where is Jefferson?" Yet there is no real evidence that Jefferson was looked upon at this time as a quitter. He was craven only in the subtler sense of T. E. Hulme's saying, that "a non-muscular man is inevitably physically a coward."

In 1779 Jefferson succeeded Patrick Henry as Governor of Virginia. He did not make a good wartime governor, as even loyal Virginians admit. He was too timorous about overstepping his strict legal rights, even in an emergency, and in practical matters his judgment was undeveloped. And Jefferson had the sudden violence of the sedentary man. With his four thousand British prisoners he was alternately too soft and too hard—at first arranging musicales and philosophical causeries for them and opening his library to the officers, and then upon hearing of Americans abused on board British prison-ships, loading his captives with irons and preparing to treat them as common criminals until Washington intervened. In later years he showed the same bursts of violence: demanding that Aaron Burr be hanged out of hand, and in the War of 1812 proposing that if the British touched our coasts "we must burn the city of London, not by expensive fleets or congreve rockets, but by employing an hundred or two Jack-the-painters, whom nakedness, famine, despera- tion and hardened vice, will abundantly furnish among themselves." This is a strain in Jefferson's nature, supposedly mild and calm, which has never colored his legend and even been ignored by most of his biographers. Hero-worship and symbol-making call for simplifica- tions, in dealing with a man so complex as Jefferson.

In the late spring of 1781, with Virginia's treasury bankrupt and the British overrunning the Old Dominion, Jefferson desperately prepared to resign in favor of a military governor. At that juncture, the redcoats swooped down on Monticello and would have caught him but for the warning of Jack Jouett, "the Southern Revere." The head of a government should avoid capture by the enemy if he can, as many European sovereigns and premiers have lately decided. A statesman who runs away may govern some other day. No discredit should arise if he has first done his best—as Tom Paine pointed out in 1805, in defense of Jefferson. It is true that after the invasion was over Jefferson had to face a charge of insufficient preparedness; on December 19, 1781, he appeared before the Legislature, was acquitted and voted thanks. But his prestige in Virginia was clouded by the disasters of his Governorship, and by his having given up the helm in a storm. Thin-skinned to criticism, Jefferson looked forward to "the all-healing grave." It was his first and last public failure. In Virginia its memory lasted until—during his absence as Minister to France—the progressives under Madison came into local power, and loyally rehabilitated Jefferson as their master. Many years later, in Jefferson's first term as President, when a rash of newspaper libels broke out against him, the facts were deliberately twisted to make it seem that Jefferson had been rebuked by the Virginia Legislature for his cowardice, in running away from the British! The charge was absurd, but strangely passed into common belief, especially in the North. Federalists dwelt upon the spectacle of this long-legged statesman leaving Monticello with more haste than grace. Even a generation ago, the great historian Edward Channing used to lec- ture vividly to his Harvard classes about the affrighted agrarian, "coattails flying in the wind." Chronologically, this is the first libel against Thomas Jefferson.

II

In France, Jefferson was overshadowed by the remembrance of Franklin. He lacked Franklin's easy bonhomie, and quaintly enough was more of a Puritan than the great Bostonian had been. Jefferson too was a widower, but no lovely ladies found him apt at flirtation and banter, nor did any crown him with laurel at *fetes champetres*.

At forty-three he was older than Franklin at seventy-five. "A dozen years ago this scene would have amused me," Jefferson wrote to Mrs. Trist, "but I am past the age for changing habits!"

Abroad, Jefferson grew more aggressively American, seeing England as an aristocracy besotted with liquor and horse-racing, and France as a land where marital fidelity is "an ungentlemanly practice." He also loved to magnify the virtues of his native land, solemnly assuring Crevecoeur that New Jersey farmers probably learned how to make "the circumference of a wheel of one single piece" from Greek epic poetry, "because ours are the only farmers who can read Homer." Jefferson fondly imagined himself the typical American farmer.

France also confirmed Jefferson's aversion to "priestcraft" and hereditary aristocracy. At the news of Shay's Rebellion at home, he rejoiced—believing in a little blood-letting at intervals for the health of the body politic. After his return to America the full fury of the French Revolution broke. At first Jefferson hailed it with almost fanatic tranquillity: "Was ever such a prize won with so little innocent blood? . . . rather than it should have failed I would have seen half the earth desolated." Even today, conservatives who hold to "sound Jeffersonian principles" try to forget his reckless remark about watering the tree of liberty periodically with blood. Jefferson maintained that only the sickly timid tory fears the People, whereas the strong leader loves and trusts them. In later years Jefferson disliked the radial plan upon which L'Enfant had laid out the city of Washington—knowing it was designed to keep mobs from throwing up impassable barricades, while soldiers massed in its "circles" could command the approaches to the Capitol with artillery. Let the People come, he said.

Yet in practice, Jefferson was the gentlest of Girondists. Upon the eve of the Revolution the French Foreign Minister had smiled upon meetings of the disaffected in Jefferson's house, "being sure," as Jefferson wrote, "that I should be useful in moderating the warmer spirits." After Jefferson's orderly election to the Presidency (which he loved to style "the revolution of 1800"), he reassured bankers and industrialists that he abhorred the spirit of unrest bred by the "blood and slaughter" in France, and was so temperate that radicals could hardly believe their ears. Out of office he was an idealist and revolutionary; within, a conservative and opportunist. Moreover, Jefferson the agrarian, urging that we "let our work-shops remain in Europe," had as deep a fear as did Hamilton of the mobs of Old World cities. Jefferson compared such mobs to "sores" on the face of a nation. Convinced that those who labor in the earth are God's chosen people, and that tillers of the soil have an instinct for order and justice, Jefferson was ready at any time to sign up with embattled farmers. A revolution with pitchforks he understood, but pikestaves unnerved him.

Returning from France to serve as Secretary of State, Jefferson came into collision with Hamilton, and soon retired to Monticello. Shy by nature, disliking to fight hand-to-hand, he tried to convince himself that he wanted nothing so much as to plant his corn and beans in peace. "I have no passion to govern men; no passion which would lead me to delight to ride in a storm," he wrote his friend Rutledge on December 27, 1796. But events helped to draft him. Leadership was needed in the fight for "republicanism," what a later age would call democracy. An immersed scholar like John Taylor of Caroline was no vote-getter, while an eager man like Patrick Henry (already hardening into reaction) had fallen into the mud too often while scrambling for prizes and profits. The younger generation in Virginia, Madison and Monroe, frankly looked to Jefferson as their master. And the Federalists, by training their guns upon Jefferson even out of office, roused his slow-kindling anger and also drew more public notice to him. He thus became the focus for discontent. At fifty-four—still protesting he preferred "the prattle of my grandchildren and senile rest"—Jefferson began to fight. He entered upon the Vice-Presidency, under John Adams. The threat of Aaron Burr's election in 1800 could be blocked only by a man like Jefferson. His duty was clear, and success followed. And so, like many other political leaders in a land where undue anxiety for office is bad form, Jefferson was carried forward upon the shoulders of his friends. Hero-worship was quick to respond.

The first *Jefferson Almanac* appeared in 1800, for the year 1801; its publisher, George Keating, guaranteed "to give the Purchaser an Almanac for 1802 in case Thomas Jefferson is not elected President of the United States." Campaign pamphlets and thumbnail biographies of Jefferson now poured from the press by dozens. Typical is J. J. Beckley's *Epitome of the Life & Character of Jefferson* (Philadelphia, July, 1800), lauding the "ardent mind of Jefferson, eagerly pursuing the principles of the revolution" (trusting apparently that readers would assume he meant the American rather than the French one); calling him "a man of pure, ardent, and unaffected piety . . . the adorer of one God . . . the friend and benefactor of the whole human race . . . the MAN OF THE PEOPLE . . . the brightest luminary of the western world." Robert Treat Paine's lyric "For Jefferson and Liberty" was sung at innumerable Jefferson rallies and "festivals," along with Rembrandt Peale's song "The People's Friend":

> Devoted to his country's cause,
>   The Rights of Men and equal Laws,
>   His hallow'd pen was given:
> And now those Rights and Laws to save
> From sinking to an early grave,
>   He comes employ'd by Heaven.

Among the Berkshire hills of Massachusetts, Elder John Leland of Cheshire, who had preached electioneering sermons for Jefferson, conceived a magnificent victory tribute. To his Baptist flock he proposed that they should make the biggest cheese in the world in honor of Thomas Jefferson. An eye-witness reported:

> Every man and woman who owned a cow was to give for this cheese all the milk yielded on a certain day—only no *Federal cow* must contribute a drop. A huge cider-press was fitted up to make it in, and on the appointed day the whole country turned out with pails and tubs of curd, the girls and women in their best gowns and ribbons, and the men in their Sunday coats and clean shirt-collars. The cheese was put to press with prayer and hymn singing and great solemnity. When it was well dried it weighed

1600 pounds. It was placed on a sleigh, and Elder Leland drove with it all the way to Washington. It was a journey of three weeks. All the country had heard of the big cheese, and came out to look at it as the Elder drove along.*

Upon his arrival in Washington, "Leland the cheese-monger," as scoffing Federalists called him, preached on Sunday before the joint Houses of Congress, from the text, "And behold, a greater than Solomon is here"— praising the President with such zeal as one might expect from a godly man who had driven for three weeks with the largest cheese in the world. A segment of this cheese was still un-eaten in 1805; it was served at a presidential reception with cake and a huge urn of hot punch. This tribute was rivalled belatedly in 1837, when a New York admirer of outgoing President Jackson con-veyed to the White House, "with banners and bands of music," a cheese weighing 1400 pounds.

Although James Fenimore Cooper knew a Federalist parson who refused, at the font, to christen an infant "Thomas Jefferson," name-sakes quickly began to appear. Among many namesake letters found in Jefferson's private papers, now in the Library of Congress, is one written with the painful care of a hand unaccustomed to the pen. The writer, Thomas Harris, says that he is "a free black man" of Sterling, Connecticut, and that his wife has

> presented me with a pair of *twin boys*. A pair of *black twin boys* are, Sir, I believe no common sight. Such a pair however claim protection and support from me, which I fear I shall not be able to afford them. But Sir, as a testimony of my gratitude, for those principles of Justice and humanity by you so boldly advanced and ably advocated, and of the very great respect in which I hold the Father of his Country, the friend of freedom and equal rights, the benefactor of mankind, and of people of colour in particular, I have named one of my twins *Thomas,* and the other *Jefferson.*

In regard to Jefferson as the Negro's friend, one of the most popular stories circulated about him was that he had returned the bow of an old darkey, in order that a Negro "might not outdo him in polite-

---

* Harriet Taylor Upton, *Our Early Presidents* (1890), pp. 165-66.

ness." Popular in school readers a generation ago, the anecdote usually went hand in hand with one about an old wayfaring man, wishing to ford a stream, who picked out Jefferson from a company of gentlemen on horseback as "the kindest-looking person." Jefferson's benevolence toward the poor and the slave was a legitimate part of his legend, though his attitude toward slavery—as the owner of two hundred blacks himself—was never quite clear to the public. For Jefferson himself (while favoring some gradual emancipation) was loath openly to endorse abolition when asked to do so by the French Society for the Abolition of the Slave Trade. It was another issue upon which the theoretical and the practical Jefferson never quite got together.

Jefferson's fan mail, as a later day would call it, is luckily preserved in the Library of Congress but of course unpublished. It reveals some interesting things. The President's known scientific bent, for example, attracted a host of letter-writers unknown to fame or to Jefferson. They send a sample of cotton wadding made by a new process, a bit of old Peruvian earthenware, "a plan of aerial navigation" which needs Federal support, a new type of loom, an apple-paring machine, "an invention for traveling under water." American ingenuity felt that a kindred spirit was in the White House. Sometimes Jefferson's humble admirers caution him to take better care of himself, hinting that he runs the risk of assassination. Sometimes he is told that a Jefferson debating club has been formed in his honor, or a play or epic poem dedicated to him, often with the proposal that he produce or print it.

That Jefferson was, in a sense unknown to Washington and John Adams, "the People's President," here stands revealed. A mechanic writes in to say that he and his wife have had "the fever," and need a loan of $500 which they are sure the President will supply. Another laborer writes that he is averse to hard work, and so needs money to get an education and become a literary man; all credit will then belong to Jefferson. A Kentuckian reports that a dislocated shoulder prevents his doing heavy labor, and therefore he wishes $2000 to finance him while he studies law; apparently getting no answer, he repeats his request six weeks later with growing irritation. The pastor of a flock of Baptist Republicans in Lebanon, Ohio, tells Jefferson that his church has lost money in a legal dispute and needs a loan; other letters, incidentally, testify to cordial relations between

Jefferson and a number of Baptist preachers and congregations. Many petitions come from needy veterans of the Revolution, debtors, and petty offenders in jail. Perhaps the most singular demand is a letter to Jefferson from one William Esenbeck, January 11, 1806; as a citizen of the national capital, he wants the President to detail six Indians to help him hunt wild beasts around the city.

Although one finds the curious complaint, in a letter of January 25, 1801, that "you will carry on the Government in a most parsimonious manner," it is plain that Jefferson in his first term won vast popular favor by abolishing the excise (the cause of the Whisky Rebellion, in Washington's day), the land tax, stamp tax, and other direct levies which had been made during the war scare of 1798. This pruning won Jefferson an abiding place in the heart of the American farmer. But the most widely applauded act of Jefferson's regime was the Louisiana Purchase. It was a shrewd and simple bargain which everybody could understand, although Jefferson himself took little subsequent pride in the Purchase and did not number it among the great "works" listed by his epitaph—probably because he knew how unconstitutional his methods had been. But the average American, in an age of land-hunger and expansionism, felt no such misgivings, and was quick to approve Jefferson the empire-builder. A typical letter, from an unknown admirer, James Garner of Pendleton, South Carolina, June 7, 1807, relates that he has just been "taking a small view of the western Country, Natchez & Lower Louisiana":

> I Returnd Home, & having a higher (if possible) Regard & Esteem for your Personal Qualifications, in that great Acquisition of the western world & Numberless Measures mild and Advantageous to the American People in General, Excites me to write, to inform you that I never Expect to See you, & in order to Get as nigh as possible have Taken the freedom of Calling my Second and Last Son Th. Jefferson.

After Jefferson's sweeping re-election, carrying all states save Connecticut and Delaware, his reputation seems to have reached its peak. His Second Inaugural shows that Jefferson, like other great leaders in world history, had become the mouthpiece of his age. Here occurs his famous counsel of "commerce and honest friendship with all nations—entangling alliances with none." Unlike Washington,

Jefferson was an adept literary artist, and it is significant that posterity has mistakenly put into the mouth of Washington one of Jefferson's most captivating phrases.

About 1806—when Jefferson the expansionist was laying claim, incidentally, to the Gulf Stream as an American preserve, "in which hostilities and cruising are to be frowned on"—his popularity was almost overwhelming. The Embargo had not yet reared its head. As early as November of that year, and increasingly through the next twelve-months, letters poured in begging him to consider a third term. From Bergen County, New Jersey, he was told that "It is the duty of every man to submit his individual wishes to the general will"; "at a crisis when the flames of war are raging in Europe with unabated violence," added the Chenango County Republicans of New York. In Delaware the Kent County Republicans wrote: "Your services is [*sic*] necessary . . . men are ridiculing the Declaration of Independence." A few admirers dissented, one reminding him that "if JEFFERSON retiring with éclat enforces the principle of Rotation . . . what man would in future have the temerity to avow a contrary doctrine? He would be immediately and deservedly denounced, as an enemy to the sovereign People. . . . None ever can be more universally beloved." But, whether tempted or not, Jefferson followed Washington's precedent.

Sensitive to censure, Jefferson also had the shy man's dislike of being lionized. Although a great democrat, he wanted to keep popularity at arm's length. This had been evident in earlier days—when in the late winter of 1797, approaching Philadelphia to take his seat as Vice-President, he had tried to enter the city by stealth. As usual, American enterprise frustrated the scheme: "A body of troops were on the lookout for him and signalled his approach by a discharge of artillery, and, marching before him into the city, bore a banner aloft on which were inscribed the words: 'Jefferson, the Friend of the People.'" As President he made it a rule to send back even small tokens offered by admirers, lest he be suspected of taking perquisites and bribes; near the end of his second term he meticulously returned an ivory cane to Samuel Hawkins, saying he desired no reward save the "consciousness of a disinterested administration." When Boston citizens sought to make his birthday a patriotic anniversary, he disapproved "transferring the honors and veneration for the great birthday of the Republic to any individual, or of dividing them with individuals." The Fourth of July was enough glory for Jefferson. At the zenith of his popularity Jefferson looked icily upon Sullivan's proposal that he take a swing around the circle, to let the provincials have a look at their beloved chief; the President declared himself "not reconciled to the idea of a chief magistrate parading himself through the several States as an object of public gaze and in quest of applause which, to be valuable, should be purely voluntary." For all his mastery of some political arts and his secret thirst for approval, Jefferson never overcame a feeling, like that of Shakespeare's Coriolanus, about cheapening himself to court the mob, "the mutable, rank-scented many." Jefferson's self-knowledge—that kept him from any illusions about his power of oratory or his personal magnetism—may have added to this feeling. Yet it is safe to say that no man today, Democratic or Republican, could become a major political hero who showed one half of Jefferson's aristocratic diffidence.

Still, he took a very human interest in what people thought about him. Jefferson kept a personal scrap-book, now in the University of Virginia Library. The first fifty pages are filled with political songs and verses, panegyrics and lampoons, accounts of dinners and Republican picnics, bearing chiefly upon himself. One tells of a monster celebration on the banks of the Ohio near Cincinnati, on the Fourth of July, 1806, at which Jefferson was toasted as "the supporter of the rights of man . . . whose integrity and virtue will live in the remembrance of a free and enlightened people, when calumniators are buried in oblivion," and cheered in the playing of "Jefferson's March" with a two-gun salute (George Washington received only one gun). Lyrics in praise of Jefferson are set to the tune of "Hail, Columbia" and "Anacreon in Heaven" (subsequently that of "The Star-Spangled Banner"). In this album one finds "Original Thoughts on the Election of Thomas Jefferson—composed by an obscure Alien," in faltering meter but full of rhapsody. There is a satire sung at a Federalist rally on Independence Day in New Hampshire, which begins:

> Great Washington's hobby, from first dawning youth,
> Was virtue, and valor, and wisdom, and truth.
> While Jefferson's hobby, on Chesterfield's plan,
> Was to *rise* in the Statesman, but *sink* in the Man.

Beside this aspersion is the retort of a loyal Jeffersonian; he leaves the first two lines intact, but emends—

> And Jefferson's hobby (on Washington's plan)
> To unite in the Statesman, the PATRIOT and MAN—

for good measure adding that "John Adams's hobby is dullness profound."

Jefferson's album includes the verses of one brave poet who exclaims
> Huzza for the prudent Embargo!

Yet, as is well known, the Embargo Act of 1807 was the one keenly unpopular deed of Jefferson's eight years. High-handed, it infringed upon American trade, "making many smugglers and traitors, but not a single hero," as Henry Adams remarked. If this be thought New England prejudice, one may hear Mr. Albert Jay Nock, that warm Jeffersonian of our own day, call it "the most arbitrary, inquisitorial, and confiscatory measure formulated in American legislation up to the period of the Civil War." Forbidding the sailing of American ships upon the high seas lest they fall into the clutches of warring Europeans, the Embargo was humiliating to patriots and disastrous to traders. Except for theorists who shared Jefferson's hope that "economic sanctions" might come to be a moral equivalent for the War of 1812, nobody loved the Embargo. Yet, as an experiment, much could have been said for it. At the end of his very successful administration Jefferson was left temporarily discredited. Many families in the South, as well as in the Middle States and New England, were ruined by Jefferson's prudential isolation; they never forgave him, and handed to the next generation their hatred along with their insolvency. Fredrika Bremer in 1850 on a railway journey through Georgia met a man "in person not unlike a meal-sack, whose father had lost $50,000 by the Embargo; he said 'I regard Tom Jefferson as the compound of everything which is rascally, mean, wicked, dishonorable.'"

IV

Indeed, in speaking of Jefferson the hero it is necessary to take account of that obbligato of hatred heard throughout his Presidency.

Some of the First Families of Virginia had detested him since the Revolution, because he fought to end aristocratic privileges like entail, and the Episcopal clergy because he divorced Church and State. In fact, parsons and "economic royalists" were Jefferson's born enemies. In Jefferson's day the charge of irreligion was a much more effective weapon of attack, before the eyes of the common man, than the charge of economic heresy. John Adams, although as much the skeptic as Jefferson, held economic views approved by the traders of New England, and hence was never set in the public pillory among the godless. A good many politicians who did not themselves give a rap for the divinity of Christ or inspiration of the Scriptures seized upon the theological brush with which to tar Jefferson. Jefferson avoided public utterance of his gravest doubts, but at heart seems to have been a deist. He disliked all sects, but came closest to being a Unitarian. He held vague hopes of immortality, but believed above all else in the religion of progress, of human betterment, "passing over us like a cloud of light." "It does me no injury for my neighbor to say there are twenty gods, or no god. It neither picks my pocket nor breaks my leg," he wrote in the *Notes on Virginia*, in tolerant words which irritated many. Although his views had been fixed long before he went abroad, Jefferson upon returning from France found he was suspected of being "Frenchified" or "contaminated" by alien nonsense. From Virginia the prejudice spread elsewhere as soon as Jefferson began to fill Federal office.

Doctor Timothy Dwight, president of Yale, "Pope" of Connecticut, and akin by blood or marriage to those Hillhouses and Wolcotts and Wadsworths who held the purse-strings of Southern New England, led the assault. In a typical *Discourse preached on the Fourth of July* he predicted in 1800 that under Jefferson all Bibles would be burnt, children "wheedled or terrified" into singing *Ca ira*, and "we may see our wives and daughters the victims of legal prostitution." The nationalization of women, as Doctor Dwight well knew, is always a clarion call. In his later book *The Character of Thomas Jefferson* Doctor Dwight charged that this heretic was also vain, insincere, double-faced, and "would descend to the low means and artifices of a practiced intriguer and demagogue to gain favor with the lowest classes of the community." To have become the People's President was, in fact, an act of perfidy! Stephen Cullen Carpenter announced that Jefferson had denied "the right of property, marriage, natural affection, chastity, and decency." In New York the Reverend John Mason warned the American people against electing a President who "disbelieves the existence of an universal deluge." Upon Jefferson's inauguration, it was reported, pious New England housewives buried their Bibles in their gardens to keep them from confiscation.

Assaults upon Jefferson continued to mingle economics with godliness. A parson significantly named the Reverend Cotton Mather Smith charged that Jefferson had robbed a widow and her fatherless children of an estate of £10,000, entrusted him as executor. The President calmly replied that his sister was the only widow whose estate he had ever administered, and that so far as he knew she had no complaints. In the days of Jefferson's Vice-Presidency the Reverend Jedidiah Champion of Litchfield, Connecticut, had prayed with fervor for President Adams, and added "O Lord! wilt Thou bestow upon the Vice-President a double portion of Thy grace, *for Thou knowest he needs it.*" But after Jefferson's accession to the highest office, the Reverend James Abercrombie of Philadelphia declared that on account of the incumbent's atheism he was "very reluctant to read the prayers for the President of the United States, prescribed in the Episcopal ritual." Whether it were better for God to give, or withhold, His grace from Mr. Jefferson was a puzzling question.

Jefferson received scores of anonymous letters about his religion, as his private papers show. They were far more numerous during his first than his second term, by which time most people saw the absurdity of burying their Bibles. A typical letter signed "A. B." and written on January 25, 1801, tells Jefferson he is rumored to be "a kind neighbour" and "certainly a Great Man," but, says the writer, "I am afraid of your Religion & your Politicks." He confesses he is not a pious man himself, but fears that if Christianity is uprooted in the United States "oaths will be nothing, and no one will be safe in his person or property." Probably the writer had never read Swift's dry remarks on abolishing Christianity in England. Another letter, signed "a poor Afflicted Sickly bruised Reed," written May 2, 1801, exhorts Jefferson to look to the Bible for wisdom, to pass more severe laws against swearing and Sabbath-breaking. A letter from "a Youth of fifteen," on March 10 of this same year, admits the alarm felt by those "who have some Regard for Religion, Liberty, and good Order," at Jeffer-

son's efforts to destroy "the Constitution which was framed by our
forefathers." That a man so near the fountain-head of our national
life as Jefferson should have been accused of laying violent hands
upon the "forefathers" is a fact worth noting.

The dwindling of such letters during Jefferson's second term
sprang, in part, from a rather curious situation. The great mass of
his followers were humble rather than rich, farmers rather than city
folk. Tidings of Jefferson's deism reached them faintly. More surely
they knew he had eased their tax burdens, and was opening to them
a vast new frontier for settlement. In other words, he was their friend.
And it was among these people, Baptist and Methodist, that a great
wave of revivalism surged during the early years of Jefferson's Presidency—the Gasper River, Holly Springs, Red River, Flemingsburg,
and other camp-meetings which excited nationwide comment. From
the loneliness of back country and frontier they discovered the gre-
garious warmth of revivals. By the light of flickering lanterns, beneath the tents of Zion, in the muddy waters of a hundred inland
rivers, men and women were washed in the blood of the Lamb. A
generation later, in the backwoods of the Lincoln country, Herndon
found them hugging each other and singing in ecstasy that was half
religious, half sexual—

> I have my Jesus in my arms,
> Sweet as honey, strong as bacon ham.

At Newburgh, New York, *The Recorder of the Times*, August 29,
1804, like many another rural newspaper, remarked the incontestable
fact that in Mr. Jefferson's "wise and virtuous administration" God
Almighty has "poured out his spirit among the people in a manner
before unknown in America." It was a mighty rebuke to Doctor Timothy Dwight and his chilly pewholders. In fact, it became common
for the rank-and-file Jeffersonians—radical in politics, conservative
in religion—to deny as calumny any doubts of their President's piety.
To many, Jefferson's stand against "priestcraft" struck a chord of
Protestant sympathy loud enough to be heard above the thunders
of Congregational and Episcopal pulpits. One of the worst poems
ever written to praise an American hero, called *The Pudding proved*

by eating of it, printed in Monroe County, Virginia, in 1804, declares:

> His States' Work doth not depend on any Clergy Whim,
> His Bus'ness hath naught to do with a Priest-Craft System:
> His religious Opinions is but between his God and him.
>
> . . . .
>
> Better have Deist President that is of mild command,
> Than a Christian one, that is for an overbearing hand.

The great mass of Americans, then as later, refused to pay attention to the handful of militant freethinkers who tried to claim Jefferson, or to the small band of parsons who refused to bury the hatchet. Even today a few conservative Virginia dames—born and bred in a socio-economic stratum whose prejudices are well-nigh immortal— think of Tom Jefferson as the freethinker and dangerous radical, who made the Episcopal Church in Virginia "just like any other church." But in the main, Jefferson's reply in old age to a prying individual— "Say nothing of my religion. It is known to my God and myself alone"— has been respected by his average hero-worshippers.

Some charges made against Jefferson early and late by his ene-mies—that he chattered like a French monkey, loved flattery, and practiced vivisection for cruelty in the name of science—were such distortions of a silent, dignified, kindly man that they had not enough vitality to live. Even Washington Irving's portrait of "William Kieft" in his *Knickerbocker's History* in 1809— dressed in "cocked hat and corduroy small-clothes" and mounted on "a raw-boned charger," who invented carts that went before horses and weathercocks that turned against the wind, who lived in "a sweet sequestered swamp" on an estate "commonly known by the name of Dog's Misery," and who punctuated counsels of state with thunderous blasts of his nose blown into a red cotton handkerchief—is funny, but even more unrecogniz-able than Maxwell Anderson's picture of Peter Stuyvesant as Frank-lin Delano Roosevelt. *The Jonnycake Papers* later burlesqued such caricatures by recalling that "Tom Jefferson . . . was nothing but a mean-spirited, low-lived fellow, the son of a half-breed Indian squaw, sired by a Virginia mulatto father, as well known in the neighborhood where he was raised wholly on hoe-cake (made of coarse-ground Southern corn), bacon and hominy, with an occasional change of fricasseed bullfrog, for which abominable reptiles he had acquired a taste during his residence among the French at Paris." Such hostile nicknames as "Thomas the Magician" or "Thomas Conundrum," seeking to suggest political skulduggery, never caught on. The public indeed had decided that Jefferson's was white magic.

The rankest canard which flew about Jefferson was that his taste ran to colored mistresses. It seems to have been invented in the North, where to some Federalists the fact was perhaps incredible that a Southern gentleman might own a hundred female slaves without claiming a *droit de seigneur*. In *The Portfolio,* issued in Philadelphia in October, 1802, one finds this lyric about the President of the United States:

A SONG

Supposed to have been written by the Sage of Monticello.

Et etiam fusco grata colore Venus. — Ovid.
"And Venus pleases, though as black as jet."

Tune: "Yankee Doodle."

Of all the damsels on the green,
On mountain or in valley,
A lass so lucious ne'er was seen
As Monticellian Sally.

Chorus: Yankee doodle, who's the noodle?
What wife were half so handy?
To breed a flock of slaves for stock,
A blackamoor's the dandy.

What though she by the glands secretes;
Must I stand shil — I, shall — I?
Tuck'd up between a pair of sheets
There's no perfume like Sally.

The little poet Tom Moore, visiting Washington in 1804 and presented at the White House by the anti-Jeffersonian Merrys, was irked by the tall President's failure to take special note of the greatest living Irish bard. To the joy of Federalists he published his verse epistle to Thomas Hume, describing the chieftain in Washington who

> retires to lash his slaves at home;
> Or woo, perhaps, some black Aspasia's charms,
> And dream of freedom in his bondmaid's arms.

James Fenimore Cooper's old schoolmaster "cracked his jokes daily about Mr. Jefferson and Black Sal, never failing to place his libertinism in strong relief against the approved morals of George III." The rumor has no known basis in fact. Jefferson, so scrupulous to answer charges which had a grain of truth, never troubled to quash this story.

Yet it had a long subterranean life. During the campaign of 1860 enemies of Abraham Lincoln, trying to damage him with the liberal as well as the Southern vote, claimed he had said Jefferson was a slaveholder who "brought his own children under the hammer, and made money of his debaucheries." Also that one of Jefferson's dusky daughters "was sold some years ago at public auction in New Orleans, and was purchased by a society of gentlemen who wished to testify by her liberation their admiration of the statesman who 'dreamt of freedom in a slave's embrace.'" Lincoln branded this supposed speech of his "a base forgery." "Old Martin," who for many years rang the campus bell of the University of Virginia, proudly boasted that he was a great-grandson of Thomas Jefferson. Although some of the Jeffersonians of Charlottesville thought he might have been a wild oat sown by one of the statesman's "fast" Randolph grandsons, one suspects the projection in time of an old legend. The University founded by Jefferson has always been very proud of him, never prone to apologize for either his real or imaginary vices. In fact it is a roosting-place for the more fantastic rumors about him—such as, that he laid out its serpentine walls while drunk, and that he built a row of small houses back of pavilions to serve as collegiate brothels. Quite without truth, it is sometimes said that in the charter of the University of Virginia Jefferson provided for licensed prostitution, upon the theory that such an outlet was better for young bullocks than vice without regulation. As recently as 1930 Mr. John Cook Wyllie of the University Library received a series of inquiries, asking for a copy or photostat of the charter, from the Public Library of St. Louis. After some coyness it came out that a patron of the St. Louis Public Library had been greatly upset by hearing this ancient rumor.

The remaining charges against Jefferson's morals stem from the year 1802 and the vilification of a Scotchman named James Thomson Callender. The facts are ironic. Callender, who had fled his own land after libelling the British Government, was first thought by the credulous Jefferson to be a misunderstood, mistreated democrat. So Jefferson gave him secret patronage. This journeyman of slander soon began to attack the Federalist Party, Adams, and Hamilton. His snapping at Hamilton's heels forced that statesman to clear himself of suspected unfaithfulness to public trust, at the expense of revealing his adultery with Mrs. Reynolds—a brave but most humiliating disclosure by Hamilton. The Jeffersonians were gleeful. Attacks upon President Adams, however, sent Callender to a Richmond jail for nine months. Upon Jefferson's inauguration Callender was pardoned and his fine of $200 was remitted. But a delay in the return of this money so angered Callender that he turned against Jefferson, and bedaubed him with the same mud with which he had spattered Hamilton. In 1802 in the Richmond *Recorder* he printed charges against Jefferson whose stain can never be quite forgotten by those otherwise disposed to hate the third President. Callender was a maudlin drunkard who often threatened to commit suicide, and in 1803 was found drowned in three feet of water in the James River; but his work lived long after him. A swarm of pamphlets took up the charges, newspapers printed sniggering allusions to them, and early in 1805 they were aired upon the floor of the Massachusetts Legislature by Congressman John W. Hulbert.

The charge of cowardice in Revolutionary days, and Jefferson's alleged statement that belief in God was "of no social importance," were spiced with accusations of sexual error, in the Callender-Hulbert libels. Jefferson admitted the truth of only one charge—that as a young man he had made improper and unsuccessful advances to Mrs. John Walker, wife of a lifelong friend and neighbor. This memoir of his dead life must have caused exquisite pain to the sensitive aristocrat. It was singular to find him writhing upon the same barb, driven by the same hand, which had pierced Hamilton. Jefferson penned a confession "that when young and single I offered love to a handsome lady—I acknoledge [*sic*] its incorrectness," and circulated it among his intimate friends and cabinet officers, with denial of the other charges. Jefferson had the misfortune at this time to become involved with the talkative, none-too-sympathetic Lees,

Henry Lee serving as go-between for Jefferson and the unhappy husband—who in 1806 requested in Jefferson's hand a statement of "his, & his lady's entire exculpation" for publication if the scandal ever reappeared. It is safe to say, as Douglas S. Freeman remarks, that Jefferson was no hero in the eyes of the Lee family or the idealistic Robert E. Lee; they and related Virginia families have tended to look upon Jefferson with contempt. Americans at large, however, have long forgotten this episode, buried among the rotten timber of Callender's libels. It is probable that a score of modern Virginians have heard about Jefferson's mythical taste for octoroons to one who has heard the real story of poor Mrs. John Walker.

Critical students of Jefferson have long been troubled by an aspect of his personality which makes less inflammable tinder for scandal, but comes closer to the real man. It is akin to the only serious blemish of Franklin, a pliant expediency. Were it not for the stalwart example of Washington, cynics might conclude that the greatest heroes of the early Republic were men who succeeded because of their resemblance to Sam Slick. Washington alone towered above the fogs of opportunism, and did all his work without recourse to occasional backstairs stratagems. He alone had a scrupulous code beyond that of the practical politician, and deservedly is the greatest hero of our early Republic. Franklin and Jefferson generally contrived to compromise issues without compromising themselves, but here and there they slipped a trifle. Clearly below them, in a descending scale, were men like Patrick Henry—who, as Jefferson knew, was a rather shady individual—and Robert Morris, so-called "financier of the Revolution." (Although Morris is still in patriotic favor, with hotels and credit associations named for him, it is now clear, as Professor Abernethy remarks, that the Revolution financed Robert Morris, and that he embraced the cause of independence as a heaven-sent speculative opportunity. But remarkably few, indeed, are the unworthies who have slipped into the fold of American hero-worship.)

The deeps of Jefferson's character are not easy to plumb. In the first place, he was a very amiable gentleman. He liked to please people. In the days of his Ministry to France he obliged a large circle of friends and acquaintances by shopping for them: even Mrs. John Adams wrote asking him to buy her daughter "two pairs of corsets," somehow assuming that Mr. Jefferson without being told would know the right size. Jefferson came close to being a born victim of that

American phrase, "let George do it." He was a natural committeeman, and if destiny had not drafted him for a higher role he would have made the ideal Vice-President. He wished to say what people wanted to hear, and (despite his authorship of a great document of defiance) he dreaded to provoke criticism, offense, personal friction. The rigors of debate had no appeal for him. Although he might collect gossip about his enemies with the calmness of research, he was reluctant to make aggressive use of it. Only when goaded did he fight back; even then he was quick to offer the olive-branch. One of his most characteristic utterances was the statement of his First Inaugural, "We are all republicans—we are all federalists."

In his talk and his letters Jefferson usually let others set the topic and tone, often restating their opinions with his own greater literary finesse. Once this habit brought him to the brink of political ruin. This was at the time of his flowery outburst, in the Latin vein, to Mazzei on April 24, 1796, during Washington's administration and pointed at the President, about those Americans "who were Samsons in the field and Solomons in the council, but who have had their heads shorn by the harlot England." Jefferson was deeply shocked when this letter bounced back in the public eye, and did all he could to unsay it. A little later, proof reached Washington that Jefferson's nephew living at Monticello had forged a letter of flattery, in disguised handwriting under the fictitious name "John Langhorne," hoping to trap Washington into private utterances which might be used against him politically. Whether Jefferson had a hand in this naive ruse cannot now be proved, in black and white, but Washington himself and some of his later partisans have so believed. Most people know nothing of this incident, and the biographers of Jefferson strangely do not mention it—though they like to tell how Jefferson, one later spring, placed upon the bust of Washington at Monticello a wreath of immortelles a French admirer had sent the philosopher to wear on his own birthday.

Jefferson the man was easy to know, but impossible to know well. Many called him "a trimmer." Sometimes it appeared that he steered a circuitous course, catching the prevailing winds as he went along, to reach in the end a wholly honorable port. John Quincy Adams, naturally inclined to overstate the case, said that Jefferson had "a memory so pandering to the will that in deceiving others he seems to have begun by deceiving himself." More sympathetically, one must say that Jefferson had been forced to learn the arts of expediency. As a young Governor, his scrupulosity over legal points had been the prime reason for a failure he never forgot. Later he was prone to believe that the end justified the means. In his most important decision, the Louisiana Purchase—in which he privately admitted that he had "done an act beyond the Constitution" in not waiting for the cumbersome machinery of democracy—certainly the result was splendid, and vindicated by all patriotism and good sense. Justifying his high-handed methods in the Burr conspiracy, free to admit that democracy is too slow in crises, Jefferson the President wrote (in words so alien to Jefferson the Governor): "Should we have ever gained our Revolution, if we had bound our hands by manacles of the law?" It was significant that President Roosevelt, in his message to Congress on September 3, 1940, apropos of the "swap" of fifty old destroyers for eight naval bases for defense of the Western Hemisphere, should have buttressed himself with the precedent of Jefferson's "unconstitutional" bargain with Napoleon—calling his exchange "the most important action in the re-enforcement of our national defense that has been taken since the Louisiana Purchase." The American people, it appears, approved both.

Jefferson's was a complex brain—the brain of a dreamer and idealist, trained by experience into a shrewd, adaptable, hard-headed politician—and it let him see all sides of a subject. His very penetration bred contradictions, and led him sometimes into passing inconsistency. (He has been quoted for and against states' rights and the right of secession, for and against restricted immigration, for and against the spoils system, for and against a big navy and preparedness.) Though some of these contradictions are more apparent than real, it must be admitted that Jefferson's intellect—far from being a single-track mind like Washington's—was a whole switch-yard. But the most vital fact remains to be added. Jefferson's devotion to the United States, above all other interests private or public, selfish or partisan, was superbly consistent. There he never wavered. Hamilton's intrigues with the British Crown in 1792, which carried him perilously near to treason, have no counterpart in the Jefferson pattern. Only to political dogmas or exclusive economic interests did Jefferson fail to show a fixed loyalty. There he allowed himself to blow hot and cold, depending upon occasions.

Of course the average American on the basis of his vague knowledge, in early times as well as today, could not be expected to rationalize all these things. He was simply disposed to accept Jefferson as "the People's friend," and this trust was not ill placed. Jefferson's contribution to the United States, as statesman and President, was not an airtight or even very logical political system. It was chiefly a faith—faith in the long run in the dependability, wisdom, and honesty of the common literate individual, as represented in his day by the agrarian majority. Woodrow Wilson said: "The immortality of Thomas Jefferson does not lie in any one of his achievements, but in his attitude toward mankind." This verdict, whether endorsed by a great modern liberal or by the man in the street, is the core of the Jefferson cult.

v

Through the long sunset years between Jefferson's retirement in 1809 and his death in 1826, he became an oracle and patriarch. He was one of the last surviving symbols of the Revolution, the sage on the hill-top, who (as a visitor wrote in 1816), after "having filled a seat higher than that of kings, succeeds with graceful dignity to that of the good neighbor." A typical English visitor to America, Isaac Candler, grew bored with being told that Jefferson was "the most learned man in the world," and with hearing Jefferson's opinions on art and literature quoted to end all discussion. (The mantle of versatility was already being cast about the shoulders of great Americans.) Jefferson's growing financial embarrassments were neglected by his native state, but brought generous gifts from citizens of New York, Philadelphia, and Baltimore. In June, 1826, Jefferson declined on the score of health an invitation to become the city of Washington's guest of honor on the Fiftieth Birthday of the Declaration of Independence. His reply, traced with a feeble hand, but stating with his old fire the conviction that "the mass of mankind has not been born with saddles on their backs," was published immediately as a broadside. It was his last pastoral charge. Shortly after noon of that Fourth of July—the date upon whose prime validity Jefferson had so long insisted—the statesman breathed his last. Every schoolboy knows that John Adams, expiring on the same day in Massachusetts, faintly murmured, "Thomas Jefferson still survives." Many Americans felt a sentiment thus expressed by a Virginia newspaper: "In this most singular coincidence, the finger of Providence is plainly visible! It

hallows the Declaration of Independence as the Word of God, and is
the bow in the Heavens, that promises its principles shall be eternal."
But at least one jealous Jeffersonian, who lived in Albermarle County,
thought that John Adams's death on the same day "was a damned
Yankee trick."

In death, as in life, Jefferson remained second to Washington.
Daniel Webster, in his great joint eulogy on Jefferson and Adams at
Faneuil Hall in 1826, exclaimed: "Washington is in the clear upper
sky. These other stars have now joined the American constellation;
they circle round their center, and the Heavens beam with new light."
It was plain that none could rival the glory of Washington, who
had fought for and won the liberty that Jefferson and Adams had
phrased. The first to hold highest office and the first to die, Washington was divorced more completely than they from sections and
parties. It was also clear that to the country at large Jefferson was a
greater hero than Adams. His single deeds—from the Declaration to
the Louisiana Purchase— had been more splendid, and his policies
had struck deeper root. The Adamses have always served America
well, but their vanity, coldness, and knack of doing the gracious
thing "in the ungracious way" have kept them in a class inferior to
the heroes—the worthies.

It was Jefferson's good luck, and the nation's, that his loyal pupils
Madison and Monroe for sixteen years carried on his will and testament. The liberalisms of later men, who in various ways tried to re-
vive the faith of Jefferson—Jackson, Lincoln, Woodrow Wilson—were
uprooted more quickly by falling into hostile hands. Jeffersonianism
enjoyed a long fruitful summer of increase; it became a name and
philosophy of rich American associations. Even the Whigs, Jackson's
enemies and Webster's friends, who had taken all there was to salvage
from the shipwreck of the anti-Jefferson Federalists, in 1841 after
their Log Cabin campaign, as a New York newspaper noted, "have
of late years repeatedly declared themselves true Jeffersonian Democrats." Henry S. Randall, in a devoted three-volume life of Jefferson
in 1858, remarked that although Jefferson was still secretly assailed
"by class and hereditary hate," yet no orator dared publicly attack
the two greatest Americans, Washington and Jefferson, "the one
who was the Sword of his country, and the other the Pen."

Walt Whitman—who had younger brothers named Thomas Jefferson and Andrew Jackson Whitman—spoke of the two agrarian

statesmen as "the sainted Jefferson and Jackson." In youth the poet of
"the Divine Average" had hailed Jefferson as "the Columbus of our
political faith," and in old age still cherished him as "among the
greatest of the great." With the storm of Civil War darkening, Jefferson, as author of the affirmation that all men are created free and
equal, began to receive fresh honor in the North. The new Republican Party, dressing its ranks for a great crusade, looked to Jefferson
the idealist. Lincoln, replying on April 6, 1859, to an invitation to a
Jefferson birthday rally in Boston, was moved to grave mirth by the
shifting of old party lines. He told the story of two drunks who got
into a fight: each fought himself out of his own coat and into that
of the other fellow. Lincoln remarked that Jefferson's land, the South,
now held that personal liberty was nothing in comparison with
property rights, while "Republicans, on the contrary, are for both
the man and the dollar, but in case of conflict the man before the
dollar." That was Jeffersonianism. "The principles of Jefferson are
the definitions and axioms of free society," Lincoln added. "All honor
to Jefferson—to the man who, in the concrete pressure of a struggle
for national independence by a single people, had the coolness, forecast, and capacity to introduce into a mere revolutionary document
an abstract truth, applicable to all men and all times."

Jefferson as hero waned somewhat after the Civil War. New idols
like Lincoln and Grant tended to dim the galaxy of the Revolution.
The unity symbolized by the amended Constitution now appeared
more precious than the ringing defiance of the Declaration. Jefferson's memory had neither its Weems nor its John Hay: his very character was too deep an enigma for conventional biography. Orators,
novelists, and poets seemed to pass him by; even Monticello grew
shabbier, more neglected, with each passing year. His liberalism
fell upon deaf ears in the era Vernon Parrington has called "the Great
Barbecue." Only here and there were men to whom Jefferson was a
magic spirit. The most ardent of them was Henry George, shocked
over land-grabbing in the West and the growing slums of Eastern
cities. Henry George believed in Jefferson's God—the Author of
Nature who had created the earth for men to till, and to exercise the
gift He had given them of life, liberty, and the pursuit of happiness.
George conceived the Single-Tax as an offshoot of Jefferson's philosophy, as a safeguard against exploitation of the soil. But he was in
the minority.

The Democratic Party, reviving slowly after the Civil War, made Jefferson its patron saint; but the national leadership of Jefferson's region, the South, had been shattered. The dominant party, the Republicans, had forgotten Jefferson since Lincoln's day. A semi-liberal like Theodore Roosevelt (who shared the historical loyalties of his Federalist friend Lodge) detested Jefferson. The only thing he could approve was the Louisiana Purchase; in all else Jefferson was a weakling. Roosevelt's most blasting damnation of Bryan was a comparison with Jefferson—well-meaning, shallow, cheap, vacillating, possessing "Jefferson's nervous fear of doing anything that may seem to be unpopular with the rank and file of the people." Thus he wrote to Taft on September 4, 1906. Indeed, Jefferson was out of fashion with more simon-pure liberals than Roosevelt. One of the most powerful books of that decade, Herbert Croly's *The Promise of American Life* in 1909, offered stinging epithets about "Jefferson's intellectual superficiality and insincerity." Even in his champions Jefferson was unfortunate: in the muckraking era, William Randolph Hearst took up "Jeffersonian democracy" as his favorite shibboleth.

Wilson had marked intellectual sympathy for Jefferson, but no warm personal admiration; he once told Colonel House that Alexander Hamilton "was easily the ablest" statesman of the early Republic.

After the Great War, Jefferson was often quoted on "entangling alliances," approved as an isolationist and lover of peace. In view of Red Russia, little was said of Jefferson the radical. Upon another tack, in 1928, it was asserted direfully that the election of a Catholic President would "roll back the progress of Democracy of Jefferson and Jackson."

VI

Jefferson did not come into his own until the New Deal. Whether consciously or not, he has been built up to offset Lincoln, as a symbol of the Democratic Party, and to give the new liberalism its sanction by tradition. The great Jefferson Memorial now being completed in Washington, the reawakened cult at Monticello, the three-cent stamp, the new Jefferson nickel, and the massive face which Gutzon Borglum has carved upon Mount Rushmore—all proclaim that he is our newest Federal God in the highest degree. Some of these tributes might have come at all events; together, they show an unmistakable drift.

Franklin D. Roosevelt as candidate for President, at St. Paul in the spring of 1932, declared that Benjamin Franklin, Jefferson, and Theodore Roosevelt were the three great Americans who knew best the cross-currents of our folk life, the hopes and fears of the common people—"and of these three Jefferson was in many ways the deepest student. . . . His, after all, was the essential point of view that has been held by our truly great leaders in every generation." (The exclusion of Lincoln was perhaps a political one, since he, rather than the "progressive" Theodore Roosevelt, was embedded so deeply in Republican myth.) A few months later in San Francisco, making his notable speech on Progressive Government, Franklin D. Roosevelt ranked Jefferson first on the roll-call of American liberals, followed by Theodore Roosevelt and Woodrow Wilson. As President, on July 4, 1936, at Monticello, he glowingly praised Jefferson's "consecration" to social justice and to "the freedom of the human mind." Mr. Roosevelt has quoted George Washington a little gingerly, even on so safe a subject as popular education, lest he be contradicted by other passages "from the somewhat voluminous writings and messages of the First President"—but of Jefferson's mind, which many regard as more perilously self-contradictory, Mr. Roosevelt has always spoken with assurance. In a more personal view, the parallel between the master of Monticello and the squire of Hyde Park, another gentle radical, is too good to miss. In July, 1937, it was reported that a portrait of Jefferson painted by the Polish patriot Kosciuszko, and carried at that time from the Polish Embassy to the White House, bore a striking resemblance to Mr. Roosevelt. Certainly the thirty-second President feels at home in the milieu of the third. At the University of Virginia on June 10, 1940, the day of Italy's entry into the War, the President welcomed an occasion to speak his mind in "this university founded by the first great American teacher of democracy." That Thomas Jefferson is Mr. Roosevelt's political hero one can hardly doubt, or that his ideals have tinged the philosophy of the New Deal.

Claude G. Bowers, admirer and biographer of Jefferson, was made Ambassador to Spain by President Roosevelt in 1933. From Madrid, to the Democratic campaign of 1936, Mr. Bowers contributed his

book, *Jefferson in Power: The Death Struggle of the Federalists.* It
described the career of a liberal aristocrat through eight years of
serene triumph, winning the people's love, engaging in vast public
works, and readily crushing his enemies who had "fought with far-
seeing cunning from behind the protecting shield of the Supreme
Court." Mr. Bowers pointed his moral by saying, "the story is offered
as a warning to all succeeding political parties and politicians that
public opinion cannot be defied with impunity." (Dissenters remarked that Mr. Bowers had nothing to say about Jefferson's dictum
that "the best government is that which governs least.") While Mr.
Bowers, here and elsewhere, implies that Jefferson would applaud
the New Deal, Mr. James Truslow Adams in *The Living Jefferson*
(1936) states that Jefferson would have hated it. Needless to say,
both men agree with Jefferson.

The enemies of Jefferson are dead, or in hiding. Nowadays no
such words are uttered publicly as those of Bishop Henry Codman
Potter, "shepherd of the Four Hundred," at the Washington Inaugural Centennial of 1889 in New York: "We have exchanged the
Washingtonian dignity for the Jeffersonian simplicity, which was in
truth only another name for the Jacksonian vulgarity." Under the
new liberalism, the Federalist heirlooms of the Republican Party
have been locked away in the cupboard. Since Andrew Mellon was
called "the greatest Secretary of the Treasury since Alexander Hamilton," the name of Jefferson's bitterest enemy has scarcely been
heard in American politics. Republicans, like the Whigs of Webster's
day, now invoke "sound Jeffersonian principles." Nobody can raise
many votes with sound Hamiltonian principles.

Conservatives may also claim the hereditary honors, as it were, in
having among their ranks the lineal descendants of Jefferson, the
Coolidges of Boston. This family presented Jefferson's writing-desk
to the nation in 1880, has served on the trusteeship of Monticello
and the new Federal memorial, and takes unfailing pride in Jefferson's memory. Thomas Jefferson Coolidge, banker and member of
the Somerset Club, served as Under-Secretary of the Treasury early
in the New Deal, but it was apparent that he was no scourge of the
vested interests. Harold Jefferson Coolidge in 1937 published a slim
volume called *Thoughts on Thomas Jefferson: Or What Jefferson Was
Not.* He there pays his respects to " 'Jefferson Clubs' whose leaders
are politicians of the type of 'Al' Smith, 'Jim' Farley, or James M.

Curley. These are the men who talk most about Jefferson." Mr. Coolidge, one gathers, is a little irritated, knowing that by any other
name the wild Irish rose would smell as sweet.

Today three great shrines to Jefferson are being repaired or built.
The first is Monticello, where Jefferson lavished ingenuity over wind-
vanes and double-action doors and experimented with new seeds and
cuttings, and where, as he wrote, "all my wishes end." Thousands
of pilgrims, in Jefferson's later years, called to pay their respects; the
sage's hospitality to them helped to drive him bankrupt. After his
death Monticello fell into strangers' hands; less reverent visitors,
seeking souvenirs, broke open the high iron gates and chipped pieces
from Jefferson's obelisk. At its lowest ebb the estate was bought by
a Jewish commodore in the Navy, Uriah Levy. His nephew, Jefferson
Monroe Levy, a New Yorker who had made millions in Canadian
Pacific Railway and had a taste for politics, inherited it and took some
pride in possession. In 1923 he sold Monticello for half a million
dollars to the newly formed Jefferson Memorial Foundation—which
immediately turned it into a national shrine. Only 19,414 visitors
came in the first year, and the outlook, with a staggering mortgage,
was not bright. But through the following years popular interest in
Jefferson quickened; new biographies were printed, orators invoked
Jefferson more warmly, magazines published articles on Jefferson
and the New Deal. Last year more than 100,000 visitors paid a half
dollar each for admission to the shrine—even though Monticello is
more remote from large cities and major highways than are Mount
Vernon, Franklin's grave, the Hermitage, or Grant's tomb. Chairman
of the Foundation and most enterprising of Jeffersonians is Mr. Stuart
Gibboney, a direct descendant of Patrick Henry, veteran of the
Spanish-American War and the Boxer uprising, and New York attorney for Angostura Bitters. Mr. Gibboney, a good friend of the
Jefferson Coolidges, takes pleasure in sending them—with something
of a twinkle in his eye—copies of their great ancestor's more inflam-
matory utterances.

Jeffersonians have long regretted the lack of a great Federal shrine,
comparable to the Washington Monument and the Lincoln Memorial.
Through the efforts of Mr. Gibboney and the Foundation, aided by
sympathy from the Democratic Party, Congress in June, 1934, created a Jefferson Memorial Commission. Its choice of a site is significant of Jefferson's new hero-rank. When the Lincoln Memorial was

built to complete an axis running from the Capitol through the Mall, and past the Washington Monument to the river bank, it was seen that at some future date the general cruciform plan would be finished by an intersecting axis drawn from the White House through the Washington obelisk to the tidal basin, where hundreds of cherry trees bloom in the spring. This site, long awaiting some memorial to match Washington's and Lincoln's, is that of the new $3,000,000 shrine to Jefferson. A circular temple of white marble, in the Palladian style of dome and colonnade that Jefferson introduced to America, will house a heroic standing figure of Jefferson yet unmade. President Roosevelt broke ground in December, 1938, and in November, 1939, laid the cornerstone, saying, on the latter occasion: "He lived as we live, in the midst of a struggle between rule by the self-chosen individual or the self-appointed few, and rule by the franchise and approval of the many. He believed as we do, that the average opinion of mankind is in the long run superior to the dictates of the self-chosen."

The third project is in St. Louis. The state of Missouri has always had a special affection for Jefferson. Even though he narrowly missed having a state as namesake, when Jefferson Territory was rechristened Colorado, in Missouri Jefferson has received more official honors than in his native Virginia. Jefferson, it is not forgotten, bought from Napoleon the inland empire of Upper Louisiana, of which St. Louis was the capital, and described this commonwealth as "choice country with room enough." The St. Louis Exposition of 1904 was held to celebrate this Purchase and to honor Jefferson. Missouri's capital is Jefferson City, and the statesman's statue rises above the capitol steps. In 1883 the University of Missouri asked for, and received from the Jefferson heirs, the original tombstone discarded from Monticello; it has been ever since the most prized possession on that campus. (Some years ago, President Richard H. Jesse of the University of Missouri caused a furore among loyal Missouri Jeffersonians when, at a dinner of the Knife and Fork Club of Kansas City, he mentioned the old darkey who claimed descent from Jefferson, and other "intimate" rumors which Jesse as a Virginian was disposed to believe.) From Missouri Jefferson has received many miscellaneous tributes: In 1856 the Legislature commissioned the state's best artist, George Caleb Bingham, to copy the Stuart portrait of Jefferson for the senate chamber of the Capitol. In Missouri oratory, Jefferson's name has always carried something of the same finality as Webster's in Massachusetts or Lincoln's in Illinois; Senator George Graham Vest—greatest of Missouri spellbinders and best known for his "Tribute to a Dog"—once exclaimed, "For myself, I worship no mortal man living or dead; but if I could kneel at such a shrine, it would be with uncovered head and loving heart at the grave of Thomas Jefferson."

In 1931 Jefferson's birthday was made a legal holiday in Missouri. The Jefferson Highway, joining Canada and Louisiana, runs the length of the state, where an extensive new park has been reserved in Jefferson's honor.

In Jefferson's lifetime the city of St. Louis, in 1824, sent him an honorary membership in her Agricultural Society. Later the city set up a Thomas Jefferson Museum. Pilgrimages from St. Louis to Monticello have been popular. In October, 1901, "the Jefferson Club of St. Louis" (organized in 1892, and soon counting 6000 members) invited "all those persons who believe in the principles and teachings of Thomas Jefferson" to go to Monticello on a chartered train and set up a block of Missouri granite near his tomb. On Jefferson's birthday in 1939 some 600 Missourians, headed by their Governor, called at Monticello. Early in the Depression, when PWA and WPA funds were flowing, St. Louis conceived a monster project to honor Jefferson the expansionist. Her politicians persuaded Congress to appoint a commission—which recommended that a tract of eighty acres, in the slums along the St. Louis waterfront, be bought and cleared as the site for a $33,000,000 "Jefferson National Expansion Memorial," with a great park, fountains, a dome-capped temple, and in the center a huge granite shaft. Today, in the colder light of economy, the project "is down to about $9,000,000, and the city of St. Louis is paying part of the cost," as Representative Cochran reported in 1939. Even so, the project was attacked by Congressman Schafer of Wisconsin: "The New Deal has strayed far from the fundamental principles and policies of government expounded and practised by Thomas Jefferson. Our New Deal friends, no doubt, ease their consciences by spending millions of dollars to erect a great memorial in honor of the man whose principles and policies they have repudiated." A park has taken the place of the slums, but the fate of the Memorial as planned is still uncertain.

At all events the cult of Jefferson marches on. He has attracted the

the worship of more statesmen and political thinkers than of artists, dramatists, and poets. The absence from the halo of Thomas Jefferson of Washington's military glory, Jackson's rugged picturesqueness, or Lincoln's tenderness and pathos, is responsible no doubt for the slower growth of his legend. Jefferson's greatest deeds—the Declaration of Independence, the abolition of class privilege in Virginia, the Louisiana Purchase, the fostering of secular education in America—grew increasingly less dramatic and pictorial. By no homely incident, no single gesture, can the maker of myths evoke for every man the essence of Jefferson. His appeal is more reflective, more intellectual. Doubtless this has handicapped the lovability of the man. In art, even Jefferson's arch-enemy Hamilton has fared better—in romantic novels of which Gertrude Atherton's *The Conqueror* is best, in John Drinkwater's play *Hamilton,* and in statues usually found among the marts of trade and finance. But, with his lack of glitter and "theatre," and his quiet life unmarked by Hamilton's aura of martyrdom, Jefferson is beyond question the greater American symbol. The drafter of documents and policies that stand beside the well-spring of our national life, Jefferson remains (as his most scholarly biographer Gilbert Chinard calls him) "the apostle of Americanism." He is the first great democrat, the people's friend. The stature of no traditional figure has grown taller than his, in the last generation. His fame is slow-ripening but solid. Undoubtedly, as John Adams said, Thomas Jefferson still survives.

INDEX OF AUTHORS

INDEX OF AUTHORS

Date Due